The Inflation of House Prices

Lexington Books Special Series in
Real Estate and Urban Land Economics

William N. Kinnard, Jr., Editor

James H. Boykin, *Financing Real Estate*

D. Barlow Burke, *American Conveyancing Patterns*

James R. Cooper and Karl Guntermann, *Real Estate and Urban Land Analysis*

Gene Dilmore, *Real-Estate Counseling*

Leo Grebler and Frank G. Mittelbach, *The Inflation of House Prices*

Gaylon E. Greer, *The Real-Estate Investment Decision*

Austin J. Jaffe, *Property Management in Real Estate Investment Decision-Making*

Irvin E. Johnson, *The Instant Mortgage-Equity Technique*

Irvin E. Johnson, *Selling Real Estate by Mortgage-Equity Analysis*

William N. Kinnard, Jr., *Income Property Valuation*

William N. Kinnard, Jr., *Principles and Techniques of Real Property Appraising*

William N. Kinnard, Jr., and Stephen D. Messner, *Effective Business Relocation*

Robert A. Sigafoos, *Corporate Real Estate Development*

Leonard P. Vidger, *Borrowing and Lending on Real Estate*

The Inflation of House Prices

Its Extent, Causes, and Consequences

Leo Grebler
Frank G. Mittelbach
University of California,
Los Angeles

Lexington Books
D.C. Heath and Company
Lexington, Massachusetts
Toronto

Library of Congress Cataloging in Publication Data

Grebler, Leo.
  The inflation of house prices, its extent, causes, and consequences.

  Includes index.
  1. Housing—prices—United   States.   2. Inflation   (Finance)—United
States. I. Mittelbach, Frank G., joint author. II. Title.
HD7293.G685   338.4'369'080973   78-20272
ISBN 0-669-02708-1

Published simultaneously in Canada.

Printed in the United States of America.

International Standard Book Number: 0-669-02708-1

Library of Congress Catalog Card Number: 78-20272

Contents

List of Figures ix

List of Tables xi

Acknowledgments xv

Chapter 1   Introduction and Summary   1

The Setting   1
Purpose and Main Findings of the Study   3

Chapter 2   The Upward Thrust of Prices   11

Methodological Problems   11
List of Price Data   13
Nationwide Price Movements   14
Regional Price Movements   23
Price Changes in Local Areas   24
Historical Sketch of House Prices   32

Chapter 3   The Homebuyers   37

Recent Growth of Home Purchases   37
Income and Wealth Constraints on Various
    Groups of Buyers   39
The Burdens of Downpayment and High
    Interest Rates   51
The Speculators   58

Chapter 4   Characteristics, Motivations, and Expectations
             of Recent Buyers: Local Surveys   69

Characteristics of Homebuyers   71
Features of Houses Purchased in 1975 and 1977   74
Previous versus Current Residence   76
Reasons for Purchase   79
Homebuyers' Expectations   83
Summary   85

Chapter 5   **Factors Associated with the Price Escalation**   89

                 Manifestations of Excess Demand   89
                 Reasons for Excess Demand—The Conventional
                     Approach   99
                 The Role of Inflationary Expectations   116

Chapter 6   **An Exploratory Model of House Prices**   129

                 General Framework   129
                 Stock-Flow Relationships   131
                 The Model   135
                 Methods   139
                 Results   143

Chapter 7   **The Outlook for Price Adjustments**   157

                 Supply and Demand Variables in the Market
                     for Homes   158
                 General Economic Conditions   161
                 The Lesson of Previous Experience   162
                 A Summary Judgment   164
                 Beneficiaries and Victims of House Price Inflation   165

Chapter 8   **The Role of Public Policies**   171

Appendix A   **Tables on House Prices Analyzed in Chapter 2**   181

Appendix B   **Methods Used for Locally Generated House
                 Price Data**   187

Appendix C   **The Price Data of the Community Analysis
                 Bureau of the City of Los Angeles**   189

Appendix D   **Historical Price Series**   191

Appendix E   **Analysis of Downpayments**   197

Appendix F   **Advertisements for Unfurnished Homes for
                 Rent in Four California Areas, 1976-1977**   201

Appendix G   **Rationale of Speculation**   203

Appendix H   **Homebuyer Surveys in Contra Costa and
                 Orange Counties, California: Methods and
                 Responses**   209

Appendix I   **Tables on Sales and Inventories of Merchant
                 Builders**   223

Appendix J   Liquidation of Home Equities in Recent Years   229

Appendix K   Formula for the Composite Index of
                    Borrowing Costs   235

Appendix L   Terms of Credit Composite Index for Conventional
                    Home Loans Made by Major Types of Lenders in
                    Two California Areas, 1970-1977   237

                    Index   239

                    About the Authors   243

List of Figures

2-1   Average Prices of New Homes Sold by Builders and of Existing Homes, 1968-1977   15

2-2   Average Prices of New and Existing Homes Reported for Transactions Financed with Conventional Mortgage Loans, 1968-1977   17

2-3   Average Prices for New and Existing Homes Financed with FHA-Insured Mortgages, 1968-1977   18

2-4   FHA-Estimated Market Price of Sites per Square Foot of Lot, 1968-1977   19

2-5   Observed Average House Prices in the City of Los Angeles Compared with Prices "Predicted by CPI," 1965-1976   30

3-1   Average Downpayment as a Percentage of Average House Price, Conventional Home Mortgage Loans, 1968-1977   52

3-2   Average Downpayment as a Ratio of per-Capita Disposable Personal Income, Conventional Home Mortgage Loans, 1968-1977   53

5-1   Unsold Completed Houses as a Percentage of All Completed New Single-Family Houses in Seven-County Area of Southern California, December 1974 to June 1977   92

5-2   New One-Family Houses Sold, for Sale, and Number of Months' Supply at Current Sales Rate   94

5-3   Median Number of Months New Single-Family Houses Have Been on the Market, United States Benchmark Data, 1969-1977   96

6-1   Plot of Actual and Fitted Values of Home Prices, 1968-1977   145

6-2   Plot of Actual and Fitted Values of Quarterly Rates of Change in Home Prices, 1970-1977   150

List of Tables

2-1   Annual Rates of House Price Increases in Selected
        Periods, United States, 1968-1977   20

2-2   House Price Increases Compared with Increases
        of Other Prices and Income, United States, 1968-1977   21

2-3   Annual Rates of House Price Increases in Four Major
        Census Regions and the United States, 1968-1976   23

2-4   Percent Changes in Average Purchase Prices of New
        and Existing Homes Financed with Conventional
        Mortgage Loans, 18 Metropolitan Areas, 1974-1976
        and 1976-1977   25

2-5   Annual Rates of Price Increases for Existing Homes
        in Three Major California Areas, 1968-1977   28

2-6   Annual Rates of Price Increases for Existing Homes
        in Seattle and Montgomery County, Maryland,
        1968-1977   29

2-7   Average Sales Prices of Single-Family Dwelling Units
        in the City of Los Angeles and Four Subareas,
        1967-1976   31

3-1   Sales of Existing and New Single-Family Houses and
        Total Volume of New-Home Acquisitions, United
        States, 1968-1977   38

3-2   Sales of New and Existing Homes in the West,
        1968-1977   40

3-3   Schematic Illustration I of Three Successive Purchases
        of New Single-Family Houses by the Same Household,
        1965-1977   42

3-4   Schematic Illustration II of Three Successive Purchases
        of New Single-Family Houses by the Same Household,
        United States, 1965-1977   44

3-5   Selected Financial Characteristics of Home Purchases
        under the FHA System, United States, 1965-1977   47

3-6   Selected Financial Characteristics of Home Purchases
        Financed with Conventional Loans Insured by a Major
        Private Mortgage Insurance Company, January through
        September 1977   48

3-7   Recent Movers into Owner-Occupied Units, by Tenure
        in Previous Unit, United States, 1973, 1974, and 1975   50

3-8   Changes in Effective Interest Rates on Conventional
        Home Loans Compared with Changes in Per-Capita
        Disposable Personal Income, United States, 1968-1977   55

3-9   Illustrations of Real Interest Rates for Homebuyers in
        Specified Years Selling the Property in Designated Years   56

4-1   Selected Housing Market Indicators, Contra Costa and
        Orange Counties, California, 1970-1977   70

4-2   Summary of Major Characteristics of Recent Home-
        buyers, Contra Costa and Orange Counties, California,
        1975 and 1977   72

4-3   Reported Home Purchase Price: Recent Homebuyers,
        1975 and 1977   75

4-4   Selected Characteristics of Current Residence: Recent
        Homebuyers, 1975 and 1977   76

4-5   Selected Characteristics of Previous Residence: Recent
        Homebuyers, 1975 and 1977   77

4-6   Location of Previous Residence of Homebuyers, 1975
        and 1977   78

4-7   Reasons for Purchasing Current Home, Contra Costa
        County Respondents, 1975 and 1977   80

4-8   Reasons for Purchasing Current Home, Orange County
        Respondents, 1975 and 1977   81

4-9   Percent of Respondents Agreeing or Disagreeing with
        Statement that Home Was Purchased Because of
        Further Expected Price Increases, 1975 and 1977   84

5-1   Unsold Inventories of New Homes in Seven-County
        Area of Southern California, 1970-1977   90

5-2   Unsold Inventories of New Homes in Nine-County
        San Francisco Bay Area, 1971-1977   93

5-3   Idle Electric Meters as a Percentage of Total Residential
        Meters in Selected Areas of California, 1970-1977   98

5-4   Residential Vacancy Rates in the United States and
        Four Major Census Regions, Quarterly, 1974-1977   99

5-5   Estimated Increase in California Civilian Population,
       Its Main Components, and Its Relation to U.S.
       Civilian Population Increase, 1964-1977   102

5-6   Percent Changes in Consumer Income in the United
       States and California, 1966-1977   103

5-7   Net Increase in Mortgage Debt on One-to Four-Family
       Houses, United States, 1971-1977   105

5-8   Net Increase in Mortgage Loan Holdings of FSLIC-
       Insured California Savings-and-Loan Associations,
       1970-1977   107

5-9   Terms-of-Credit Composite Index for Conventional
       Home Loans Made by Major Types of Lenders in the
       United States, 1968-1977   108

5-10   Index of Monthly Payments on Conventional Home
       Loans Made by Major Types of Lenders in the United
       States Compared with Composite Index of Cost of
       Borrowing, 1970-1977   110

5-11   Index of Monthly Payments on Conventional Home
       Loans Made by Major Types of Lenders in Two
       California Areas Compared with Composite Cost of
       Borrowing, 1970-1977   111

5-12   Index of Debt Service on Single-Family Houses
       Financed with FHA-Insured Loans, United States,
       1970-1977   112

5-13   Cumulative Percent Increase of Starts of Single-Family
       Houses in the United States during Four Expansion
       Periods   113

5-14   Cumulative Percent Increase of Building-Permit
       Authorizations for Single-Family Houses in California
       during Three Expansion Periods   114

5-15   Consumers' General Price Expectations, United
       States, 1973-1977   119

5-16   Consumers' Opinions on House Purchase, United
       States, 1973-1977   120

5-17   Price Changes for Selected Variable-Price Assets,
       1968-1976   123

6-1   Number of Existing Homes Sold per Quarter, United
           States, 1968-1977   151

6A-1   Variables in U.S. Housing Price Model, 1968-1977   155

8-1   Key Data for Two Graduated-Payment Mortgage
           Plans and the Fixed-Payment Plan   174

Acknowledgments

This monograph was prepared as a project of the Housing, Real Estate and Urban Land Studies Program at the UCLA Graduate School of Management. The project was supported by the California Department of Real Estate, which made funds available for research and clerical assistance. The authors are indebted to the department and to the many executives of organizations operating in the single-family home and mortgage markets who were interviewed to obtain insights into the subject matter and furnished materials. We owe thanks to the sources which have permitted the use of copyrighted information, including the data compiled by the National Association of Realtors (a federally registered trademark).

We benefited greatly from incisive comments on a preliminary draft by Lawrence B. Smith, John C. Weicher, and our colleague John M. Clapp. We are grateful to David F. Seiders for data and suggestions concerning appendix J. As usual, the reviewers should be exonerated of any responsibility for the final product, however. We acknowledge also the helpful advice of Larry Kimbell and other colleagues on the model presented in chapter 6.

We owe special thanks to Rose Altman who saw this volume through various drafts as efficiently and cheerfully as she did so many other publications over the past 20 years, and to Nancy Kawata for intelligent and careful secretarial work. Both of them prepared the index.

Dan Cole and John E. Marsteller provided significant and continuous research assistance during the study. Bret Bernard, Pamela Hamway, Richard Hogeboom, and Rebecca Lee also contributed to the project at various phases, and we are grateful to all of them.

1 Introduction and Summary

The Setting

The sharp price increase for single-family houses became top news in early 1977, receiving wide and sometimes overdramatic coverage in daily papers, national business and general journals, and other media. Its genesis can be traced to the spring of 1975, however, when house prices in major urban centers of California began to rise at greatly accelerated rates. Since that time price escalation has been experienced in many other areas. The news coverage reflected unusually keen interest of the general public and at the same time served to promote it. House prices became a prominent topic of conversation among actual and would-be homeowners.

The price surge did not constrain the demand for homes. On the contrary, purchases of new houses and transactions in the resale market have increased rapidly since 1975, although activity in some areas, especially in California, began to recede in the second half of 1977. New homebuilding soared. In the fall of 1977, the number of single-family house starts in the United States reached the highest level since 1959 when starts by type of structure were first recorded. Many developers could easily sell their prospective output long before the houses were completed or even before they were started.

In California some of the manifestations of a buying spree at fast-rising prices were quite unusual and seemed to border on hysteria, so they were reported in great detail. "Traffic" on the sites of many new home projects reached unprecedented proportions. In some cases buyers willing to sign a purchase contract and make the requisite deposit lined up in long queues, sometimes camping out overnight. Builders who had advertised their products at fixed prices resorted for a while to lotteries for allocating their limited supply. The case of The Irvine Company's Woodbridge project in Orange County illustrates the frenzy although it cannot be considered typical:

> We opened the first phase of our 10,000 unit Woodbridge Village planned community in the City of Irvine on June 20, 1976. . . . We had only 220 homes available in the first phase, and requests from more than 3,000 families to buy them. In the face of such intensive demand, it was obvious to us that a first-come, first-served sales policy would result in chaos. So we organized public drawings. . . . Some 12,000 people showed up to see who would get those 220 homes. . . . I might note here that the homes sold that day took four years to plan and

1

process through government, four months to build, and four hours to sell.[1]

In the market for existing houses, the time lapse between offer and sale was drastically shortened. The main problem of real-estate brokers became to secure listings rather than to effect sales.

Boom conditions similar to those initially observed in California appeared in an increasing number of other single-family house markets. In the spring of 1978, when sales activity and price increases in California had moderated, buyers were reportedly camping out at the opening of desirable new tracts in the Miami-Fort Lauderdale area. Some builders in Phoenix were selling out homes before they put in streets and curbs. Phoenix, Denver, Minneapolis-St. Paul, and Seattle, which all set records for single-family permits in 1977, reached new peaks in early 1978. Increases in house prices were still accelerating in many areas. Prices were rising at annual rates of 20-25% in Denver and Phoenix and 15-20% in Chicago, Dallas, and Houston.[2]

"Speculation" was soon singled out as the culprit, at least in California where it was most notable. The queues at new home developments were said to include large numbers of buyers who intended to resell rather than occupy the property. Likewise, a substantial portion of transactions in the market for existing residences was claimed to represent speculative purchases for quick sale to owner-users. In both cases the acquisitions rested on the expectation of still higher prices in the near future—a few days or weeks or months. Builders and mortgage lenders proceeded with attempts to curb speculative buying or loans to nonoccupants. The hectic market activity and especially its speculative ingredients caused the Federal Home Loan Bank of San Francisco on April 22, 1977, to raise its interest rates on advances to savings-and-loan associations by a full percentage point and to suspend the variable-rate provisions for long-term advances. The action was designed as a general warning signal and intended specifically to induce greater caution in the lending practices of associations in the bank's district (California, Arizona, and Nevada).[3]

As one would expect, the escalation of home prices evoked calls for government intervention. Concern over ever-increasing numbers of people being priced out of the market, simmering for many years, was becoming acute. "Affordability" appeared with ever greater frequency in the public debate of housing problems.[4] During 1977 bills were introduced in the U.S. Congress to subsidize the purchase of homes by middle-income families. Further, there was growing apprehension that the price bubble would burst, with adverse effects on recent homebuyers, the single-family house market, mortgage lenders and mortgage insurance companies, and indirectly on the general capital market and the economy as a whole. Antispeculation measures were proposed in California.

Purpose and Main Findings of the Study

This study seeks to document and measure the price rise, to indicate its geographic extent beyond California, and, perhaps most important, to attempt to explain it. Explanation would be simple if the price surge was part of general inflation, with house prices moving up more or less apace with other prices. This was not the case. As will be seen, house prices in 1973-1974 when general inflation reached double-digit proportions increased less than the consumer price index (CPI). Paradoxically, it was after the rate of general inflation was moderating that house prices rose faster than the CPI and displayed *their* double-digit escalation. Of course, the 1973-1974 period was marked by a severe business recession and a slump in the demand for single-family houses. The period since 1975 has been one of economic expansion. Yet the dissymmetry in the movement over time of house prices and general prices remains somewhat of a puzzle and calls for extensive investigation.

Another purpose of the analysis is to outline the probable consequences of the price surge for single-family houses. Will the boom be followed by a bust or by smooth transition to price stability? Indications of a softening market in California may signify the "beginning of the end" of price escalation, but what kind of end? At this writing, the market adjustments cannot be foreseen with any degree of certainty. The factors bearing on the outcome can be specified, however, and their analysis allows some admittedly fallible judgment on the outlook.

Some parts of the study focus on California. This emphasis is warranted because the inflation of house prices originated and has been most pronounced in California. Also, price information and related data seem to be more fully developed for major California areas than for regions outside the state. Finally, California was the principal locale of speculation in single-family houses, and as already mentioned, it seems to be the first part of the nation to experience market reactions to the price surge.

Chapter 2 lays the foundation for the analysis by recording and measuring price movements for single-family houses between the late 1960s and 1977. Average prices are reported from a variety of sources for the United States, major census regions, and some local areas. To our knowledge, this represents the most comprehensive price information brought together in one place. Generally, the data show substantial price advances throughout the period and a notable acceleration in 1976-1977. The acceleration began somewhat earlier and was greatest in large metropolitan centers of California, but it was soon noted in many other areas as well. Thus the study deals with a geographically widespread phenomenon, although the timing and the rate of price inflation in the single-family house market have varied from place to place. The chapter includes a comparison of house price changes in the country as a whole with those of other prices, consumer income, homeowner expenses, and rents. The average increase in house prices exceeded the average increase of general consumer prices in the entire period 1968-1977, but the excess over gains in consumer income was confined to 1975-1977.

Chapter 3 turns to the recent homebuyers. Since the price escalation was accompanied by rapid growth of purchases of both existing and new single-family dwellings, there is the obvious question of who could afford to buy? An answer is attempted in light of the income and wealth constraints faced by two broad groups: (1) the owner-buyers who sold their property and acquired another, and (2) the first-time home purchasers. Owner-buyers generally experienced no wealth constraints; they obtained the downpayment for a more expensive house from capital gains on the sale of their previous residence. But the transaction often required that a larger share of income be allocated to current housing outlays. It seems that many owner-buyers were willing to incur larger periodic outlays in the expectation of income increases or of future capital gains from resale. As for first-time buyers, the evidence suggests that their access to the market has not deteriorated as much as the prophets of doom allege, especially when purchases of existing property are considered. Nevertheless, first-time buyers have accounted for a declining share of total purchases in recent years.

The chapter proceeds to investigate the "burden" of downpayment, miscalculated in much of the literature, and the impact of high interest rates on homebuying. When various alternative yardsticks are used to convert nominal to "real" rates, the latter turn out to be moderate or low. Recent home purchasers seem to have developed an instinctual feeling for the interest-rate illusion under inflationary conditions. The notion of repaying debt with cheaper dollars has gained ground. That high nominal rates have not acted as a brake on homebuying in recent years confirms this hypothesis.

Finally, chapter 3 addresses the unusual appearance of speculation in the single-family house market. Speculative activity of any consequence was confined to California and lasted just about a year. It was more of a symptom than a cause of the price surge. The discussion deals with the magnitude of speculation, the efforts of builders and mortgage lenders to restrain it, and the rationale of speculators. As for the impact on the market, the classic argument for speculation as a stabilizing force is shown to be largely inapplicable. The ingredients that generate stabilizing effects in the prototype speculative operations, say, of the commodity, foreign exchange, and securities markets, are lacking in the single-family house market. However, final judgment must be reserved until the current liquidation of speculative holdings has run its course.

In view of the paucity of information on the characteristics, motivations, and expectations of recent homebuyers, a sample survey of 1975 and 1977 purchasers was undertaken for this study in two California counties. The main results are presented in chapter 4. One of the most notable findings is the importance attached by owner-occupant respondents to the investment component of the decision to buy. The single-family dwelling as a hedge against inflation loomed large in the minds of most buyers. The same is true for the anticipation of further price increases, especially by the 1977 purchasers. Many respondents considered the acquisition of a home in either 1975 or 1977 as their "last chance to buy." A high percentage also assigned great importance to the income-tax benefits of homeownership, although such benefits were already available to owner-buyers who represented a large and growing proportion of all buyers. On average, the respondents held high and probably unsustainable expectations of future property appreciation.

The purchasers were typically in their mid-thirties or a little younger, which conforms to the normal pattern. They included an unusually large percentage of households with two breadwinners, however. The typical income of 1977 and 1975 buyers was about the same when adjusted for general inflation. Since house prices in the intervening period moved up more sharply than general prices, the typical price-income ratio for 1977 purchasers exceeded substantially the ratio for 1975 buyers. Further, current housing expenses for the properties acquired in either year averaged considerably more than for the previous residence occupied by the respondents. For that matter, the units bought in either year tended to be superior on several specified criteria.

Chapter 5 focuses on short-run excess of demand over available supply as the cause of the price surge for single-family houses. Excess demand first manifests itself in a decline of unsold homes held by builders and in falling vacancies in the housing stock. Drastic changes of this type occurred before and during the initial phase of price escalation in California, but they were less pronounced in the country as a whole. This helps explain why California led the house price inflation. Turning to the reasons for excess demand, the chapter distinguishes between "normal" market factors considered in conventional analysis and the emergence of inflationary expectations among homebuyers as an additional cause of the boom in purchases and prices. A review of conventional variables suggests that they provide an insufficient explanation of the house price surge of 1975-1977. Demographic changes favored the demand for homes for some time before 1975. At best, one can speculate that demographic forces were subdued during the recession of 1973-1974 and were reactivated in the subsequent recovery, with the combination of pent-up and current demand generating unusual pressures on the inelastic short-run supply. Gains in consumer income since 1975 have been on a par with those in previous periods of economic expansion. While home mortgage funds were plentiful until late 1977, there was no decline in the cost of borrowing, measured by a newly devised composite index that takes account of non-interest loan terms as well as interest rates. The increasing regulatory constraints on homebuilding in many areas had probably a minor impact on the volume of new supply, although they will become a more serious obstacle in the future. This judgment is consistent with the fact that the 1975-1977 rate of expansion in single-family house starts compares well with the rate observed in previous upswings. The cost of additional regulations may have contributed to builders' shifts to higher priced homes, but the evidence on this point is not strong.

One of the conventional variables favoring the demand for homes was influenced by special circumstances in the 1975-1977 period. The growing labor force participation of females, a long-term trend, became a potent market force when legislation adopted in 1974 and 1975 required mortgage lenders to cease their previous practice of discounting the income of females including married women. Even if one allows for some dilution of the new rules in the marketplace, the legislation meant that additional families could meet the income standards for home-purchase loans or qualify for larger loans that enabled them to buy more expensive houses. Households with two earners have indeed accounted for a rapidly growing proportion of recent home purchasers. Two additional changes affected California: the renewed increase of in-migration and some stretching of mortgage loan terms.

Nevertheless, there remains a strong presumption that inflationary expectations played a significant role in the homebuying spree and the attendant price escalation. The national consumer polls of the Michigan Survey Research Center and the local surveys discussed in chapter 4 lend considerable support to this hypothesis. Among the two principal components of the decision to acquire a house or a more expensive dwelling for owner-occupancy—the desire to obtain superior housing services and the desire to make a "good investment"—the latter has become increasingly important in recent years. This change has paralleled the public's general search for "inflation-proof" investments as fears of inflation persisted. In comparison with other investments accessible to the broad public, the 1968-1977 record of the single-family house as an asset with steady appreciation potentials is indeed impressive. The nationwide phenomenon of inflationary expectations in the past few years interacted with diverse conditions in local markets in such fashion as to generate different rates of advance in house prices in various areas. In other words, there is no contradiction between the expectations hypothesis and locally differentiated price movements.

To supplement the foregoing investigation of forces bearing on the price surge, chapter 6 adds a quantitative analysis. The chapter develops and tests a national model of home prices and price changes from 1968 to 1977. The findings affirm that prices and their movements have been significantly associated with demand factors. Permanent income and the increase in the general price level are prominent variables explaining home prices and their rates of change. In addition, the model identifies the persistent influence of seasonal factors on prices of single-family dwellings. Direct measures of inflationary expectations, which are difficult to quantify, have low explanatory power, but recent rates of home price changes have a strong influence on current rates of change. Also the combined price of new and existing homes is directly related to the CPI minus its shelter component, lagged by one quarter. These findings suggest that substantial and broadly sustained price increases were generating expectations of further house price escalation. On the supply side, the relative ease of mortgage credit had an effect on house prices in one version of the model. The stock of occupied homes, on the other hand, was not significantly related to prices or price changes. This result may reflect the short-run inelasticity of supply or technical difficulties in quantifying the stock variable.

Chapter 7 deals with the probable market adjustments to the recent boom in home purchases and prices, already noticeable in California where the volume of transactions and the rate of price increase have been slowing down since mid-1977. The analysis considers first the forces operating within the single-family house market itself. One factor concerns the actions of builders. Will they repeat their historical performance of overshooting the market and thereby add to competitive downward pressures on prices? Another factor in the outlook is the tightening of home mortgage credit since late 1977. Further, one must expect some distress sales by recent homebuyers for owner-occupancy who have overextended themselves. Likewise, liquidations by speculators caught at the end of the line and unable or unwilling to extend their holding period will have a dampening effect on prices in California. To the extent that inflationary expectations caused anticipatory homebuying by owner-occupants, future demand will be lessened. Moreover, purchases of previous homeowners, which were the main support of the new-home market in the past few years, are unlikely to continue at recent rates. First-time buyers can fill the gap only if builders are able to adjust the product and price mix to their needs.

The adverse effects of these forces, however, will be mitigated by continued strength of the underlying demand for single-family dwellings, which comes from demographic factors and a further beneficial impact on the market of the upward trend of families with two earners. Also even those recent homebuyers who find their current housing outlays untenable have to protect their usually subtantial downpayments and will therefore sell rather than "walk away" from their properties. Finally, the market adjustments are likely to occur in local succession rather than simultaneously, following the pattern of the boom itself.

The outlook for the single-family house market depends also on external circumstances, especially on general economic conditions and the rate of general inflation in the near future. Taking account of the possibility of continued expansion or a recession, and after examining previous boom-bust experience in the residential markets of three local areas, we conclude that the adjustment problems following the recent escalation of house prices will be of moderate proportions. Their severity will range between a "hard landing" and the "soft landing," which the vast majority of practitioners seem to expect. In any event, however, the adjustment process will take considerable time. A major market imbalance of the type that generated the recent surge of house prices is hardly ever followed smoothly by equilibrium. More often than not, a disequilibrium leads to another before market balance is achieved. This does not necessarily mean a fall in *average* house prices but may involve a more moderate rate of increase accompanied by actual price declines from the 1976-1977 level for individual properties or small neighborhoods.

Price inflation for any kind of asset is associated with redistribution of wealth. The concluding part of chapter 7 seeks to identify the groups that have benefited from the recent surge of house prices and those that have become its victims.

The final chapter reviews public policy issues that have surfaced in the wake of the house price inflation. Attempts in California to impose an antispeculation tax on various classes of real estate have been abortive but may yet be revived. In the context of this study, the discussion is confined to a special capital-gains tax on short-term holdings of single-family houses, and its merits appear highly dubious. Another issue, the speculative purchase and sale of homes by real-estate brokers and their personnel in California, seems adequately covered by existing regulation. However, the authorities could have allayed public impressions of wrongdoing by broader dissemination of the rules when speculation was in its heydays. The critical problem of reduced access of moderate-income people and especially young families to homeownership has triggered two types of policy proposals: (1) official sanction of alternative mortgage payment plans that reduce the borrowers' initial monthly outlays and increase the later payments to remove the "deficit," notably the graduated payment program; and (2) expanded federal subsidies to specified groups of homebuyers or income tax benefits for savings accumulated for downpayments, possibly combined with the first proposal. These proposals suffer from several debilities. Among others lower initial mortgage payments would reduce lenders' cash flows and therefore their lending capacity. Expanded subsidies to moderate-income people raise serious questions about social priorities at a time when federal housing aid to the poor is highly disproportionate to the need. Further, should the proposed measures be adopted and used on any significant scale, their effects on the demand for homes could add to future inflationary pressures on house prices and cancel some if not most of the intended benefits.

Improved access to homeownership of moderate-income groups, especially first-time buyers, calls for more fundamental policy changes that deal with the causes of the problem rather than its symptoms. One of the required changes is a more effective and sustained containment of general inflation. As was shown, widespread inflationary expectations have contributed to the escalation of house prices. While the previously discussed market adjustments will dampen these expectations, failure to demonstrate the nation's capacity to reduce inflationary pressures may well generate another round of sharp house price increases. For that matter, the longer inflation above the "tolerable" level of 2 or 3% a year persists, the greater the danger that consumers as well as other decision units will seek investments held to protect them against it—if not single-family houses, then other assets. Such shifts could generate sizeable distortions and inefficiencies of our economic system. Another major policy change requires a revision of the costly additional restrictions on homebuilding that were imposed in recent years at the local level. As usual, when a new policy objective supported by a popular movement appears on the scene, the pendulum in favor of environmental concerns has swung too far. A better balance is needed between environmental and housing desiderata. The interests of those parts of the public that benefit from constraints on new construction, usually the "haves," must be reconciled with the interests of others who carry the burden by being unable to buy homes they can afford, typically the "have-nots."

This study, written while the price surge for single-family houses was continuing in many parts of the country and accelerating in some, can offer only a preliminary appraisal of its dimension and its probable aftermath. A final assessment turns on the future course of general inflation. If economic policy succeeds in bringing about a substantial and sustained reduction in the rate of overall price increases, the recent experience in the house market will appear as an episode. Even so the ratchet effects of the price escalation are likely to leave a lasting imprint on the level of home prices. If there is a resurgence of inflation and the public's concern over the possibility of its containment gathers fresh momentum, the belief of large groups of consumers in the single-family house as the most suitable and accessible hedge against erosion of the dollar's purchasing power will be reinforced. Under this condition, disproportionate price increases for homes are in danger of becoming a more continuous feature of the market. Income and wealth constraints or a greater response of homebuilding to the demand pressure will ultimately put an end to the spiral, but market adjustments will become more painful when inflation is eventually brought under control. An alternative though perhaps less likely scenario is a persistent acceleration of general inflation, in the pattern observed in some foreign countries. This course of events would entail such massive change of the nation's socioeconomic fabric that its effects on the single-family house market defy projection.

Notes

1. Testimony by Frank E. Hughes, Vice President, Residential Division, The Irvine Company, before the Homeownership Task Force of the U.S. House of Representatives, Long Beach, California, January 17, 1978.

2. *U.S. Housing Markets*, issued by Advance Mortgage Corporation and Citicorp Real Estate, Inc., May 19, 1978.

3. For the bank's action, see its Bulletin No. 95 to the district associations. For an authoritative interpretation, see the interview with Maurice Mann,

president of the Federal Home Loan Bank of San Francisco, in *National Thrift News*, May 12, 1977, and Dr. Mann's remarks at the Quarterly UCLA Business Forecast Update Conference, Los Angeles, June 16, 1977, entitled "The California Housing Boom—Where Is It Going?" In response to some moderation of the boom, the bank reduced its rates by 25 basis points on July 22, 1977. Subsequent rate changes were related to general money market conditions.

4. For examples, see use of this term in the text of U.S. Congressional Budget Office, *Home Ownership: The Changing Relationship of Costs and Incomes, and Possible Federal Roles* (January 1977); John C. Weicher, "The Affordability of New Houses," *Journal of the American Real Estate and Urban Economics Association,* Summer 1977; and "The Controversy over Homeownership Affordability," *Journal of the American Real Estate and Urban Economic Association,* Fall 1977. For further references to the literature on affordability and a comprehensive discussion, see also Donald M. Kaplan, "Homeownership Affordability: A Summary of the Issues and A Point of View," paper presented in *The Cost of Housing*, Proceedings of The Third Annual Conference of the Federal Home Loan Bank of San Francisco, December 7, 1977. Another contribution by Craig Swan, entitled "The Affordability of Unaffordable Housing," is awaiting publication. The most extensive and highly critical study of the subject appears in John C. Weicher, "New Home Affordability, Equity, and Housing Market Behavior," scheduled for a forthcoming issue of the *Journal of the American Real Estate and Urban Economics Association.* One of the author's main points is that measures of affordability have concentrated on income and ignore wealth. If the latter is taken into consideration, the level of affordability is raised substantially, and the results conform more closely to the actual market behavior of households.

2 The Upward Thrust of Prices

Although this study focuses on house prices in 1974-1977, the data in this chapter extend back to the late 1960s or early 1970s, depending on their availability or relevance. Obviously, the price movements between 1974 and 1977 cannot be properly assessed without reference to earlier price changes. The background of these changes will serve to clarify what chapter 1 described as a "surge" or an "escalation" of prices. Average prices of both new and old single-family houses have tended to increase ever since World War II, at varying rates and with some usually short interruptions, as did those for most goods and services. To what extent does the recent period distinguish itself from earlier experience? To clarify this question, *price escalation* may be defined alternatively as (1) an acceleration of rates of increase over those recorded in previous years and (2) a sustained excess of the rate of house price advances over gains in consumer income or the rise in the consumer price index (CPI).

Methodological Problems

The definition of the product is quite straightforward. The data reported here cover detached as well as attached residences (including so-called townhouses), but only those with one dwelling unit in the structure. Although it has become customary to consider mobile homes in statistics on housing starts or the total housing supply, they are not included in the price data. As an aside, it may be noted that the price surge for conventional houses since 1975 has not been accompanied by an expansionary trend of mobile home shipments. In other words, consumers did not turn increasingly to the "lower priced" product as a substitute for the regular house.[1]

Beyond the general product definition, the measurement of home prices poses numerous problems. There is no single, authoritative price index like the consumer or the wholesale price index (WPI) for a fixed market basket or a fixed group of commodities, with components weighted according to their importance in the total dollar volume of purchases or transactions. Hence this chapter draws on a great many different sources using different methods for the compilation of house prices nationally and locally. The problem is also complicated by the extreme heterogeneity of the product. Apart from the distinction between new and existing homes, the properties may range from small and moderately equipped if not substandard homes in poor locations to the modern equivalent of mansions on sites of several acres. The "product mix" may change from year to year in terms of the average size of lots, the average floor area of the structure, the number of bedrooms and baths, and the internal home equipment. Such changes may be the function of shifting consumer preferences, family budget constraints under varying economic conditions, builders' notions of what kinds of new houses will yield quick sales, and lenders' judgments concerning desired property and borrower characteristics. The increasing proportion of townhouses in the mix of newly constructed homes during recent years illustrates the impact of product shifts on average prices. Price movements from year to year may also reflect concessions by sellers in periods of economic recession. Finally, the reported data are affected by changes over time in the locational pattern of home purchases. The mix of transactions responds to interregional migrations and the growth or decline of urban areas and subareas.

The ideal basis for price measurement may be a standard house. We shall present data for *new* homes approximating this ideal. Even so, homebuyers' preferences change quite rapidly from period to period, and the standard house of, say, 1967, may become quite unimportant in the market mix of 1976. In any event, the standard house concept is difficult to apply to existing residences, which constitute a market far exceeding the number and dollar volume of new houses. Analysts have constructed "hedonic" house price indexes for local areas, which are designed to measure prices and price changes abstracting from product variations. Further research along this line is desirable but faces conceptual and statistical problems.[2]

Most of the data in this chapter are based on actual transactions. In these cases, price movements reflect changes in the product and location mix as well as the many demand and supply factors that produce "pure" price changes. Despite the methodological deficiency, however, there is considerable merit in tracing price movements for the properties people were actually buying over the years. Other, locally generated data come from periodic surveys of a fixed sample of used homes by experienced appraisers, regardless of whether they change hands but taking known transaction prices for similar houses in similar locations into account. This method minimizes the problem of changes in product mix, but the results depend on the accuracy of appraisals. Besides, price series derived from a fixed sample of resale homes may be flawed by capital improvements between survey dates such as additions of rooms or garages or modernized kitchens on the one hand, and by the possibility of neighborhood or property obsolescence on the other. This is true for any group of older dwellings irrespective of whether price reports are based on transactions or appraisal surveys.

In sum, price aggregations for any number of homes suffer from the familiar index problems, and the resulting defects are probably more severe than those for older, more established price indexes that have benefited from sophisticated statistical work performed over several decades. Hence the reader will find that some of the house price series coming from different sources show varying rates of change in the same area and for the same period. The discrepancies can often but not always be explained by market segmentation. Thus data drawn from

FHA reports pertain to homes at the lower end of the price spectrum while the price statistics of the Federal Home Loan Bank Board relate to transactions financed with conventional home loans and include a much larger portion of the spectrum. On the whole, however, we believe that the quality differentials between house price and other price data can easily be overdrawn. Researchers are more aware of statistical weaknesses in their area of concentration than of those in other areas. The continuous clamor for improvement of the older, well-recognized price indexes testifies to *their* persistent problems. Thus the U.S. Bureau of Labor Statistics is begining to issue CPIs for urban consumers as a group to supplement the previous indexes that are confined to a "market basket" for wage earners and clerical workers.

Finally, price aggregations can be expressed in terms of average (mean) or median. The level of mean prices tends to exceed the level of median prices, but there is no such systematic tendency for percentage changes from one period to another. Mean prices are presented throughout this chapter for the reason that some of the important sources do not report medians. For the measurement of price changes we use compound rather than arithmetic rates when comparisons extend over several years such as 1974-1976 as against earlier groups of years. The analysis in this chapter focuses on price *changes*. The underlying price statistics are in appendix A.

List of Price Data

The analysis begins with aggregate price data for the *United States*, using the following sources:

New houses: U.S. Department of Commerce (Census Bureau) for homes sold by merchant builders; Federal Home Loan Bank Board (FHLBB) for homes financed with conventional loans made by major types of lenders; Federal Housing Administration (FHA) for homes financed with insured loans under Section 203b, which excludes houses built under various subsidy programs administered by the agency.

Existing or resale houses: National Association of Realtors; FHLBB and FHA, as described previously.

The U.S. analysis is followed by data for four major census *regions*: the Northeast, North Central, the South, and the West.[a]

The chapter proceeds to *local area* statistics as follows:

---

[a]FHA statistics are available for individual states. They are not included here because FHA operates in a limited segment of the market, no supplemental data for other market segments are available for states, and it was held desirable to keep the materials within manageable proportions. For similar reasons and because of the small number of FHA insurance cases in many metropolitan areas, no local FHA data are presented.

Eighteen metropolitan areas throughout the nation, for which FHLBB price data on new and resale homes are available: These include the Los Angeles and San Francisco Bay areas. The area coverage was recently expanded, but the additional data allow no comparison with previous periods and are therefore omitted.

Locally generated price data for existing houses, covering several counties in southern California and in the San Francisco Bay area, Sacramento, Montgomery County (Maryland), and Seattle: Separate price information is presented for the city of Los Angeles.

The local price data are supplemented for recent periods by information obtained from the area underwriters of two mortgage insurance companies. The reports reflect judgments of underwriters intimately familiar with developments in their jurisdiction rather than an independent set of statistics. They are used to fill gaps in available area data and to trace more fully the geographic spread of major price increases and their sequence over time.

Nationwide Price Movements

The first three charts show indexes of house prices since 1968 which serves as a base year. No matter which one of the several series is considered, there is a clear upward movement throughout the period, sporadically interrupted by small declines. As is evident from figure 2-1, the trend holds for new houses regardless of whether one uses the yardstick of prices of homes actually sold each year or the prices of the nearest equivalent of a standard house (the kinds of houses sold in 1967).[3] In the 1968-1977 period as a whole, the price rise for existing property has been more steady and somewhat greater than that for new houses. Between the base year and 1977, average resale prices advanced from $22,300 to $47,900, or by 115%, as against $26,600 to $54,200, or 104%, for new homes actually sold. The ratio of existing to new home prices, .83 at the beginning of the period, approximated .88 at the end, though it varied in the intervening years. To some extent, the greater increase for existing property may reflect the fact that the stock of houses becoming available for sale over a 10-year period includes larger numbers of recently built and therefore relatively expensive houses while losses from the stock are probably concentrated among homes at the lower end of the price spectrum.

But the most significant observation drawn from figure 2-1 is the recent acceleration of house prices. In 1976 average prices for existing homes rose by a little over 8%, within the range of immediately preceding annual rates of change. In 1977 the price increase reached double-digit proportions—11.3%. For new houses actually sold, there was an acceleration from 9.5% in 1975 to nearly 13% in 1976 and another 13% a year later. The price escalation is all the more remarkable since it occurred in a period of reduced general inflation compared with the 1973-1974 experience.

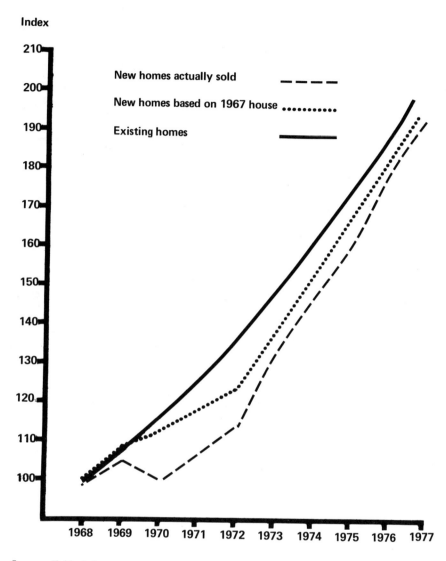

Source: Table A-1.

Figure 2-1. Average Prices of New Homes Sold by Builders and of Existing Homes, 1968-1977 (1968=100)

The 1970 decline in the series for new homes actually sold warrants brief comment because the unusual phenomenon of price reduction for newly constructed houses in one year has become a matter of controversy in the debate about "affordability." Some analysts who assert a growing disproportion between house prices and income have developed their argument from statistics based on 1970 as a benchmark year. The price decline was occasioned by the fairly large volume of home sales under FHA subsidy programs, mainly under Section 235, which were enacted in 1968 but became effective in subsequent years, reaching a peak in 1970 and being suspended in January 1973. If the relatively low price of 1970 is used as a base, price increases in later years are overstated. Thus the 1970-1972 data in figure 2-1 for actual sales of new homes are flawed by the influence of the subsidy programs. Interestingly, the price gyrations of 1968-1970 in this series do not appear in the statistics for the new dwelling of the 1967 kind nor in those for resale units.

The data in figure 2-2 portray price movements of single-family houses financed with conventional mortgages written by major types of lenders. Here recent annual rates of increase have substantially exceeded those of 1970-1972, the preceding period of a booming housing market. For existing houses, they were 10-11% in 1974 and 1975, fell back to 8% in 1976, and reached 11.5% in 1977. Prices for new houses rose by 8% in 1974, over 11% in 1975, more than 8% in 1976, and 12% the next year.[b] In the 1968-1977 period as a whole, the price increase for existing property (85.5%) again exceeded that for new residences (76.9%). The ratio of existing to new home prices, .83 at the beginning of the period, was .87 at the end, a change quite similar to the ratios derived earlier from two independent sources. Here again, however, the ratio did not move up steadily. An analysis of possible cyclical variations in the price relationship between old and new houses is beyond the purview of this study.

Figure 2-3 turns to FHA-financed transactions under Section 203b. These represent a lower price segment of the market. In 1977, for example, the FHA sales price for existing homes averaged $28,900 as against $47,500 for conventionally financed property. Similar differentials obtained throughout the period for both new and resale homes. As the chart indicates, a notable price escalation for FHA-financed single-family houses as early as 1974 and 1975 was followed by a more moderate price increase. This is at variance with the evidence in figures 2-1 and 2-2 and may be explained by belated legislative adjustments of FHA mortgage ceilings[c] coupled with the agency's reluctance to recognize the recent rise of house prices in its rather conservative underwriting practice. Over the 1968-1977 period as a whole, average FHA prices for existing homes, the bulk of the agency's activity, have advanced from $16,200 to $28,900, or by 78%. This was a lower rate of increase than that reported in the previous statistics. Average prices for new houses rose from $19,700 in 1968 to $36,800 in 1977, or by 86.8%. During the period, FHA's share of the total market has declined, and it was quite small in recent years.[4]

---

[b]The 1973 decline visible in figure 2-2 for both new and existing homes and the sharp increases in 1974 and 1975 are probably in part attributable to a revision in the FHLBB series. Among other things, the coverage of reporting lending institutions was broadened to include a larger number of small lenders located outside major metropolitan areas. As a consequence, the data for 1973 and later years give greater weight to such lenders than the pre-1973 figures. The revision should not affect the price changes between 1974 and subsequent periods, however.

[c]For example, it was only in 1977 that the mortgage ceiling of $45,000 was raised to $60,000. At the same time downpayment requirements were lowered. The changes were made in the Housing and Community Development Act of 1977.

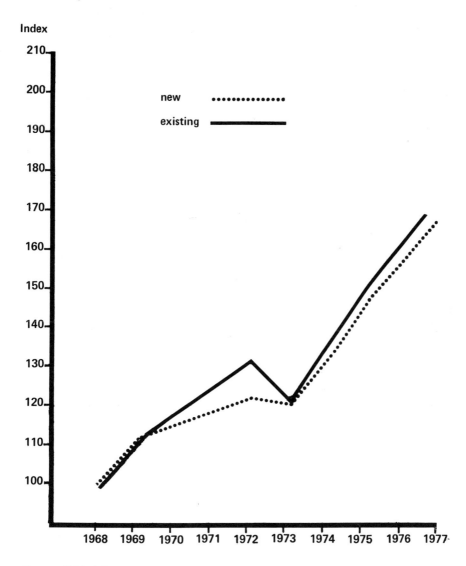

Figure 2-2. Average Prices of New and Existing Homes Reported for Transactions Financed with Conventional Mortgage Loans, 1968-1977
(1968 = 100)

In the case of FHA, data are available on changes in some important
characteristics of homes having a bearing on house prices. The most significant
of these are the FHA-estimated market prices of sites, the lot size, and the
average price of sites per square foot of lot. The latter are shown in figure 2-4;
the underlying figures are given in appendix table A-2 together with other

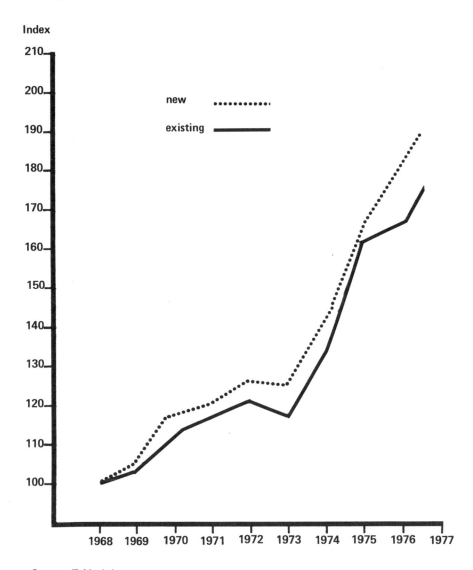

Source: Table A-1.
Figure 2-3. Average Prices for New and Existing Homes Financed with FHA-
Insured Mortgages, 1968-1977 (1968 = 100)

characteristics of FHA-financed homes.[5] The chart portrays the much discussed
increase in the unit price of sites. Between 1974 and 1977, it rose by 25% for
both new and existing houses. The increase since 1968 was 100% for new and
81.6% for old property. As is evident from table A-2, the average lot size of new
homes declined from about 9,600 sq. ft. in 1969 to less than 7,500 sq. ft. in
1974 and rose again to 8,100 sq. ft. thereafter. The lot size of existing homes

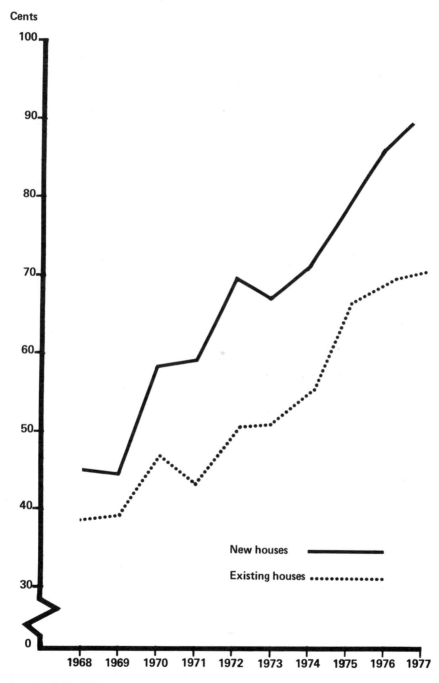

Source: Table A-2.

Figure 2-4. FHA-Estimated Market Price of Sites per Square Foot of Lot, 1968-1977

shows also a decline from 1969 to 1973 and a subsequent increase without regaining the level of the late 1960s. As for other characteristics, the improved floor area of new FHA-financed houses moved up from about 1,200 sq. ft. in the initial period to more than 1,300 sq. ft. in recent years, but it changed little for existing property. Still more remarkable is the fact that of late about 60% of the new homes had central air conditioning as against 23% in 1968. This statistic and larger floor areas indicate product improvement even in the lower price segment of the market for new houses while smaller lots for both new and old property signify greater density, that is, a decline in quality.

Table 2-1 summarizes the price data for all the nationwide series. All series except FHA show annual double-digit rates of increase in 1975-1977. Four of the seven series exhibit such rates for 1974-1976, and only one for 1972-1974. Excepting again FHA, these are clear indications of an accelerated price rise in 1975-1977 over 1974-1976 for both new and existing properties. In the 1968-1977 period as a whole, prices increased at average annual rates of about 6-9%, depending on which one of the series is considered. Average rates per year in the 1970-1976 period were in about the same range, except for prices of new homes sold by builders (Commerce Department). In this case, the price rise computed from the 1970 base exceeded that calculated from the 1968 base by a considerable margin, confirming the previously mentioned distortion that results from the relatively low 1970 value in this particular series.

Has the rising trend of house prices been out of line with the movement of

Table 2-1
Annual Rates of House Price Increases in Selected Periods, United States, 1968-1977
(compound rates)

| | New Houses | | | | Existing Houses | | |
| | Commerce Department | | | | | | |
Periods	Current Houses	1967 House	FHLBB	FHA	NAR[a]	FHLBB	FHA
1968-1970	b	5.6%	7.5%	8.5%	7.4%	8.3%	6.0%
1970-1972	7.1%	5.6	2.5	3.3	8.2	5.5	3.7
1972-1974	12.9	9.9	3.7c	5.8	9.1	1.9c	5.1
1974-1976	11.1	10.0	9.9	13.0	8.6	9.1	11.5
1975-1977	12.8	11.2	10.3	6.4	10.8	11.5	5.0
1968-1977	8.2	8.3	6.5	7.2	8.9	7.1	6.6
1970-1977	10.7	9.0	6.3	6.8	9.3	6.8	6.8

Source: Appendix table A-1.

[a]National Association of Realtors.

[b]The rate was zero, with prices averaging $26,600 in both 1968 and 1970. The 1969 figure was $27,900. The statistical fluke of identical prices in 1968 and 1970 is discussed in the text.

[c]Influenced by revision of the series in 1973; see note b on page 16.

general prices, the housing component of the CPI, and measures of consumer income? Table 2-2 presents data relevant to this question. It is not our intent, however, to join in the already extensive debate over the issue of homeownership affordability (see chapter 1).

Since the seven series on house prices in table 2-1 themselves vary, two have been selected for comparison: prices for new homes of the 1967 kind and those for existing homes reported by the National Association of Realtors.d To facilitate analysis, item 3 in table 2-2 shows weighted average price increases for

Table 2-2
House Price Increases Compared with Increases of Other Prices and
Income, United States, 1968-1977
(compound annual rates)

Item	1968-1977	1968-1970	1970-1972	1972-1974	1974-1976	1975-1977
1. New houses (1967 kind)	8.3%	5.6%	5.6%	9.9%	10.0%	11.1%
2. Existing houses (NAR)	8.9	7.4	8.2	9.1	8.6	10.8
3. Weighted average for (1) and (2)a	8.7	6.9	7.6	9.3	8.9	10.9
4. CPIb	6.4	5.6	3.8	8.6	7.4	6.1
5. GNP deflatorc	6.2	5.2	4.6	7.9	7.2	5.4
6. Housing component of CPId	6.9	6.8	4.2	8.0	8.5	
a. Rent	4.6	3.7	4.1	4.7	5.3	5.7
b. Homeowner expenses	7.6	10.3	4.4	7.9	8.4	6.2
7. Disposable personal income	9.2	8.1	8.5	10.7	9.4	9.9
8. Same, per capita	8.3	6.9	7.1	10.0	8.9	9.0

Sources: Appendix table A-1 for items (1) and (2); U.S. Bureau of Labor Statistics for (4) and (6); and U.S. Department of Commerce for (5), (7), and (8).

aRates of price increases for new and existing houses were averaged for each period by using weights for each type derived from the directly reported dollar volume of existing home sales and the computed dollar volume of new home sales (number of homes times average sales price). The weights for existing houses are 78 for 1968-1977, 75 for 1968-1970, 76 for 1970-1972, 78 for 1972-1974, 81 for 1974-1976, and 80 for 1975-1977. The weights for new homes are the reciprocals of these numbers.

bAll items including the housing component, shown separately under (6). The weight of the housing component in the total CPI has increased in recent years. Computed from "old" CPI.

cThe GNP deflator is a broader measure of price changes than the CPI. It reflects price movements for investment goods, export and import goods and services, and government purchases of goods and services, as well as those for consumption.

dTotal housing component including rent, homeownership expenses, fuel and utilities, and household furnishings and operation.

---

dPrices for new homes of the 1967 kind were selected for this analysis because they minimize the problems of changes in the product mix and because of the statistical fluke of a zero price increase between 1968 and 1970 for houses actually sold in these two years. The NAR data for existing homes, covering the entire universe of the used-house market, should be less affected by product mix than are the other series on existing property or those for new houses.

new and old residences combined, and this item will be used in the following discussion.

The rate of house price increases in 1974-1976 was well in line with the rate of income gains (items 7 and 8), but it exceeded the latter in 1975-1977. In each of the previous biannual groups of years, house prices rose less than DPI, a finding that warrants emphasis when the recent adverse relationship is considered. In the 1968-1977 period as a whole, house prices advanced at a somewhat lower rate than DPI but at a slightly higher rate than per-capita DPI. In sum, if house price escalation is defined as a rate of increase in excess of consumer income gains, it emerges as a phenomenon limited to 1975-1977.

Comparison of the movements of house prices and general consumer prices (CPI) yields quite different results. The former increased at a higher rate than consumer prices in all the periods under review (item 4). The excess of house price increase over CPI was especially great in 1975-1977 when the average rate of general inflation was declining. The price escalation for single-family homes occurred in the face of moderating general inflation. The divergence of house price and overall price increases is even greater when the latter are expressed by the GNP deflator, a more general measure of price movements than the CPI. One can speak of a surge in house prices on the ground that the price advance for residences has exceeded the advance of overall prices.

Throughout, house prices have also risen more sharply than consumers' current housing outlays, measured by the housing component of the CPI (item 6). This is true not only for rent, which has moved up at moderate rates, but also for homeowner expenses, except for the 1968-1970 period. Among other things, homeowner expenses reflect higher purchase prices through larger mortgage amounts and debt service payments for new homeowners. However, expenses of existing homeowners weigh heavily in the index. Among these expenses, fuel, gas, and electricity have shown by far the greatest rate of increase—60% between 1972 and 1976.

Homeowner expenses, in turn, have not risen faster than disposable personal income. In all subperiods except 1968-1970 as well as for the entire 1968-1976 period, DPI increased at a rate exceeding that of homeownership outlays. This relationship prevailed also between 1950 and 1965,[6] and its continuance in the face of recently accelerated advances in house prices warrants notice.

Considering just the period of house price escalation from 1974 to 1977, there has been a remarkable divergence between the rise in rents on the one hand and in homeowner expenses and house prices on the other. Rents increased by 17.5%, homeowner expenses by 25.5%, and house prices, weighted as in item 3 of table 2-2, by 34.3%. Yet the unfavorable relationship between the rise of house prices or homeowner outlays and rents did not deter home purchase at a fast growing rate. Data on homeownership and rental vacancies, presented in later chapters, indicate no sizeable shift away from the tenure that was becoming more expensive relative to renting. Our subsequent analysis will, among other things, deal with the hypothesis that investment considerations fueled by persistent house price increases and inflationary expectations have been among the factors explaining consumers' preference for the "superior good" of the owner-occupied house, even in the face of relatively low rents.

Regional Price Movements

The geographic disaggregation of house price changes begins with the four major regions of the nation as defined by the U.S. Bureau of the Census. In terms of housing market activity, the West[e] is dominated by California. As is evident from table 2-3, the West has led the other regions in the average rate of price increase for new dwellings since 1972-1974. For new houses of the 1967 kind, the West is the only region to show an annual double-digit rate (12%) in 1972-1974, which accelerated to 13.5% in 1974-1976 and 16.3% in 1975-1977.

Table 2-3
Annual Rates of House Price Increases in Four Major Census Regions and the United States, 1968-1976
(compound rates)

Period	Northeast	North Central	South	West	United States
New Homes (1967 House)					
1968-1970	7.1%	4.8%	5.9%	5.4%	5.6%
1970-1972	7.6	4.4	6.0	4.5	5.6
1972-1974	8.0	9.0	8.5	12.0	9.9
1974-1976	7.5	10.1	7.9	13.5	10.0
1975-1977	5.7	10.1	8.8	16.3	11.2
1968-1977	7.4	7.5	7.3	10.0	8.3
1970-1977	7.4	8.3	7.6	11.3	9.0
Existing Homes					
1968-1970	8.3%	6.6%	7.2%	4.3%	7.4%
1970-1972	8.8	6.6	9.1	8.6	8.2
1972-1974	8.7	9.1	9.7	9.9	9.1
1974-1976	7.5	8.3	6.3	13.6	8.6
1975-1977	6.1	10.2	7.7	19.7	10.8
1968-1977	8.1	8.1	8.3	10.8	8.9
1970-1977	8.1	8.6	8.6	12.7	9.3

Sources: U.S. Department of Commerce for new homes, National Association of Realtors for existing homes.

---

[e]In addition to California, the West includes Arizona, Colorado, Hawaii, Idaho, New Mexico, Montana, Nevada, Oregon, Utah, Washington, and Wyoming.

The average annual price rise in the South and the North Central region was more moderate during recent periods, yet reached nearly 9% in the former and slightly more than 10% in the latter during 1975-1977. The Northeast, in contrast, recorded a deceleration of price increases since 1972-1974. Over the longer span of years, 1968-1977 and 1970-1977, the West also shows the highest average rate of price advance, of the double-digit variety. The rates for all other regions range between 7% and 8%, still a substantial increase per year. In this long-term computation, the recent deceleration of price rises in the Northeast is offset by high rates in the late 1960s and the first half of the 1970s.

A similar pattern holds for existing dwellings. Here the price increase in the West clearly outpaced the other regions in 1974-1976 and in 1975-1977, with an average annual rate of nearly 14% and almost 20%, respectively. The price rise in the South and North Central region from 1974-1976 to 1975-1977 was again more moderate. Here too the Northeast shows declining rates of price advances since 1972-1974, probably reflecting its slower demographic and economic growth relative to the rest of the nation. Once more, the West ranks first in the rate of price increase over the longer periods of 1968-1976 or 1970-1976.

Thus there have been substantial regional variations in the extent of house price inflation, as one would expect. The forces accounting for regional differences will be sketched in the discussion of variations in local price changes where they appear even more strongly, reflecting the localism of housing consumption markets.

Unfortunately, the data available for California do not lend themselves to analysis. Since July 1975, the California Association of Realtors has released monthly figures on sales and prices of existing houses in the state. Apart from the relatively short period covered, the data are subject to large sample variations. The number of reporting local Real Estate Boards has ranged from 23 to 34 for each month through 1977 and has generally declined from the initial to the later period. The FHA's state series of prices covers only the low-price part of the market and is subject to other qualifications already mentioned in the discussion of nationwide movements of house prices. Besides, FHA plays an even more marginal role in California than elsewhere, reflecting the great strength of savings-and-loan associations in the state and their concentration on conventional lending.

Price Changes in Local Areas

The richest source of home purchase prices in metropolitan areas is the Federal Home Loan Bank Board, which includes average prices in its periodic reports on terms of conventional home mortgage loans made by all major types of lenders. The local data cover 18 metropoles in all parts of the country. To simplify and structure the mass of figures, table 2-4 presents average annual rates of price change for 1974-1976, classifies the areas by the rate of increase in this period,

Table 2-4
Percent Changes in Average Purchase Prices of New and Existing
Homes Financed with Conventional Mortgage Loans, 18 Metropolitan
Areas, 1974-1976 and 1976-1977

Area[a]	Percent Increase per Year, 1974-1976[b]		Percent Change 1976-1977	
	New	Existing	New	Existing
A. *Average Annual Increase of 10% or More for Both New and Existing Homes in 1974-1976*				
Denver-Boulder SMSA	13.2	11.8	22.0	14.0
Los Angeles-Long Beach-Anaheim SCSA	12.8	20.2	10.0	18.0
San Francisco-Oakland-San Jose SCSA	16.0	12.2	16.2	18.1
B. *Average Annual Increase of 10% or More for Either New or Existing Homes in 1974-1976*				
Baltimore SMSA	15.8	3.6	0.0	14.0
Cleveland-Akron-Lorain SCSA	12.9	7.7	14.6	6.2
Dallas-Fort Worth SMSA	7.7	10.4	5.8	−1.8
Houston-Galveston SMSA	11.4	1.6	7.3	6.3
Miami-Fort Lauderdale SMSA	16.5	7.1	−15.6	3.2
Minneapolis-St. Paul SMSA	n.a.	13.3	n.a.	6.2
Philadelphia-Wilmington-Trenton SCSA	12.7	7.3	3.4	7.0
Seattle-Tacoma SCSA	10.9	7.7	4.4	14.6
St. Louis SMSA	12.0	6.0	14.0	27.6
Washington, D.C.-Maryland-Virginia SCSA	9.6	10.8	13.0	11.5
C. *Average Annual Increase of 5 to 9.9% for Both New and Existing Homes in 1974-1976*				
Atlanta SMSA	5.7	7.1	4.1	4.2
Chicago-Gary SCSA	6.8	8.8	19.9	14.2
D. *Other Areas*				
Boston-Lawrence-Lowell SCSA	n.a.	5.2	n.a.	3.7
Detroit-Ann Arbor SCSA	6.3	4.1	7.9	6.2
New York-Newark-Jersey City SCSA	7.4	4.7	16.5	10.3

Source: Table A-3. One of the revisions in the U.S. "new" series beginning 1973 does not affect the local data, that is, the greater weight to small lenders outside major metropolitan areas.

n.a.: Data not reported for several months of a year.

[a]SMSA: Standard metropolitan statistical area; SCSA: Standard consolidated statistical area.

[b]Compound rates.

and traces price developments between 1976 and 1977. Actual prices are shown for each year since 1970 in appendix table A-3, and average annual rates of change for selected periods back to 1970 in table A-4.

Three of the 18 areas exhibit average annual price increases of 10% or more in 1974-1976 for both new and existing houses (category A). Two of these are the Los Angeles and San Francisco complexes. They report the highest rates of price rise, ranging from 13% to 16% for new units and from 12% to 20% for existing property. The price rise accelerated between 1976 and 1977 in San Francisco but not in Los Angeles. The two areas also show the highest price *levels* among the 18 for which data are available. In 1977 the averages were in the $72,000 to $75,000 range for new homes and happened to be $71,000 for existing units in both places. Only the New York area, with an average of nearly $70,000 for new and $61,000 for existing houses, and the Washington metropolis approximated the California levels. The third case in category A is Denver where price advances in 1974-1976 were more moderate than in Los Angeles and San Francisco but accelerated sharply between 1976 and 1977.

In 10 areas, the average annual price rise for 1974-1976 was 10% or more for either new or existing units (category B). In most cases, the stipulated range of increase applied to new homes. Between 1976 and 1977, however, the price rise decelerated for new homes in 6 of 9 reporting areas, with Miami showing a decline probably attributable to a substantial change in the product mix or locational pattern of new homebuilding. For existing property, 5 of the 10 reporting metropoles experienced accelerated price increases, which were quite sharp in Seattle and Saint Louis. There was a small decrease of average prices of existing houses in Dallas following a double-digit rise in the 1974-1976 period.

Only the Atlanta and Chicago areas registered an average annual price increase in 1974-1976 of 5% to 9.9% for new and existing residences (category C). Of the 2, Chicago shows a notable price acceleration between 1976 and 1977 for both types.

Category D in table 2-4 lists three areas that meet none of the previous classification criteria. The most noteworthy case is the New York region where the relatively moderate price rise of 1974-1976 accelerated substantially in 1977, reaching double-digit proportions.

Of course, this array of data confirms the ancient observation that the consumption markets for single-family homes as well as other types of housing are local. The price movements described here result from area-differentiated demand and supply forces such as population changes, especially inmigration and outmigration, economic growth and consumer income, temporary shortages or surpluses of new homes reflected in builders' inventories, and housing vacancies generally. Since the price data come from lending institutions, they may also be influenced by lenders' shifting preferences for the quality and location of homes they finance. Such shifts can account for temporary differences in the price movement for new and existing houses in the same metropolis. It is impossible within the framework of this study to explain the various rates of price change in 18 areas. It *is* possible, however, and relevant to our purpose to examine the question of whether extraordinary price increases have been confined to certain regions of the country or, to be more concrete, to California. We proceed to investigate this question by reference to the 68 observations of price changes in table 2-4, including both the 1974-1976 and the 1977 data,[f] and by defining extraordinary rates of increase as 10% or more per year. Of the 68 observations, 32 reveal increases of this magnitude for either new or old homes or both. The areas recording such rates of price advance are located in the East (Washington and its environs, Baltimore, Philadelphia, New York), the Midwest (Cleveland, Saint Louis, Chicago), Texas, as well as the West (Denver, Los Angeles, San Francisco, Seattle). Although the price surge began in California, it was soon experienced in many other metropoles including some that are not noted for rapid population or economic growth such as Cleveland, Philadelphia, and Saint Louis. Further, the rates of price increase accelerated in 1977 over those of 1974-1976 in 15 of the 18 areas for either new or existing houses or both, without necessarily reaching double-digit proportions.

According to the regional underwriters of two private mortgage insurance companies, also operating in the conventional home finance segment, several areas not covered by the FHLBB statistics have also experienced substantial price increases. In a midwest region,[7] for example, average prices for existing homes reportedly rose 10% between the spring of 1976 and the spring of 1977, and those for new houses by 15% as against only 5% a year earlier for both types. In the Kansas City area, the price advance in 1976-1977 is estimated at 11%. In a region centered in Connecticut, prices increased by 7% for existing and by 10% for new homes. In the Portland, Oregon, area prices for existing property escalated by 19% and those for new units by 12%. Although these are "soft" data, they reflect observations by practitioners in close touch with the market, bolstered in some cases by locally collected statistics on actual transactions. They reinforce the earlier finding that the price escalation has not been limited to California.

Turning to locally generated data, table 2-5 shows annual rates of price increase for existing homes in three major California areas. In all three cases, the increase, moderate in 1968-1970 and 1970-1972, accelerated at a rapid pace thereafter. In the 1974-1976 period, the annual average price rise reached well over 16% in northern and southern California and nearly 13% in Sacramento. Acceleration continued in 1977 when prices shot up by over 30% in the South, 28% in the North, and 19% in Sacramento. The enormous escalation in the North and South translates into price increases of about 2.5% per month. These data do not, or not yet, reveal the softening of the market reported by trade sources in the course of 1977. Because the dramatic price surge of recent years followed more moderate upward movements in the earlier years, the overall advance was "only" in the range of 9 to 11% per year in the 1968-1977 period and 11 to 14% in 1970-1977.

The average annual price increase of 1974-1976 in the San Francisco Bay area and southern California is broadly consistent with the FHLBB-reported rise

---

[f]The potential number of observations is 18 × 4, or 72. However, data for four of the cells in the table are not available.

Table 2-5
Annual Rates of Price Increases for Existing Homes in Three
Major California Areas, 1968-1977ª

Period	San Francisco Bay Areaᵇ	Sacramento County	Southern Californiaᶜ
1968-1970	1.2%	1.1%	4.3%
1970-1972	3.8	5.0	4.2
1972-1974	10.4	8.2	7.9
1974-1976	16.7	12.8	16.5
1976-1977	28.1	19.1	30.6
1968-1977	11.0	8.8	11.6
1970-1977	12.8	10.9	13.7

ªCompound rates for groups of years, arithmetic rates for 1976-1977. Since price data are published semiannually in April and October, the percent figures are based on the October reports.

ᵇIncludes the following nine counties: Alameda, Contra Costa, Marin, Napa, Solano, Sonoma, San Francisco, San Mateo, and Santa Clara. Source for this column and Sacramento: Reports of the Real Estate Research Council of Northern California.

ᶜIncludes the following seven counties: Los Angeles, Orange, Riverside, San Bernardino, San Diego, Santa Barbara, and Ventura. Source: Reports of the Real Estate Research Council of Southern California.

for existing houses (table 2-4), but the magnitude of additional escalation in the 1976-1977 period is not. In the first place, the two series differ in geographic coverage. Second the data in table 2-5 are derived from appraisals of a more or less fixed sample of properties whereas the FHLBB figures are based on transactions. Third the samples of appraised properties are quite small—153 in the case of the seven-county area of southern California. Hence the figures in table 2-5 may reflect sample biases. These probably stem primarily from the small size of the sample and the quality of appraisals; as far as one can judge, the cases seem to be appropriately distributed by property location and price class. Detail on the samples and methods used for locally generated price data is discussed in appendix B. Because of the small size of samples, price statistics for subareas or by price ranges and age of property included in some reports issued by the data sources are not reproduced here.

Table 2-6 shows price increases for existing homes in Seattle, also derived from appraisals of a relatively small sample of properties, and in Montgomery County, Maryland (part of the Washington, D.C., complex). The data are again broadly consistent with those reported by the FHLBB, including the spectacular price escalation in the Seattle area in the 1976-1977 period. The small 1970-1972 increase in Seattle is explained by a local economic slump; more will be said about this phenomenon in chapter 7. Price advances in Montgomery County have been more steady, at high annual rates equal to an average of 11%

Table 2-6
**Annual Rates of Price Increases for Existing Homes in Seattle
and Montgomery County, Maryland, 1968-1977**

Period	Seattle[a]	Montgomery County[b]
Annual Average[c]		
1968-1970	4.7%	5.9%
1970-1972	0.9	11.2
1972-1974	5.8	13.6
1974-1976	8.8	8.3
1968-1976	5.0	9.7
1970-1976	5.1	11.0
Annual[d]		
III-1975-III-1976	13.1	7.6
III-1976-III-1977	29.3	10.0

[a]Seattle-Everett metropolitan area. Source: Reports of the Seattle Real Estate Research Committee.

[b]Source: Reports issued and kindly made available by Alfred W. Jarchow, Rockland, Maryland.

[c]Compound rates, based on April figures for Seattle.

[d]October to October for Seattle, third quarter to third quarter for Montgomery County.

in the 1970-1976 period, and have reflected the strong growth of the federal government in Washington, D.C.

Finally, the Community Analysis Bureau of Los Angeles began in 1975 to publish sales price data for single-family houses in the city as a whole and four major subareas, carried back to 1965. The data include both existing and new dwellings, but the former category predominates. Although the series suffer from some deficiencies, they are notable in two respects. First their coverage is so broad that the figures for subareas can be accepted whereas the samples used in other local surveys are too small for area disaggregation (see appendix C for detail on the series and their limitations). Second the data show that the increase in citywide average house prices through 1975 lagged behind the rise of the CPI for the metropolitan area. Only in 1976 was this relationship reversed. The Community Analysis Bureau compares the house prices in current dollars with those that would be "predicted" by application of the CPI. As is evident from figure 2-5, the change of citywide average house prices between 1967 and 1972 lagged behind the rise that would fully reflect the CPI increase. It moved apace with the CPI from 1973 to 1975, and it was only in 1976 that house prices advanced more than the CPI.

Third just as the recent price escalation was first experienced in California and then in other regions of the nation, the price rise in Los Angeles has spread

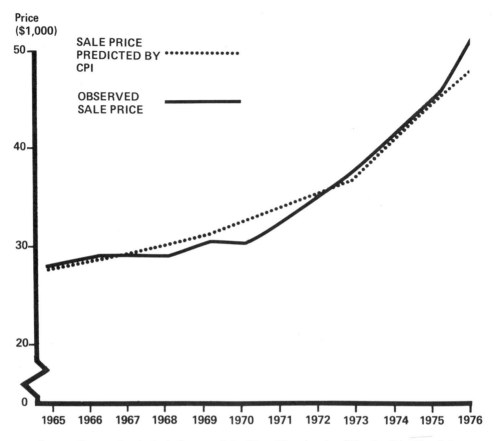

Source: Community Analysis Bureau of the City of Los Angeles, "Housing Price Trends in the City of Los Angeles, 1975-1976" (July 1977).

Figure 2-5. Observed Average House Prices in the City of Los Angeles Compared with Prices "Predicted by CPI," 1965-1976

from the west Los Angeles area to other areas of the city where average price *levels* have always been lower than on the Westside, the preferred residence location of higher income groups (table 2-7). In 1976 this extension of the upward price movement reached the point where the percentage increase in west Los Angeles, smaller than in any of the preceding four years, was greatly exceeded by that in the other three areas. The data for groups of years at the bottom of table 2-7 show price acceleration in 1972-1974 over 1970-1972 for the city and three subareas, the central district being the exception. Acceleration continued in 1974-1976 over 1972-1974 everywhere except the Westside. On the whole, the record suggests the conclusion that recent price increases of double-digit proportions have spread throughout the city. Of course, the

Table 2-7
Average Sales Prices of Single-Family Dwelling Units in the City of Los Angeles and Four Subareas, 1967-1976

Year	Prices (thousands of dollars)					Annual Percent Change				
	City	Valley[a]	West L.A.	Central	Harbor	City	Valley[a]	West L.A.	Central	Harbor
1967	28.7	28.7	41.5	23.9	23.6	—	—	—	—	—
1968	29.0	29.3	42.5	23.5	22.8	1.0	2.1	2.4	-1.7	-3.4
1969	30.1	30.5	46.0	24.2	24.0	3.8	4.1	8.2	3.0	5.3
1970	30.1	30.8	47.3	23.9	24.4	0	1.0	2.8	-1.2	1.7
1971	32.4	31.4	48.7	27.5	25.6	7.6	1.9	2.9	15.1	4.9
1972	35.0	33.1	52.4	29.8	27.6	8.0	5.4	7.6	8.4	7.8
1973	37.6	35.6	58.9	31.4	29.7	7.4	7.5	12.4	5.4	7.6
1974	41.6	39.1	66.3	35.0	33.9	10.6	9.8	12.6	11.5	14.1
1975	44.8	42.3	77.3	36.0	37.1	7.7	8.2	16.6	2.8	9.4
1976	51.1	48.2	82.1	43.5	42.8	14.1	13.9	6.2	20.8	15.4
	Dollar Increase in Selected Periods					Percent Increase in Selected Periods				
1970-1972	4.9	2.3	5.1	5.9	3.2	16.3	7.5	10.8	24.7	13.1
1972-1974	6.6	6.0	13.9	5.2	6.3	18.8	18.1	26.5	17.4	22.8
1974-1976	9.5	9.1	15.8	8.5	8.9	22.8	23.3	23.8	24.3	26.2
1970-1976	21.0	17.4	33.8	19.6	18.4	69.8	56.5	73.6	82.0	75.4

Source: Community Analysis Bureau of the City of Los Angeles, "Housing Price Trends in the City of Los Angeles, 1975-1976."
[a]San Fernando Valley.

subareas themselves are so large that price movements in smaller districts may have varied a great deal.

The citywide data show recent rates of price rise substantially below those reported for southern California (table 2-5). However, comparison is unwarranted since the geographic coverage differs enormously, the results for southern California are based on a small sample of existing homes, and the survey periods are not identical.

Historical Sketch of House Prices

Some statistics on trends in housing prices are available for historical periods not included in the foregoing analysis. The information is limited in scope and accuracy, covering different periods for various localities, and is based on diverse methods of constructing home price series. Nevertheless, the materials serve to place recent price increases in a broader perspective. They suggest that house prices tended to decline or increase at low rates whenever they had been pushed up to unusually high levels. Internal market forces sometimes combined with external factors (such as the removal of backlogs after wars) have served to generate adjustments eventually leading to or approximating equilibrium conditions. The duration of the adjustments has varied greatly from one price cycle to another. At the same time one must note that the historical price fluctuations rarely occurred in a context of prolonged general inflation comparable to that of the past five or six years and the expectations induced by persistent inflation.

Only major price developments are sketched out here. Series on home prices back to the beginning of the twentieth century and, in one case, to 1890 are available from several sources (appendix table D-1). These include a 22-cities index for one-family owner-occupied houses in 1890-1934; asking-price indexes for Los Angeles (1900-1953) and Washington, D.C. (1918-1947); and three-year moving averages of prices paid for a new six-room frame house and lot in Cleveland (1907-1930) and Seattle (1909-1930).

The 22-city index shows sharp annual fluctuations in home prices between 1890 and 1905 with a peak in 1894. In 1893-1894 home prices advanced 17%, but this was followed by sharp declines in the following two years. Around the turn of the century prices began to advance again until 1904 except for a sharp downturn in one year—1900-1901. The Los Angeles data beginning in 1900 show prices in 1903 to be 69% above those in 1900, followed by more moderate increases through 1907.

The year 1907 apparently represented a watershed in the 22 cities and Los Angeles. In the 22 cities, prices had advanced in 1906 and 1907 by 19 and 10%, respectively, but fell in the two subsequent years and moved irregularly between 1910 and 1913. The 1907 peak was not attained again until 1914. In Los Angeles the prices prevailing in 1907 were not realized again until 1919. The declines after 1907 may have been associated with the financial crisis of that year.

On the other hand, new home prices in Cleveland, reported first in 1907, increased at annual rates of 9-10% in 1909 and 1910 and at more moderate rates until 1917. The Seattle index, beginning in 1909, shows a more erratic pattern, with 1918 home prices 17% above those of 1909.

Price escalation attributable to war and postwar conditions began in either 1917 or 1918 depending on the area. Home prices jumped by about 10% in both 1919 and 1920 in the 22 cities. Los Angeles asking prices more than doubled between 1918 and 1921. In 1920 alone prices rose by 53%. The Washington, D.C., series beginning in 1918 shows annual double-digit increases in asking prices for three years. Cleveland's new-home price index also rose at a double-digit rate for three years starting in 1917, and so did the Seattle index in 1919-1920. All the series show more moderate price changes after 1920 or 1921, probably due to the severe though short business recession of that period and the attendant decline in the general price level. New peaks were reached everywhere in the 1924-1926 period. After the mid-1920s home prices began a decline prolonged by the Great Depression, reaching bottom in 1933 or 1934.

The upward movement of house prices beginning in the mid-1930s was irregular until 1940. Thereafter Los Angeles and Washington, D.C., the only areas for which consistent data are available, experienced steady increases in prices. Los Angeles shows double-digit escalation starting in 1943, culminating in a 48% increase of asking prices in 1946. In Washington, D.C., double-digit rates of price rise are recorded for 1945 (17%) and 1946 (25%). Asking prices dropped in Washington, D.C., in 1946, and the series ceases at this point. Los Angeles asking prices declined between 1947 and 1949 and increased steadily thereafter.

The house price movements of the 1940s in Washington, D.C., and Los Angeles reflect, of course, the influence of a war and postwar economy on the market. This influence appears also in a nationwide series: the estimated values of FHA-financed single-family houses (appendix table D-2). Value increases were moderate during the war but reached double-digit proportions in the three years 1947 to 1949 for existing homes and in 1947-1948 for new homes, at a time when the removal of wartime controls had pushed up the general price level. The sharp house price increases of the immediate postwar years were followed by less dramatic advances for existing property and by small declines for new houses in 1949-1950. The increases in the immediate postwar years were associated with rising value-income multiples, but even the highest multiples exceeded two by only slight margins. Between 1946 and 1954, values moved up by 90% for existing houses and by only 56% for new ones, suggesting that the main forces for price escalation came from the demand side rather than from increased costs of new supplies. Of course, the FHA data, as well as those in table D-1, reflect changes in the "product mix" and may therefore be subject to error.

Finally, it is instructive to review the complete house price index from 1944 to 1977 for Los Angeles County. The data in appendix table D-3 reveal an upward trend over several decades that was punctured by rare reversals. Most newcomers to the Los Angeles area since World War II were quickly informed that they could count on steady appreciation of market values when they bought homes. One can assume that a population experiencing a long-term rise in residence prices was especially responsive to the recent price escalation and was more readily inclined to plunge into home purchase for fear of future price increases. A population less conditioned by a strong upward trend in market values may respond more sluggishly when prices rise at an accelerating rate, as they did in 1976-1977. At the same time one notes that the long historical series for Los Angeles County in table D-3 shows no precedent for the sustained and accelerating double-digit price rise recorded in the four years from 1974 to 1977. Only in two previous years, 1945 and 1946, did house prices jump at annual rates of more than 10%, and only the extraordinary 1946 increase of 52% exceeded the peak rate of the recent period—nearly 32% in 1977. Even in Los Angeles then the recent price surge has been a unique experience if seen in the perspective of the record since 1944, and this is probably true for southern California as a whole.

Notes

1. The comparison pertains to the acquisition rather than the carrying costs. Mobile home shipments declined from a peak of 576,000 in 1972 to a low of 213,000 in 1975 and recovered to 277,000 in 1977 (*Federal Reserve Bulletin*). The rate of recovery since 1975 has been far below the rate for single-family house starts or completions. The average retail sales price of mobile homes between 1972 and 1976 increased by 77% while the Commerce Department price index for new one-family houses sold rose by 57% (see Clayton P. Pritchett, "The Effect of Regional Growth Characteristics on Regional Housing Prices," *Journal of the American Real Estate and Urban Economics Association*, Summer 1977, pp. 202-203). Analysis of other reasons for the recent lackluster performance of the mobile home industry after its great expansion during the 1960s would take us too far afield.

2. See, for example, Duncan Maclennan, "Some Thoughts on the Nature and Purpose of House Price Studies," *Urban Studies*, February 1977, and the bibliography presented therein. See also Peter T. Chinloy, "Hedonic Price and Depreciation Indexes for Residential Housing: A Longitudinal Approach," *Journal of Urban Economics*, October 1977; Peter T. Chinloy, "Depreciation, Adverse Selection and Housing Markets," *Journal of Urban Economics*, April 1978; and M.G. Ferri, "An Application of Hedonic Indexing Methods to Monthly Changes in Housing Prices, 1965-1975," *Journal of the American Real Estate and Urban Economics Association*, Winter 1977.

3. The so-called standard house holds eight characteristics of homes sold in 1967 constant. These are floor area, number of stories, number of bathrooms, air conditioning, type of parking facility, type of foundation, geographic division within region, and metropolitan area location. The eight characteristics account for approximately 65% of the variation in selling price. Recently the U.S. Department of Commerce has developed an updated price series for a 1974 house. This series holds two additional characteristics constant: the square foot area of the lot and the presence of fireplaces. While annual price changes vary, trends over longer periods are remarkably similar. Between 1968 and 1976, average prices of homes actually sold each year rose by 80.4%, those of the 1967 kind of house by 81.8%, and those of the 1974 kind of house by 77.1%. Even in the recent period of III-1976 to III-1977, prices increased at similar rates: 12.3%, 12.1%, and 11.5%, respectively.

4. When the number of existing homes financed with FHA loans are compared with the sales of such homes reported by the National Association of Realtors, the share of FHA was 5.3% in 1974, 7.1% in 1975, 6.1% in 1976, and 5.9% in 1977. In 1968, the first year of reported total sales, FHA accounted for 18% of the total. The FHA share declined steadily to 4.2% in 1973. Starts of 1- to 4-family houses under FHA have also accounted for a diminishing proportion of total starts. In the context of this study, it is unnecessary to join the debate of the reasons for the declining or small FHA share in the market.

5. Changes in selected characteristics of new houses are reported on a more comprehensive basis by the Bureau of the Census and HUD (*Characteristics of New Housing, Construction Reports C25*). However, they include lot size but not lot prices. As for other characteristics, the price series for the 1967 kind of new house makes it unnecessary to refer to detail here. The FHA data have the advantage of including materials for both existing and new homes.

6. See William Gorham and Nathan Glazer, *The Urban Predicament* (Washington, D.C.: The Urban Institute, 1976), pp. 134-136, and especially figure I depicting the ratio of monthly cost of a "standard" new home to median family income.

7. The administrative region comprises parts of Illinois, Michigan, Ohio, Indiana, and Kentucky, plus portions of South Dakota, Nebraska, Kansas, and Missouri.

3   The Homebuyers

The price escalation shown in the preceding chapter raises the classic question: Who could afford to buy homes at the steeply rising acquisition costs and the incremental carrying costs that are usually associated with higher purchase prices? The answer would be relatively easy if the price inflation were accompanied by a notable decline in homebuying. In this case, which would conform to the principles of static economic analysis (higher price means lower quantity sold), homebuying would be increasingly confined to the more well-to-do or those who have a strong preference for the single-family house. In fact, however, the price surge was associated with a greatly expanding volume of house purchases. This compounds the question and complicates the answer.

Recent Growth of Home Purchases

The nationwide growth in homebuying is shown in table 3-1. In 1976 and 1977, total purchases of existing and new houses, 4 million and 4.8 million, respectively, reached unprecedented levels. In the market for new homes, the percentage increase of acquisitions in 1975-1977 nearly matched the increase recorded for the 1970-1972 housing boom when prices for single-family residences were rising at more "normal" rates. Purchases of existing homes in 1975-1977 were growing at a higher rate than in 1970-1972. In fact, the resale market exhibits a strong upward trend throughout the 1968-1977 period, interrupted just once by a slight decline in the recession year of 1974. For new-home acquisitions, the table includes not only the sales by merchant builders but also an often neglected, significant component of homebuilding: the units constructed on owners' land by contractors (custom-built homes) and by the lot owners themselves with or without assistance of subcontractors. In the period as a whole, about 63 such units were built for every 100 homes sold by merchant builders. Cyclical variations in this type of homebuilding have been much less pronounced than in sales by builders. Further, inclusion of this component changes the ratio of existing to new-home acquisitions substantially in favor of the latter although the market for old houses remains dominant and gained in dominance in recent years (columns 5 and 6 of table 3-1).

    In the context of this chapter, however, homebuilding on owners' land is most relevant for the reason that it may provide new houses for middle-income people who seem to be excluded from the market when only the prices of homes

Table 3-1
Sales of Existing and New Single-Family Houses and Total Volume
of New-Home Acquisitions, United States, 1968-1977
(1,000 units)

Period	Existing-Home Sales (1)	New Homes Sales by Merchant Builders (2)	New Homes Built on Owner's Land[a] (3)	New Homes Total Acquisitions[b] (4)	Column 1 as Ratio of Column 2 (5)	Column 1 as Ratio of Column 4 (6)
1968	1,569	490	350	840	3.20	1.87
1969	1,594	448	318	766	3.56	2.08
1970	1,612	485	308	793	3.32	2.03
1971	2,018	656	378	1,034	3.08	1.95
1972	2,252	718	401	1,119	3.14	2.01
1973	2,334	634	434	1,068	3.68	2.18
1974	2,272	519	380	899	4.38	2.53
1975	2,452	549	361	910	4.47	2.69
1976	3,002	646	406	1,052	4.65	2.85
1977	3,572	819	440[c]	1,259	4.36	2.84

Percent Change in Specified Periods

Period	(1)	(2)	(3)	(4)	(5)	(6)
1968-1970	2.7%	d	−12.0%	−5.6%	−	−
1970-1972	39.7	48.0	30.2	41.1	−	−
1972-1974	d	−27.7	−5.2	−19.7	−	−
1974-1976	32.1	24.5	6.8	18.6	−	−
1975-1977	45.7	49.2	21.9	39.2	−	−

Sources: Column 1: National Association of Realtors. Estimated sales are computed from regional data for the participating multiple listing services (MLSs) and a constant factor "to blow up" the figure to account for MLSs not participating in the surveys. The regional factors are based on measures of total market activity derived from special computer runs from the 1973 and 1974 Housing Survey tapes. Regional sales are aggregated to yield the national sales volume. Column 2: U.S. Bureau of the Census, Construction Reports C25 "New One-Family Houses Sold and for Sale," revised data for 1973-1977. Column 3: same, "Characteristics of New Housing."

[a]One-family structures for owner-occupancy on owner's land including contractor-built and owner-built units. The 1968-1970 figures denote starts and include a small number of homes built for rent. The later data denote completions and exclude units built for rent.

[b]Sum of columns 2 and 3.

[c]Authors' estimate.

[d]Not computed because of increase for existing home sales from 1972 to 1973 and decline to almost the 1972 level in 1974; similar reasons for sales by merchant builders.

offered by merchant builders are considered. This conjecture is suggested by two observations. First, 46% of the houses "built on owner's land" in 1972-1976 were constructed by the lot owners themselves. The remainder were custom-built units. Second even the custom-built units, which are usually equated with "luxury" houses, had an average contract price of only $40,100 in 1976.[1] If one makes a generous allowance of 50% of the contract price for the site cost, the total would be $60,000. It is reasonable to assume that the average cost of units built by lot owners themselves, usually in smaller cities or towns or on the fringe of metropolitan areas, was much lower. Of course, the sweat-labor of do-it-yourself builders would account for much of the difference. But the economic rationale of "opportunity costs" (the value of time alternatively spent in gainful employment) is hardly applicable. Most amateur builders consider their project a worthwhile leisure activity yielding psychic as well as material benefits. In fact, a few construct homes for sale, which are not reported in the sales of merchant builders.

Information on the growth of home acquisitions in California, the "hot market" of recent years, is much more fragmentary than for the United States. There are no state data for builders' sales or units built on owners' lots. However, sales of both new and existing houses are reported for the western region, which is dominated by California (table 3-2). Sales of new houses in the West increased at a fast pace after the trough of 1974; their 1977 volume was 84% higher than the 1974 level and exceeded substantially the previous peak of 1972. Moreover, they accounted for a growing portion of total sales in the United States. Sales of existing units in the West rose by 42% from the trough of 1974 to 1977 and were twice as large in 1977 as in 1968-1970. Relative to total U.S. sales, however, transactions in the West declined after 1975; the turnover of existing property expanded faster in other regions.

Income and Wealth Constraints on
Various Groups of Buyers

The combination of increasing sales and sharply rising prices of residences in recent years warrants a review of the financial constraints faced by homebuyers. Under any circumstances, home purchase is limited by income (from which periodic ownership expenses must be met) and by wealth or assets (the source of the downpayment). One would expect these constraints to become more severe when house prices rise faster than consumer income, as they did in 1975-1977 (see table 2-2); income serves as the base not only for recurring housing outlays but also for the prices buyers can afford to pay. As a general, time-honored rule of thumb, the house price should not exceed 2 to 2½ times the annual income, depending on the income-tax bracket and other individual circumstances of purchasers. This multiple is one of the financial ratios examined with some care by mortgage lenders before they approve loans, and it is at least vaguely familiar among shoppers for homes. Have the ordinary constraints remained operative, or have they been altered?

Table 3-2
Sales of New and Existing Homes in the West, 1968-1977
(1,000 units)

Period	New Homes		Existing Homes	
	Number	*Percent of U.S.*	*Number*	*Percent of U.S.*
1968	121	24.7%	308	19.6%
1969	114	25.4	308	19.3
1970	121	24.9	292	18.1
1971	176	26.8	389	19.3
1972	187	26.0	473	21.0
1973	161	25.4	446	19.1
1974	139	26.8	434	19.1
1975	150	27.3	491	20.0
1976	199	30.8	591	19.6
1977	256	31.2	615	17.2

Sources: New homes: U.S. Bureau of the Census, Construction Reports C25, "New One-Family Homes Sold and For Sale." Existing Homes: National Association of Realtors.

The Case of Owner-Buyers

The answer varies with the type of purchaser, particularly with regard to wealth constraints. The upward trend of house prices has minimized these constraints for households that already own a home, sell it, and buy another. Generally, this class of purchasers—labeled here "owner-buyers"—has obtained a large capital gain on their equity in the house they sold, and their total equity at sale was sufficient to make a downpayment on the typically more expensive property they bought. In fact, the capital gain in quite a few cases has yielded proceeds leaving cash in the seller's hands over and above the required downpayment on the newly purchased residence. The extra cash could be used to help defray the larger periodic outlays for the second house or for any other purpose. The process involved in owner-buyer transactions is often described as "upgrading." This is not always so. Owner-buyers may acquire a smaller though still more expensive unit suited to the needs of families whose children have left home. Or they may buy another house because of job transfer, other changes in employment location, divorce, or retirement. Some may purchase a property in the same or even a lower price class than the one they sell.[2] However, owner-buyers often face income constraints even when wealth constraints are nil.

Tables 3-3 and 3-4 present schematic illustrations of these points based on successive purchases of *new* homes financed with conventional loans on the average terms reported by the FHLBB for home mortgages made by all major types of lenders. Average prices of houses sold by merchant builders are available since 1963, while those for existing one-family units do not begin before 1968.

Hence illustrations for the acquisition of new houses make it possible to trace successive transactions between reasonable occupancy periods—six years between the first purchase (which may be thought of as a change from renter to owner status) and the second purchase, and another six years between the second and third. The illustrations are based on actual data and estimates specified in the footnotes to the tables.

Table 3-3 assumes that the same household bought new homes in 1965, 1971, and 1977 at the average price reported for sales by merchant builders in each period. This involves some moderate "upgrading" as a new house was exchanged for property that was six years old. According to the illustration, wealth constraints in the second and third purchase were nonexistent. The equity of the owner buying in 1965 and selling in 1971 was $11,000 at sale and exceeded the initial outlays (downpayment plus closing costs) of about $8,000 required for the purchase of the new 1971 house. The estimated net sales price of the property (after brokerage commission of 6% and another 6% discount allowing for the fact that the new house of 1965 was no longer new in 1971) was only 16% higher than the original purchase price. However, the owner's equity almost doubled in the six-year period.[a] The equity of the owner who sold in 1971 was also more than ample to buy the new house of 1977—$29,000 as against the $14,700 required for the initial outlays. In both successive purchases, then, there was indeed cash left over for other purposes. The market value of the property in the 1971-1977 case appreciated by 70%, but the owner's equity tripled.

At the same time table 3-3 reveals tolerable income constraints. Income is estimated from purchase prices on the assumption that the price-income multiple was two in the first purchase and 2.2 in the second and third (see footnote h for detail). The average annual homeownership expenses of the 1965 buyer are less than 20% of his income at the time of purchase, a quite "normal" relationship. This does not allow for income gains over the six-year holding period exceeding increases in annual ownership expenses. Since mortgage payments are fixed and represent the major portion of total outlays, increases in the latter would be moderate, applying mostly to property taxes and, since 1973, to fuel.

Between 1965 and 1971, the owner's required income before tax rises from $10,750 to nearly $13,000, or 20%. This is a moderate gain compared to personal income statistics. Annual outlays after the 1971 purchase move up to 25.6% of income, still not an extreme relationship. Between 1971 and mid-1977, the owner's income would need to have increased from about $13,000 to almost

[a]The data do not provide for "opportunity costs" of the amount of downpayment, that is, the yield forgone if the amount had been placed in an alternative investment. Most homebuyers do not seem to make such calculations. Besides, the omission may be more or less offset by the omission of income-tax savings in "total annual outlays" for owners who itemize deductions of mortgage interest and property taxes. Nor do the data provide for prepayment penalties on the mortgage loans repaid after six years.

Table 3-3
Schematic Illustration of Three Successive Purchases of New
Single-Family Houses by the Same Household, 1965-1977

Item	First Purchase	Second Purchase	Third Purchase
Dates of purchase	Mid-1965	Mid-1971	Mid-1977
Purchase price[a]	$21,500	$28,300	$54,700
Initial outlays	6,255	8,119	14,661
Downpayment[b]	5,610	7,270	13,020
Closing costs: 3% of price[c]	645	849	1,641
Annual outlays			
Mortgage payments[d]	1,200	1,890	3,670
Other[e]	900	1,400	3,000
Total before income-tax saving	2,100	3,290	6,670
Mortgage balance at sale	13,800	19,000	–
Net sales price[f]	24,900	48,100	–
Percent of property appreciation	16%	70%	–
Owner's equity at sale[g]	11,100	29,100	–
Excess of equity over downpayment	5,490	21,830	–
% of equity appreciation	98%	200%	–
Owner's required income at purchase[h]	10,750	12,860	24,860
Annual outlays as % of owner's income before tax saving	19.5%	25.6%	26.8%
Memo: Owner's annual occupancy costs (outlays reduced by equity appreciation)	1,180	–340	–

[a]For mid-1965 and mid-1971, annual average price of new houses sold by merchant builders during the year. For mid-1977, average prices for sales in II-1977.

[b]Based on average annual loan-price ratios reported by FHLBB for conventional loans on new homes in 1965 and 1971, and the ratio reported for July 1977. The ratio was 73.9% in 1965, 74.3% in 1971, and 76.2% in July 1977.

[c]A survey of FHA and VA loans for a congressional report in 1972 showed sellers' average settlement costs of $1,483, or 7.6% of the average sales price of $19,397. Settlement costs included sales commission, accounted for in "net sales price" in the table. The 3% represents the reported closing costs plus prepaid items. Discount payments on mortgage loans are not included because they are less frequent in conventional than in FHA- or VA-loan transactions. Besides, when discount payments are borne by sellers, they are usually recaptured in the sales price. See *Mortgage Settlement Costs, Report of HUD and VA to the Senate Committee on Banking, Housing and Urban Affairs,* 92nd Congress, 2nd sess., March 1972, p. 35. Closing costs are transaction costs not considered in the subsequent calculations of owner's equity.

[d]Level payments derived from annual average effective interest rates and maturities for 1965 and 1971 and those for July 1977, applied to the mortgage loan (difference between purchase price and downpayment). Rounded figures. Effective interest rates used are 5.75% instead of 5.81% actual in 1965, 7.75% instead of 7.74% actual, and 9.0%, which conforms to actual. Actual maturities at the three dates were 25 years, 26.2, and 27.9, respectively. Maturities used in the calculations are 25, 26, and 28 years, respectively, with extrapolations from the standard tables showing maturities in 5-year intervals.

[e]Based on FHA annual data in dollars for property tax, maintenance and repairs, hazard insurance, and heat and utilities. The sum of these items equaled 3.9% of sales price in 1965-1977, 4.0% in 1968-1970, and rose thereafter to 4.8% in II-1977. Assuming that at least some of these items would be somewhat higher relative to sales price for conventionally financed homes because of location affecting property-tax rates or for other

Table 3-3 continued

reasons, the dollar figures in the table average 4.2% for the 1965-1971 period and 5.0% for the 1971-1977 period, and the figure for the mid-1977 purchase was estimated at 5.5%. All figures are rounded.

fAverage price of new homes sold by merchant builders in year of sale minus 6% sales commission and minus 6% discount to allow for fact that the new house of mid-1965 was no longer new in 1971, and that of mid-1971 no longer new in mid-1977. Total deductions: 12%.

gNet sales price minus mortgage balance.

hBased on ratio of house price to before-tax income of 2.0 for first purchase and of 2.2 for second and third purchase. Unfortunately, actual ratios are only known for FHA transactions where they averaged 1.7 to 1.8 in 1965-1976 for new homes. Ratios are assumed to be higher for conventionally financed purchases. According to special tabulations of the 1973 National Housing Survey, the median ratio was 1.9 for home purchasers who were previous renters and 2.2% for those who were previous owners (National Association of Realtors, *Profile of the Single-Family Home Buyer*, 1977, p. 25).

$25,000, or 93%, if the assumed house price-income ratio of 2.2 were to be maintained. This gain exceeds the 77% rise in personal disposable income.[3] Annual outlays would equal nearly 27% of the required income. Both buyers and mortgage lenders seem to have been willing in recent years to stretch the customary price-income multiples and housing expense-income ratios. In any event, the income constraints inferred from the data are not severe.

Table 3-3 shows still another relationship in *memo* form: the owner's annual occupancy costs if his outlays are retroactively reduced by the appreciation of his equity. The reduction is substantial. In the 1965-1971 period, the annual ownership expenses are cut from $2,100 to $1,180, or 11% of income. In 1971-1977, the capital gain on the equity wipes out the annual outlays, that is, current expenses were nil. These calculations highlight the important difference between homeowners' periodic cash outlays and true occupancy costs. The latter take account of equity appreciation (or depreciation) and can therefore be determined only after sale of the property. The calculations have a significant bearing on home purchase under conditions of inflationary expectations. Some recent buyers who recognized that they were overextending themselves in terms of their income expect that capital gains will ultimately help reduce high ownership outlays provided they can in the interim allocate cash to meet the expenses by reducing other consumption or savings or by other means. Under this kind of calculus, of course, the capital gain on equity will not be available for the downpayment on another home purchase at a higher price, but other sources of funds such as non-house investments or an inheritance may take its place. Also the retroactive consideration of annual outlays after appreciation of the equity is pertinent for households that do not intend to move to still another house, say, elderly couples or individuals who shift to rental status. In these cases, however, the amount of appreciation would be reduced by the capital-gains tax.

Table 3-4
Schematic Illustration II of Three Successive Purchases of New
Single-Family Houses by the Same Household, United States, 1965-1977

Item	First Purchase	Second Purchase	Third Purchase
Dates of purchase	Mid-1965	Mid-1971	Mid-1977
Purchase price[a]	$21,500	$42,600	$104,000
Initial outlays	6,255	12,378	28,120
Downpayment[b]	5,610	11,100	25,000
Closing costs: 3% of price	645	1,278	3,120
Annual outlays[c]			
Mortgage payments	1,200	2,900	7,800
Other	900	2,100	5,700
Total before income-tax saving	2,100	5,000	13,500
Mortgage balance at sale	13,800	28,500	—
Net sales price[d]	24,900	53,650	—
Percent of property appreciation	16%	26%	—
Owner's equity at sale	11,100	25,050	—
Excess of equity over downpayment	5,500	13,950	—
% of equity appreciation	97%	56%	—
Owner's required income at purchase	10,750	21,500	52,500
Annual outlays as % of owner's income before tax saving	19.5%	23.2%	25.7%
Memo: Owner's annual occupancy costs (outlays reduced by equity appreciation)	1,180	2,700	—

[a]Computed in second and third purchase on assumption that owner invested his total equity at sale of previous house in the downpayment and on the loan-price ratios shown in footnote b to table 3-3, rounded to 74% in 1971 and 76% in 1977.

[b]In second and third purchase, equals owner's equity at sale of previous house.

[c]Computed as in table 3-3.

[d]Assumes price increase of 33% between 1965 and 1971. This increase is reported by the Bureau of the Census for the near-standard new house (1967 house). From the resulting dollar figure, 12% has again been deducted for sales commission and discount allowing for the fact that the house sold in 1971 was no longer new.

The relationship between equity appreciation and annual outlays, especially fixed mortgage bills, reflects the "tilting" effect of inflation on any kind of fixed debt payments. Under inflationary conditions, such payments become appreciably lower in real terms when consumer incomes (or corporate earnings) rise more or less apace with the rate of general price increase.[4] Thus even initially high payments become less burdensome over time. Homeowners who bought their property years ago and still occupy it are among the beneficiaries of the tilting effect, although the benefits obviously vary with the owners' income experience (retired versus economically active persons, for example). Under conditions of inflationary expectations, many homebuyers *anticipate* that the real burden of fixed outlays will decline.

Table 3-4 makes the more extreme assumption that the household used the entire proceeds from the equity in the property it sold as a downpayment on the property it bought and that it selected a house priced accordingly, given the average loan-price ratio reported for the transaction period. Since wealth constraints are assumed away, the relevant part of the illustration concerns income constraints. On the estimated price-income multiple, income would have to double between 1965 and 1971 and to rise by 144% between 1971 and 1977 in order to make the transactions possible. Both gains are far in excess of those reported in general income statistics (see note 3). However, some groups of homebuyers may have experienced income increases of such magnitude if wives began to enter or reenter the labor force and their earnings were fully recognized for mortgage loan qualification. On the required income basis, annual outlays would rise from less than 20% for the 1965 house to 23% for the 1971 house and a little under 26% for the 1977 house—not a severe constraint. Here again, the conventional house price-income multiples have probably been revised upward in the recent years of price escalation—the process of "stretching" that was mentioned earlier. Also the households making the successive purchases are most likely to itemize deductions for income-tax purposes. On the basis of after-tax mortgage interest and property-tax payments, their annual outlays would be substantially reduced, and the income required for loan qualification would be lowered. Although the proportion of taxpayers who itemize home-owner deductions has declined, recent purchasers are generally highly motivated to do so. Actual experience probably lies somewhere between the schematic illustrations of tables 3-3 and 3-4. Also the relationships between income, house price, and homeowner expense would change if one used "permanent" rather than a specific annual income.

Table 3-4 reiterates the calculation of annual costs when cash outlays are retroactively reduced by the appreciation of the owner's equity. In this case, homeownership expenses for the 1971 house are almost cut in half, from $5,000 to $2,700, or from 23% of income to 12.6%—reflecting again in large part the tilting effects of inflation on fixed mortgage payments. To repeat, this calculation is relevant to home purchase under conditions of inflationary expectations. An increasing number of recent homebuyers seem to have been motivated by a trade-off between high periodic outlays for a more expensive property and anticipated capital gains. It appears that they are willing to allocate a larger initial share of their income to housing expenses for the sake of capital appreciation and expect the relative burden of fixed payments to decline. The trade-off has generally been validated to date. Whether it can be validated in the longer run will be discussed in chapter 7.

The Case of First-time Buyers

First-time home purchasers typically face both wealth and income constraints. The downpayment must come from the savings of a generally young family or other household, and most young households do not have sufficient income to accumulate substantial savings. In some cases, though, this handicap is overcome by parents or well-to-do relatives providing all or part of the downpayment as a gift or "soft" loan. The number of such cases is unknown, but it appears to have increased with growing affluence over the long run and with the elders' belief in homeownership as a good hedge against inflation for young couples. The income constraints of most first-time buyers require no elaboration.

The case of first-time home purchasers can be illustrated by FHA statistics available for many years and by data from a large private mortgage insurance company for 1977. Whether single-family houses bought with FHA-insured mortgage loans represent first-time or other home acquisitions is not reported. However, average prices of FHA-financed residences are substantially lower than those of conventionally financed properties (chapter 2). Since 1965 about 90% of the home mortgages insured by FHA under Section 203b were made for the purchase of existing houses, which are the major objects of first-time buyers. For these reasons, the FHA data can be used as a proxy for the experience of this group. The only drawback comes from the fact that FHA's recent share in the total market for both new and existing house purchases has been quite small.

As table 3-5 shows, the price-income ratio in FHA-financed home transactions has been remarkably stable throughout the 1965-1977 period, varying between 1.7 and 1.8 for new and between 1.5 and 1.6 for existing houses. These multiples remained unaffected by the escalation of house prices in recent years. They are also much lower than the ratios of 2 to 2.2 assumed in tables 3-3 and 3-4. The stability of the FHA price-income ratio did not result from the agency catering over time to buyers in *relatively* higher income groups. Of course, the family income of FHA purchasers increased practically each year, but the increase was, in fact, less than the gains recorded in general income statistics.[5]

The average FHA buyer's required equity investment rose relative to his income in the case of new homes—from 13.7% in 1965 to 15-16% in 1976 and 1977—but it declined for purchasers of existing homes.

Income constraints appear in the ratio of mortgage payments to income (MP/I). The ratio increased quite steadily from a little over 15% in 1965 to 20% in 1974 in the case of new homes but fell from this peak thereafter, just in the period of house price escalation. The MP/I ratio rose almost continuously in the case of existing houses. As for the level of the ratios, it should be noted that total mortgage payments under the FHA system include property tax and property insurance, which are collected pro-rata along with interest, amortization, and mortgage insurance. Income constraints appear also in the ratio of estimated total housing expense to income, which increased from about 19% in 1965 to 25-26% in 1977.

Altogether, when the recent period of escalating house prices is considered, neither the income nor the wealth constraints have been severe for that part of

Table 3-5
Selected Financial Characteristics of Home Purchases under the
FHA System,[a] United States, 1965-1977

Period	Family Income[b]	P/I Ratio[c]	Buyer's Investment[d]	MP/I Ratio[e]	HE/I Ratio[f]
New Homes					
1965	$ 9,300	1.8	$1,272	15.2	19.2
1967	10,700	1.8	1,478	15.9	19.9
1969	12,140	1.7	1,697	17.2	20.9
1970	13,780	1.7	2,249	18.3	21.7
1971	14,180	1.7	2,056	17.6	21.0
1972	13,730	1.8	2,278	18.3	22.4
1973	14,410	1.7	2,254	17.0	21.2
1974	15,970	1.7	2,843	20.0	22.8
1975	18,670	1.7	3,117	18.6	22.8
1976	19,800	1.8	3,194	19.4	23.7
1977	20,630	1.8	3,136	n.a.	26.5
Existing Homes					
1965	$ 9,110	1.6	$1,151	14.6	18.6
1967	10,150	1.6	1,167	15.0	19.0
1969	11,300	1.5	1,289	15.7	19.5
1970	12,410	1.5	1,581	16.7	20.3
1971	12,760	1.5	1,529	16.2	20.0
1972	13,070	1.5	1,573	15.9	20.1
1973	13,100	1.5	1,406	15.8	20.2
1974	14,690	1.5	1,973	17.1	21.4
1975	16,980	1.5	2,071	17.7	22.2
1976	17,400	1.5	1,789	17.9	22.7
1977	18,150	1.6	1,938	n.a.	25.1

Source: Periodic reports of the Federal Housing Administration on Section 203b Home Mortgage Characteristics.

[a]Under Section 203b, omitting subsidy programs administered by FHA.

[b]Average annual income at time of purchase, designated "annual gross family income" through 1975 and "annual family income (total claimed income)" thereafter. Figures are rounded.

[c]Price-income ratio (multiple).

[d]Downpayment plus closing cost excluding prepayable expenses, that is, total acquisition cost less mortgage amount. This is the equivalent of "total initial outlays" in tables 3-3 and 3-4.

[e]Ratio of total mortgage payments to income. Mortgage payments include interest and amortization, the mortgage insurance premium, hazard insurance, and property taxes.

[f]Housing expense-income ratio. In addition to mortgage payments specified in footnote e, housing expense includes maintenance and repair plus the estimated cost of fuel and other utility services for the first year. The 1977 ratio is somewhat overstated, since FHA's preliminary report for that year relates housing expense to "effective income" rather than "claimed income."

the market served by FHA-insured loans. But because of the declining share of FHA in the total market since 1965, the beginning year of the data in table 4-5, the representativeness of FHA information may be open to question. For this reason, supplementary data are given in table 3-6 for conventional home mortgage loans insured by one of the largest private mortgage insurance companies that operates nationwide. These companies protect lenders against loss for the top 20-25% of each loan, and lenders seek the protection mostly if not exclusively for home mortgages exceeding 80-85% of the appraised property value.b The small downpayment means that the privately insured transactions may be expected to be in about the same part of the market served by FHA, reflecting predominantly house purchases by first-time buyers. As in the case of FHA, the average age of buyers in the private insurance operation was slightly over thirty years. The companies have grown so rapidly that their new insurance written has for some time exceeded the FHA volume. Privately insured home loans accounted for 13.2% of the total amount of 1- to 4-family mortgages originated in 1976 and the first nine months of 1977.[6]

The data in table 3-6 relate only to the first three quarters of 1977, but this was a period of rapid house price escalation in many areas of the country. The data are reported not only for the United States but for regions conforming to the administrative organization of the company that supplied the information.

Table 3-6
Selected Financial Characteristics of Home Purchases Financed with
Conventional Loans Insured by a Major Private Mortgage Insurance
Company, January through September 1977
(averages for all insured loans; rounded amounts)

Item	United States	North Central	Western	South Central	South East	North-east
Sales price	$38,100	$33,900	$46,250	$38,400	$39,600	$36,650
Buyer's annual income	21,650	19,800	24,800	22,100	22,800	20,600
Loan-price ratio[a]	90.0%	91.0%	88.6%	90.6%	89.9%	88.8%
Price-income ratio	1.8	1.7	1.9	1.7	1.7	1.8
Buyer's investment[b]	$3,800	$3,060	$5,250	$3,600	$3,800	$4,100
% of income	17.5%	15.4%	21.1%	16.3%	16.6%	19.8%
Computed monthly mortgage payment[c]	$280	$255	$334	$287	$288	$265
% of monthly income	15.5%	15.4%	16.1%	15.5%	15.2%	15.4%

[a]All ratios and percentages are computed from unrounded figures.

[b]Sales price minus loan amount.

[c]Computed by authors from reported average interest rate, loan maturity, and loan-price ratio.

---

[b]Among other things, lenders seek the protection because of loan-resale restrictions. Both the Federal National Mortgage Association and the Federal Home Loan Mortgage Corporation buy conventional home mortgages exceeding a specified loan-value ratio only if they are insured by qualified mortgage insurance companies.

Some of the figures under private mortgage insurance come close to the FHA statistics. Others indicate that home purchases with privately insured loans are made by buyers of somewhat superior financial means yet falling into the broad moderate-income group served by FHA. The annual income of buyers under private mortgage insurance in the first three quarters of 1977 was $21,650 as against $18,250 under the FHA program.c The price-income ratios were 1.8 and 1.7, respectively. The buyer's average investment was larger than for FHA transactions, $3,800 compared to about $2,000. In relation to income, however, the investment was about the same, 17.5% for transactions under private insurance as against nearly 18% under FHA. The reported mortgage payment-to-income ratios are not comparable since they include pro-rata property-tax and hazard insurance under the FHA program, but the 15.5% for buyers using privately insured loans indicates no serious constraint.

As for the regional data in table 3-6, it may merely be noted that the western division throughout shows substantially larger dollar amounts as well as ratios.

The lower income range of the market, in which first homebuyers predominate, is served not only by FHA and private mortgage insurance companies but also by VA-guaranteed home loans and the activities of the Farmers Home Administration. The latter focus on rural areas but not necessarily on the financing of farm dwellings, and they extend mainly to the fringes of cities and metropolitan areas. The VA program is heavily weighted in favor of existing houses—78% of the total in 1974-1976. Although no detail on borrower characteristics is available for the operations of the other agencies, the sum of transactions under FHA, VA, Farmers Home Administration, and private mortgage insurance suggests that first-time buyers have been better served than is often alleged.[7]

Further Comment on First-time Buyers

The foregoing analysis does not complete the evidence on access of first-time homebuyers to the market. The remaining evidence is partly circumstantial and dated yet highly suggestive.

Homeownership has continued to increase. On a restrictive definition including only "regular" detached and attached single-family houses, the number of owner-occupied units rose by an annual average of 1,041,000 in the 1970-1973 period, 848,000 in 1974, 1,320,000 in 1975, and 755,000 in 1976.[8] The increase of single-family house completions from 1 million in 1976 to nearly 1.3 million in 1977, together with the expansion of builders' sales, suggests

cSince the data from the private insurance company are for new and old home purchases combined, the FHA statistics in this paragraph are weighted by the proportion of such purchases under the FHA program, which was one and nine, respectively. In the case of the private insurance company which supplied the data, the proportion was three and seven.

further substantial additions to owner-occupied units. Obviously, these net gains cannot have resulted from the transactions of owner-buyers, which generally mean a unit sold for every unit bought. Rather, the gains must largely reflect first-time purchases. The continuous growth of homeownership, though varying from year to year, seems incompatible with the notion that first-time buyers have been virtually excluded from the market, although their share in total purchases may have decreased. Data from the National Housing Surveys indicate indeed that the number of previous renters moving into owner-occupied houses[9] declined between 1973 and 1975, and so did their share in total moves to owner-units (table 3-7, item I). Whether these changes were related to adverse cyclical conditions or signified more severe income and wealth constraints on first-time buyers remains uncertain in the absence of 1976 and 1977 data. When the analysis of recent movers starts with previous renters rather than present owners, the proportion of those who shifted to homeownership also dropped between 1973 and 1975 (item II). The last item in the table serves as a reminder of the reverse shift: about 4 of every 10 movers who were previous owners became renters in 1975.

A decreasing share of first-time buyers in the total purchases of existing and new single-family houses is also evident from local information obtained in surveys conducted for the present study, which are discussed in the next chapter. In Contra Costa County (Northern California), first-time purchasers accounted for 42% of the 1975 homebuyers but only 34% of the 1977 buyers. In Orange County, the figures were 37% for 1975 and only 21% for 1977. Reduced access of first-time buyers to the market for *new* homes is apparent

Table 3-7
Recent Movers[a] into Owner-Occupied Units, by Tenure in Previous Unit, United States, 1973, 1974, and 1975
(movers with same household head in previous and present unit)

		Number of Units (1,000)			Percent Distribution		
Present and Previous Tenure		1973	1974	1975	1973	1974	1975
I.	Present unit owner-occupied	3810	3854	3400	100.0	100.0	100.0
	Previous unit o.o.	1779	1942	1775	46.7	50.4	52.2
	Previous unit r.o.	2031	1911	1626	53.3	49.6	47.8
II.	Previous unit renter-occupied	7379	7459	7009	100.0	100.0	100.0
	Present unit o.o.	2031	1911	1626	27.5	25.6	23.2
	Present unit r.o.	5347	5548	5383	72.5	74.4	76.8
III.	Previous unit owner-occupied	2744	2887	3002	100.0	100.0	100.0
	Present unit o.o.	1779	1942	1775	64.8	67.3	59.1
	Present unit r.o.	965	945	1227	35.2	32.7	40.9

Source: U.S. Bureau of the Census and U.S. Department of Housing and Urban Development, *National Housing Surveys for 1973, 1974, and 1975*, part D, table A-2.

[a]*Recent movers* are defined as households that moved into their present units within 12 months prior to the date of enumeration.

from estimates of the National Association of Homebuilders, based on information gathered in connection with the group's warranty program. According to the estimates, the share of first-time purchasers in total sales by builders has declined from about half to one-third. At the local level, Walker & Lee, one of the largest residential sales organizations in southern California, reports that previous renters represented approximately 27% of the buyers of new homes in the first half of 1977 as against 40 to 60% in the early 1970s. In principle, the usual emphasis on new homes in the debate over "affordability" seems misplaced. Most first-time buyers have always bought existing property. Further, the percentage distribution of first-time purchasers and owner-buyers does not tell the whole story. Taking builders' sales as a basis (table 3-1), let us assume that 50% of the 485,000 units sold in 1970 and only 30% of the 819,000 units sold in 1977 were acquired by first-time buyers. The number of such buyers would be about the same in both years, and their relative access to the market declined only to the extent that the ranks of potential first-time purchasers had increased in the interim. Finally, the recent growth of demand for new houses by owner-buyers may have caused builders to cater to this clientele. The product and marketing policies of builders could change within the limits of land and construction costs when the game of musical chairs played by owner-buyers slows down.

Despite these reservations, the sum total of the evidence in this section warrants the conclusion that first-time buyers have indeed encountered greater difficulty in obtaining access to home ownership in recent years.

The Burdens of Downpayment and High Interest Rates

The increasing dollar amounts of downpayments and the high mortgage loan interest rates in recent years are often singled out as evidence of constraints on home purchase. With respect to downpayments, for example, a report by the Congressional Budget Office shows that they rose from 59.3% of median family income in 1970 to 71.6% in 1975 for new houses and from 58.4% to 64.4% for existing houses. But this computation is based on an *assumed* 25% downpayment remaining constant throughout the period.[10] Thus the growing "burden" of downpayment becomes a function of median house prices increasing at a faster rate than median family income. Further, the document of the Congressional Budget Office acknowledges the lower FHA downpayments but does not refer to those under the VA and Farmers Home Administration programs and under private mortgage insurance, which, as was shown earlier, add up to a significant part of the market.

In fact, downpayment requirements for conventional home loans (implied in the 25% assumption) have varied considerably over time, as is evident from figure 3-1. According to the FHLBB reports, average downpayment as a percent of average purchase price fell from a high level in 1968-1970 to a low in 1972-1973, increased moderately through 1976, and declined in 1977. The decline was one of the indications of loan terms being stretched, as was mentioned earlier. Even in the recent periods, the downpayment-price ratios did not reach the levels of 1968-1970. In this case, percentage changes that appear

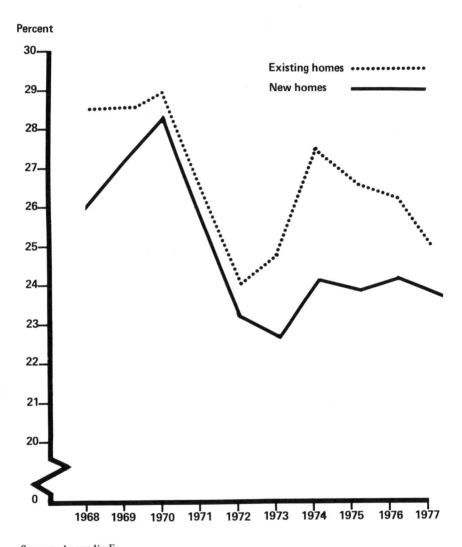

Source: Appendix E.

Figure 3-1. Average Downpayment as a Percentage of Average House Price, Conventional Home Mortgage Loans, 1968-1977

small have substantial impact on the amounts of downpayment. The latter, shown in appendix E, have increased in 1968-1977, though not regularly. Downpayments in 1977 averaged about $12,900 as against $8,000 in 1968 for new houses, and $11,800 as against $7,300 for existing residences. Consumer income was also rising, however. To express the relationship between downpayments and income, figure 3-2 shows average downpayments as a ratio of per-capita disposable personal income. This ratio declined substantially between

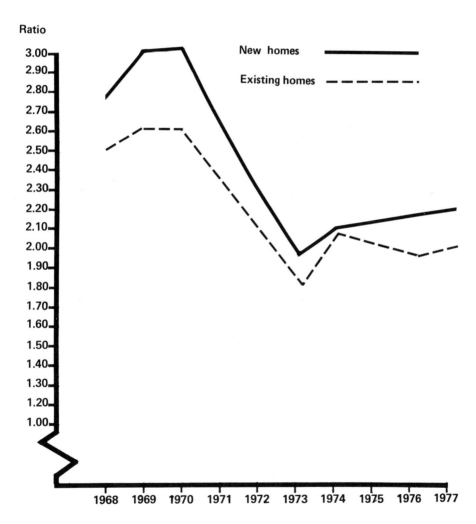

Source: Appendix E.

Figure 3-2. Average Downpayment as a Ratio of per-Capita Disposable Personal Income, Conventional Home Mortgage Loans, 1968-1977

1970 and 1973, and it increased moderately thereafter for new-homebuyers while it remained fairly stable for existing-home purchasers in the 1975-1977 period. For both types, the "burden" of downpayment in late years was far lighter than in 1968-1970 and somewhat lighter than in 1971-1972. This finding refutes the artificial computations of the Congressional Budget Office and is far more consistent with the recent growth of homebuying and the continued advance of homeownership. Nevertheless, wealth constraints on first-time home-buyers have probably become more severe. The data analyzed here do not distinguish between this group and owner-buyers.

Turning to mortgage interest rates, the borrowers' burden is substantially modified when the high nominal rates are converted to "real" rates. Under the inflationary conditions of the past few years, it has become common practice to view the nominal rates set by lenders generally as composed of two parts: a real rate of, say, 3%, presumably related to average long-run productivity, and a premium for anticipated inflation. A similar calculus, though perhaps more vaguely conceived, can be attributed to home mortgage borrowers when they become increasingly aware of continuous inflation and project nominal income gains as well as price increases into the future. High nominal mortgage interest rates under such circumstances have not deterred homebuying, as is evident from the increased purchases of existing and new houses in recent years. The notion of repaying mortgage debt in "cheaper dollars" gains ground and is applied to both the interest and principal components of debt payments. As Henry C. Wallich, governor of the Federal Reserve System, has put it in a more general context,

> if we interpret long-term interest rates in real terms, and make allowance for the fact that to most private debtors interest payments are tax-deductible, real long-term rates are indeed very low and for many borrowers probably negative.[11]

There is no information on the thought processes or intuitions through which homebuyers convert nominal interest to real interest. Hence only reasonable inferences are possible from what are presumed to be the purchasers' observations. One of the price movements they do observe are increases in consumer prices, apparent in their own shopping for goods and services even if they do not follow the news about the consumer price index (CPI). However, only the latter is available for quantitative illustrations. On the hypothesis that homeowners consider mortgage interest rates *ex post* in the light of general consumer price rises, the 1968 purchasers who on average paid a nominal rate of 7% on their mortgages paid a real rate of only 1.8% in 1977 if the intervening increase of CPI by 74.2% is taken into account (seven times reciprocal of 74.2). On the same reckoning for 1971 buyers, the average nominal rate of 7.7% of that year had been reduced to 3.7% in real terms by 1977. Even for 1974 purchasers, the average 9% nominal rate equaled a real rate of 7.8% after only three years of occupancy.[12] The calculated real rates of about 2 to 4% on loans obtained in 1968 and 1971 are low in comparison to the fragmentary historical data on rates for periods of stable price levels.

Another indicator of real interest rates on home loans is the differential change over time in nominal rates and consumer income. Although the interest rate-income ratio is an unconventional measure of real rates, it reflects direct experience of homeowners. According to table 3-8, per-capita disposable personal income more than doubled between 1968 and 1977. Interest rates on home mortgage loans increased by less than 30%. While nominal rates were about 9% at the end of the period as against 7% in 1968, the "burden" of high interest rates declined sharply. Dividing the index of interest rates by the index of income, one finds that the real rate for 1968 home purchasers who still occupied their property in 1977 was only 63% of the nominal 1968 rate, or 4.4%, if their earnings kept pace with our measure of income. The same calculation shows a real rate for 1971 purchasers equal to less than 70% of the nominal rate for that year, which was about 7.7% (ignoring the small rate differences for new and existing homes). The real rate in 1977 was 5.4%. For 1974 buyers, the nominal rate of about 9% at the time of purchase meant a real rate of less than 7% in 1977. In these calculations, the base year of the index numbers in table 3-8 is shifted to 1971 and 1974, respectively.

Table 3-8
Changes in Effective Interest Rates on Conventional Home Loans Compared with Changes in per-Capita Disposable Personal Income, United States, 1968-1977
(1968 = 100)

| | Interest Rates[a] | | Per-capita |
| | New | Existing | Disposable |
Period	Homes	Homes	Income[b]
1968	100.0	100.0	100.0
1969	112.0	111.2	106.2
1970	121.2	118.9	114.3
1971	111.0	109.1	122.4
1972	109.0	106.8	130.9
1973	114.1	113.9	146.2
1974	128.0	128.2	158.6
1975	129.3	131.0	173.3
1976	129.0	129.6	188.1
1977	129.3	128.3	205.0

[a]Based on effective interest rates on conventional home loans made by the major types of lenders, reported by the FHLBB.

[b]Based on amounts in current dollars reported by the U.S. Department of Commerce.

All these data reflect again the tilting effect of fixed debt payments under inflationary conditions, which was discussed earlier in this chapter. In terms of expectations, it is quite realistic to assume that large groups of recent home-buyers anticipate that their incomes will rise and make high interest rates (and debt payments) less burdensome. Thus about 75% of the Contra Costa respondents to our surveys of purchasers expected higher income in the year after purchase in both 1975 and 1977. In the case of Orange County respondents, 76.5% expressed the same view in 1975 and 71% in 1977. In both areas, well over 80% reported actual income gains between the year preceding purchase and the year of purchase. When expectations of increased income are combined with expectations of rising property prices the recent surge of homebuying at escalating prices and high interest rates is not astonishing.

Finally, real mortgage interest rates may be calculated by relating nominal interest payments during occupancy to realized capital gains in the sale of property. Table 3-9 shows three illustrations of the inferred real interest rate for

Table 3-9
Illustrations of Real Interest Rates for Homebuyers in
Specified Years Selling the Property in Designated Years

Item	Case I	Case II	Case III
1. Year of purchase[a]	1968	1972	1968
2. Year of sale[a]	1972	1976	1976
3. Purchase price of new house[b]	$26,600	$30,500	$26,600
4. Proceeds from sale[c]	27,400	38,400	38,400
5. Excess of (4) over (3)	800	7,900	11,800
6. Loan at purchase[d]	19,700	23,500	19,700
7. Interest rate at purchase[e]	7.0%	7.6%	7.0%
8. Interest payments during occupancy[f]	6,671	8,700	11,521
9. Excess of item (8) over (5)	5,871	800	−279
10. Inferred real interest rate[g]	6.0%	0.7%	Negative

[a]Assumes purchase at beginning of the year and sale at end of the year. Thus the occupancy period is five years for cases I and II, and nine years for case III.

[b]Average price for new houses reported by the U.S. Department of Commerce. No closing costs assumed in purchase of new homes.

[c]Average price for existing houses reported by National Association of Realtors, minus 6% sales commission and 3% closing costs, rounded. For closing costs, see note c to table 3-3. The figures omit capital-gains taxes due on property sales without acquisition of another home.

[d]The average loan-price ratio for conventional mortgages on new homes was 76.8% in 1972 and 73.9% in 1968. The dollar amounts are computed from a rounded 77% and 74%, respectively (FHLBB).

[e]Annual average effective rate for conventional mortgages on new homes (FHLBB). Rounded for 1968 when the actual rate was 6.97%.

[f]Based on interest rates in item (7) and average maturities of 27.2 years for 1972 and 25.5 years for 1968 (FHLBB). Does not provide for prepayment penalties.

[g]Item (9) divided by 5 years in cases I and II and by 9 years in case III and annual figure expressed as a percent of item (6).

homebuyers who begin and terminate ownership in specified years, based on reported average prices and nominal interest rates. The results are quite startling. The 1968 and 1972 buyers who terminated ownership in 1976 (cases II and III) obtained a capital gain on the sale of the property close to their total interest payments during the occupancy period. In other words, if the capital appreciation is retroactively applied to interest payments, the inferred real interest rate becomes insignificant or slightly negative, as is suggested in Henry Wallich's passage that was quoted earlier. The experience of the 1968 buyers' terminating ownership in 1972 was less favorable, largely because house price increases were more moderate. Even so, the nominal interest rate of 7% is reduced to a real rate of 6%. Of course, these conclusions hold only for home purchasers who terminated ownership status on sale of their property. If the sale was associated with the acqusition of another house, all or much of the capital gain would typically be used for a downpayment. But changes from ownership to rental are not infrequent. In the years 1973-1975, between 33 and 41% of "recent movers" who were homeowners became renters (table 3-7). Besides, relative capital gains on the owner's downpayment have exceeded the relative appreciation of the property, as is evident from the following figures keyed in to table 3-9:

	Case I	Case II	Case III
Proceeds from sale	$27,400	$38,400	$38,400
Loan balance at sale	$17,981	$21,859	$16,120
Equity at sale	$9,419	$16,541	$22,280
Original downpayment	$6,900	$7,000	$6,900
Capital gain on downpayment	$2,519	$9,541	$15,380
% of property appreciation	3.0%	25.9%	44.4%
% of capital gain	36.5%	136.3%	222.9%

   In sum, contrary to widespread notions, the high nominal rates of the past few years have in fact been bargains when they are converted to real rates on the basis of either general consumer price increases or income gains or price movements in the single-family house market. In terms of expectations, again, it is reasonable to assume that the experience recorded in table 3-9 has not gone unnoticed. Home shoppers keep themselves fairly well informed of house prices and mortgage interest rates in their localities, and they form expectations with respect to both from their own observations of past trends and from talks with relatives, friends, coworkers, and real-estate agents. To the extent that they anticipate capital gains from rising house prices, buyers tend to weigh such gains against the periodic cash outlays for high interest rates (or total debt payments), are willing or think they can afford to devote a larger part of their income to current homeownership expenses, or expect their earnings to rise so rapidly that housing expenses will soon bear a normal relationship to income. That some recent buyers may find their expectations invalidated and discover they have overextended themselves is a subject reserved for discussion in chapter 7.

The Speculators

The analysis to this point has been confined to purchasers of homes for owner-occupancy, hereafter labeled "occupant-buyers." But when the California news reports about escalating property prices made headlines, speculators seemed to hold the center of attention, and they were accused of causing or at least aggravating the price surge. This section of the study seeks to describe the role of speculators in the 1976-1977 market, convey some orders of magnitude of speculative house purchases, discuss measures by mortgage lenders and builders to curb such purchases, and address the question whether speculation had a stabilizing or destabilizing effect on the single-family house market. Such an attempt is made difficult not only by the paucity of facts but also by the familiar problem of defining speculation.

In conformity with definitions in other markets where speculation is a permanent activity, notably the commodity, foreign exchange, and securities markets, speculators may be said to have bought homes for resale in the expectation of a capital gain over and above transaction and holding costs plus income taxes on the gain. They usually anticipate a short holding period. In one type of operation, the "double-escrow," purchase and sale are virtually simultaneous. In other cases, speculators may or may not rent the property, but income derived from renting does not loom large in their motivations, and negative cash flows during the holding period are considered acceptable. In the case of old houses, speculators may make property improvements ranging from the cosmetic type to major modernization to enhance the potential for resale and profit. Generally, the distinction between speculators and other market participants has been drawn by M. Friedman in terms of the prices they consider in trading particular goods. Speculators determine their actions on the basis of future expected prices as well as current and past prices. Transactions by others are directly influenced by current prices only.[13] But this somewhat didactic definition is modified by the observation that in the real world each market participant is to some degree a speculator. According to Baumol, the distinction is not between pure speculators and pure nonspeculators but may involve a dichotomy between professional and amateur speculators, or perhaps conscious and other speculators.[14] This modification bears on the quality of information on which market participants act, and it is especially relevant for the recent activity in the California single-family house market. Amateur speculators seem to have joined the ranks of professionals—the real-estate practitioners—in fairly large numbers. Further, occupant-buyers themselves have been propelled into house purchase by expected future prices. Homebuyers have always considered not only the capitalized value of the periodic housing services they acquired (the consumption component) but also the resale potentials of the property (the investment component). During the recent buying spree, capital-gain expectations of owner-occupant purchasers have greatly increased in importance, as is evident from the surveys discussed in the next chapter. Thus the issue of defining speculation is extremely complex in the case at hand.

The problem is compounded by the existence of investors in single-family houses. They distinguish themselves from speculators by a longer time horizon, by definite intention to rent the property, and by greater expectation of positive net yields from operation, although they, too, may be motivated by capital-gains prospects in later resale. There has always been moderate investment activity in the single-family house market, and it seems to have increased in recent years. According to unverifiable reports, some small portion of the growing foreign investment in U.S. assets has gone into homes held for rental, especially on the East and the West Coasts, as well as apartment houses and other income property. But it would be erroneous to assume that the sizeable inventory of rented single-family dwellings owes its origin entirely to spontaneous investment. Some of these units are rented when the owner-occupant transfers to another location but expects that he may come back, or they are located in declining neighborhoods where the original owner-occupants were faced with dismal sale potentials when they decided to move.

As for the extent of speculation, mortgage lenders and builders base their impressions necessarily on the distinction between occupant-buyers and others, as evident from loan applications or purchase contracts and from the specific affidavits that lenders and builders required after they became aware of the growth of speculation. In any event, the direct information comes from the prospective buyers. As speculative purchasers noted measures by developers and lenders to restrict their activity, the documentary information became less reliable, causing a cynical executive to quip "we have two classes of buyers: owner-occupants and liars." In many cases, lenders discovered nonoccupant buyers only after the fact when borrowers gave billing addresses other than the address of the home they had purchased.

Under these circumstances, the magnitude of speculation eludes dependable measurement, but it is clear that it has been largely confined to California and was of short duration, with speculative purchases gathering momentum in mid-1976 and diminishing sharply a year later.[15] Further, speculation has been far more a symptom than the cause of the price escalation. Purchases of single-family houses for resale appeared to be profitable when the quantity of homes demanded for owner-occupancy was not matched by available supply and consumers rushed into homebuying for fear of further price increases. Indeed, speculation was vanishing in the latter part of 1977 as demand-supply relationships moved toward normalization and the frenzy of owner-occupant purchases subsided.

Estimates of the extent of speculation, obtained through interviews with mortgage lenders, builders, and home-selling organizations, vary a great deal depending on the markets in which the informants operate and on the availability and reliability of documentary evidence. In areas of especially active markets such as Orange County, estimates range up to 20% of all new-unit sales being made to nonoccupant buyers.[16] For individual projects, they run up to 30%. In the case of a large-scale developer in Orange County, two thirds of the nonoccupant purchasers were found to be holding and selling title to the property while the papers were in escrow—the double-escrow technique that was mentioned earlier. One savings-and-loan association operating throughout the state estimated that 20% of all loans on new and existing homes were made to nonoccupants at the height of speculation. Another, operating in southern California, reported 14% for 1976. The "normal" proportion was said to range up to 5%. On the whole, speculation seemed to be more widespread in transactions for new houses than in those for existing property relative to the size of the two markets, although the number of speculative purchases of old units may have exceeded those of new dwellings.

The Citizens Savings and Loan Association headquartered in San Francisco has developed a "speculation index" based on samples of ads offering unfurnished homes for rent in four California areas. The method assumes that fluctuations in speculation can be discerned from changes in the number of such advertisements, although the offerings of investor-owners of single-family houses cannot be distinguished from those of speculators who rent properties pending sale in the near future.[17] The results of this interesting though not conclusive attempt to measure the extent of speculation show a sharp increase of ads in the first half of 1977 over the same period of 1976 and some decline thereafter (see appendix table F-1), consistent with general market observations. The "speculation index" may continue for a while at relatively high levels as recent buyers for capital gain decide to rent rather than hold the property vacant, or rerent when their tenants move out.

Speculative purchases have decreased markedly not only because changed market conditions made them less profitable but also because of efforts by builders and mortgage lenders to curb speculation. Lenders imposed larger downpayment requirements and higher interest rates on nonoccupant buyers, and some of them eventually rejected loan applications by such buyers. In the process, two-party unrelated purchasers were increasingly considered nonoccupants. Builders did not accept purchase contracts with persons on behalf of others unless they presented signed power-of-attorney documents. Buyers were disqualified if they wanted to acquire more than one property in the same development. None of these methods were foolproof, nor were the affidavits declaring that the house would be occupied by the purchaser.[18] Nevertheless, the measures taken by builders and lenders tended to discourage speculation. Builders were strongly motivated to exclude speculators. As one developer put it, it was painful to see a product he placed on the market for $50,000 resold within months for $20,000 more. Also, the speculators tended to delay closing while arranging for resale. Their for-sale signs could unnerve potential buyers in a new tract.[19] Mortgage lenders expected that, on average, credit to speculators would be more risky than loans to owner-occupants.

Why did builders fail to raise their prices to a level approximating the prices obtained or anticipated by speculators and thus capture the latters' capital gains? Why did some of them resort to lotteries to allocate the supply instead of using the time-honored price mechanism or the auction method (applied in very few cases)? On the whole, one would expect builders or at least the larger firms to be at least as well informed about market conditions as were the speculators as a group. This precludes inferior knowledge as an explanation. One answer to our questions lies in the traditional merchandising method of the merchant builder. He constructs a few model houses, advertises their prices and opens the project or a substantial section to the public, and then schedules the rate of construction on the basis of purchase contracts. He seeks to minimize price risks by fixed-cost arrangements with contractors or subcontractors or by anticipating increases in dwelling construction costs when prices are set. Under ordinary circumstances, this is an entirely rational procedure. It provides the builder with flexibility in rates of completion and with information on the kinds of houses in greatest demand, and it is a device for economizing on scarce working capital. The risks of offering the "wrong" mix of products and the capital requirements would be far greater if the developer *completed*, say, 100 homes, and opened his project and set prices at that point. Commitments of construction and mortgage loans, an essential ingredient of merchandising houses, would be difficult to obtain under such a procedure. Besides, early price announcements avoid pointless and costly dealings at the site with potential buyers of, say, $50,000 houses, when the units in the project are priced at $80,000 to $120,000, or vice versa.

Moreover, builders' customary method of pricing seems to be based on cost plus profit, with the cost calculation providing for anticipated increases when homes are sold before completion. Amidst the fast-moving market developments in 1976-1977, many builders found it difficult to deviate from traditional practice even if they recognized that they were underpricing their product. Alternatively, the cost-plus approach militated against close observation of the market, that is, builders were indeed less well informed about obtainable prices than were the speculators. In addition, builders are always concerned with fast turnover of units in a project so they can begin to repay construction loans and move on quickly to the next project. Under volatile conditions, many tend to sell below the market for fear that higher prices would slow the pace of sales. In other words, profit maximization may take account of factors beyond the prices set for a given quantity of houses placed on the market at one time.

Most builders, especially those planning future projects or sections on adjoining or nearby sites, were also concerned over their reputation and long-term sales prospects if they raised prices above the advertised amounts. In addition, they were uncertain whether the speculators' prices were sustainable. If not, there might be an unusual number of buyers defaulting on their mortgages, giving the developer a "black eye" in future dealings with lenders. As for lotteries, it seems that the publicity given to the first cases caused some other builders to use this method of allocation simply to attract attention to their projects.

Of course, conditions in the California market for new single-family houses between the summer of 1976 and the summer of 1977 were not ordinary. It took time for builders to recognize the appearance and extent of speculation, and their actions were then confined to efforts to control it. Meanwhile, traditional ways of doing business militated against any radical change in merchandising technique, although some developers were reported to delay price announcements. On the whole, it seems that relatively few and typically small builders pursued a price policy that attempted to capture the gains obtained or expected by speculators. Others adjusted themselves to the situation by curtailing the size of project sections opened to the public at set prices.

According to close observers of the market, one of the remarkable characteristics of single-family house speculation in California was the widespread participation of nonprofessionals as well as real-estate practitioners: accountants, lawyers, dentists, doctors, and so forth. In some cases the nonprofessionals bought homes for resale; in others, they acquired property for owner-occupancy but held their old house for capital appreciation, renting it or trying to rent it in the interim. Among the professionals, real-estate brokers and salespersons were in a unique position to spot offers below current or expected market prices and made purchases in their own name. Small builders or interior decorators joined their ranks and specialized in short-term transactions typically accompanied by alteration or other work to enhance the market value of existing homes—a type of activity well known before the recent wave of speculation. Participation ranged from "one-shot" deals to repetitive operations.

Considering the speculators' rationale, one must note that their expectations of price increases for individual properties were apt to exceed the *average* price rise shown in chapter 2 for several localities. This is consistent with the wide dispersion of price advances in specific neighborhoods or for homes in specific price classes or size groups, age categories, or equipment characteristics. On the other hand, even unsophisticated speculators had to anticipate that some part of the price appreciation would be absorbed by transaction expenses, the holding costs between purchase and resale, and income tax on their capital gain. Hence their proceeds were less than the difference between purchase and resale price. Appendix G presents some hypothetical cases of speculative transactions in Los Angeles. They show sizeable profit potentials, but realized gains depend greatly on transaction and holding costs and on tax treatment of profits as well as the tax bracket of the speculator.

Was the recent speculation in single-family houses a parasitic or economically useful activity? This is an old question with respect to commodities, securities, and foreign exchange in which speculation has long been an institutional and continuous feature of the markets. The question has also been raised in connection with raw or improved land, although the market is less organized, the turnover less frequent, and the average holding period longer than the position taken by speculators in the prototype speculative markets. It is a novel issue for the single-family house market. The public debate of house speculation and the attempts to constrain it suggest a negative view of its economic function, conforming to the prevailing popular disapproval of any kind of speculation.

On the other hand, economic analysis has demonstrated that speculation can and often does have beneficial effects in a competitive economy. The analysis applies for the most part to the commodities, foreign exchange, and securities markets so long as speculation is nonmonopolistic, that is, does not "corner" a market. In the view of economists, speculation tends to smooth cyclical fluctuations, that is, stabilize prices and improve the relationship between the supply and final demand for the goods or assets traded. Taking the classic case of wheat, for example, the speculator operating in the futures market assumes the price risk that the producers would bear in the absence of speculation; and the farmer can "hedge" against uncertain future price changes (often seasonal as well as cyclical for agricultural commodities). When informed speculators anticipate rising wheat prices and step up their futures commitments, they bring on price increases sooner than would otherwise be the case. This encourages more planting and production and discourages wheat consumption in favor of substitutes. The opposite changes are induced when speculators expect prices to decline. Such adjustments would be delayed in the absence of speculation, that is, the market would function less efficiently. It should be noted that the beneficial effects rest on the existence of specialists who make it their business to collect and analyze information and on the availability of information. The latter is indeed comprehensive and up to date in the commodities, securities, and foreign exchange markets to the point of published daily quotations. Also the stabilizing effects come from speculators operating on both the upside and the downside of the market, depending on their price expectations. Finally, the objects of trading are relatively homogeneous.

The case of land speculation is more complicated because land is highly heterogeneous, information far poorer and less accessible, sales are more sporadic, and market adjustments much slower. The recent analyses by Lawrence B. Smith and others indicate that land speculation can be stabilizing or destabilizing, that is, can cause the amplitude of price fluctuations to either increase or decrease. Among other things, a destabilizing tendency may result from the effects of speculators' activity on the price expectations and the demand curve of land purchasers for final use.[20]

The principal question for an assessment of the effects of the recent house speculation is the relevance of the standard analysis applied to the classic speculative markets. The product is heterogeneous. The single-family house market is highly imperfect and poorly organized. Information on transaction prices is spotty, usually based on individual cases or observations of varying accuracy, and difficult to generalize even for narrowly defined areas. This is a crucial matter, for the stabilizing effects attributed to speculation in commodities, securities, and foreign exchange rest largely on the high quality of

information available to market participants. The knowledge of amateur speculators is generally inferior to that of the professionals. The distinction between the
two types is therefore of some importance, although it is heuristic rather than
categorical. Depending on the specialized skills in determining when and where
to buy, individuals might be classified along a continuum running from pure
dilettantes to persons with considerable sophistication.

Equally crucial is the virtual absence of house speculation as a continuous
activity. Although there may have been sporadic speculative activity in earlier
housing booms, evidence of unbroken and significant participation of speculators in the single-family house market is totally lacking. Even the rudiments of
an institutional framework for speculation, so highly developed in the other
markets, do not exist. Futures contracts and hedging are unknown. There is no
market mechanism for transferring the price risk from builders to other parties.
In fact, homebuilders have historically been the only large group incurring price
risks, and they were indeed labeled "speculative builders" before the more
dignified term "merchant builders" came into use. Moreover, the recent
speculation occurred only on the upside of the market, within a brief span of
time, and it simply petered out when the market was softening. It is difficult to
see how speculation on the downside could become an operable and profitable
activity. Houses have never been "sold short." Finally, unit transaction costs in
the purchase and sale of single-family houses are high in comparison to those in
the classic speculative markets.

Thus the house speculation of recent vintage lacks all the important
ingredients of speculative operations in the prototype markets analyzed by
economists for their stabilizing or destabilizing effects. It was a temporary
"bubble" consisting of price arbitrage.[21] Professional and amateur arbitragers
entered the market when their more or less sketchy information led them to
believe that some houses available for sale—new or existing—were "underpriced."
Even the arbitrage function varied from its counterpart in the typical speculative
operations in one important respect. In the latter, small and sometimes miniscule
differences between prices in two separate places, say, the dollar in London
versus Tokyo, or between spot and future prices give rise to arbitrage because
the trading volume is large. In the single-family house sector, the spread between
asking price and the speculator's perception of the true market price must be
lumpy to evoke arbitrage. This is the result of high transaction costs for each
property combined with the difficulty of trading in large numbers of properties
at the same time.

Market-correct pricing is an important economic function because it
channels goods or services to those who use them most effectively and thus helps
to allocate resources efficiently. But one must question whether this general
principle holds demonstrably for housing services. Does a house buyer who pays
$80,000 to a speculator instead of $60,000 to a builder or owner of an existing
property use the unit more effectively? The housing services rendered by the

property are largely fixed by its size, age, and design and by the neighborhood amenities associated with its location. There is no reasonable presumption that the household paying $80,000 is larger than that of the buyer who would have spent $60,000 for the same house, that is, that intensity of occupancy varies with price. The condition is quite different in most of the prototype speculative markets. If speculators in silver, for example, accelerate an ongoing price rise, smaller quantities of the metal will be used in some of the innumerable product combinations in which silver is one of the components such as jewelry; or silver-plating may be substituted for pure silver.

Nevertheless, it is instructive to pursue some other points made in favor of speculation as a stabilizing force. By raising prices sooner or more sharply than would otherwise be the case, speculators are said to stimulate production and restrain consumption of a particular good. The output argument could hold for homebuilding in the 1975-1977 period. To the extent that speculation accelerated increases in house prices, builders may have been encouraged to step up their activity. But the short-term effects on the total market supply of homes would be quite marginal since about three existing units are offered for every new unit. Thus if speculation in California induced a 10% rise in new construction, the total available supply would be augmented by only 2.5%. The impact is quite different in markets where the supply at any given time is dominated by new output.

As for constraints of consumption, it is quite dubious whether house price increases brought on or sped up by the recent speculation have served such a purpose. House purchases by final users, that is, owner-occupants, were growing sharply and reached extraordinarily high levels despite the marginal price effects of speculation. Speculators were not needed to hold an inventory of houses until it was required to meet final user demand—one of the related functions attributed to speculation in other markets. Instead of restraining user-demand, it is much more likely that speculative activity *stimulated* purchases by owner-occupants because it reinforced the latter's inflationary price expectations. To a large extent, these expectations were emulative. When potential homebuyers observed not only hectic purchases by other final users but the much publicized entry of speculators, their fears of future price increases became aggravated.[22]

From the present vantage point, it appears that the classic argument for a stabilizing influence of speculation is largely inapplicable.[23] Final judgment on whether the recent speculation in the California single-family house market had a net stabilizing or destabilizing effect must await the ongoing liquidation of speculators' holdings. For example, sales by speculators may help dampen the rate of price increase if their disposition of property is timed so as to anticipate the peaking out of prices. Also the speculative activity may have had a beneficial side-effect on the rental market. It served to increase at least temporarily the supply of houses for lease when speculators rented properties pending sale; thus upward pressures on rents may have been somewhat reduced. In any event, the moderate overall volume of speculation means that its consequences will turn out to be marginal except in local subareas where it was of more substantial magnitude.

Notes

1. Data from Bureau of the Census, *Construction Reports C25*, "Characteristics of New Housing," 1976.

2. Of the owner-buyers in 1973, 70% purchased houses priced above the ones they sold; 17% bought in the same price class, and 13% in a lower price class. National Association of Realtors, *Profile of the Single-family Home Buyer* (1977), p. 26. The data are based on special tabulations from the *Annual Housing Survey 1973* (Bureau of the Census).

3. Personal disposable income increased by 58%, and the per-capita equivalent by 48% between 1965 and 1971. The corresponding increases for 1971 to mid-1977 are 77% and 69%, respectively.

4. For the tilting effect and illustrations, see Donald Lessard and Franco Modigliani, "Inflation and the Housing Market: Problems and Potential Solutions," In Modigliani and Lessard (eds.), *New Mortgage Designs for Stable Housing in an Inflationary Environment* (Federal Reserve Bank of Boston, Conference Series No. 14, 1975), pp. 15-18.

5. The average family income of FHA purchasers (table 3-5) rose by 122% in the case of new homes and nearly doubled in the case of existing homes between 1965 and 1976. The gains during the same period were nearly 177% for personal disposable income and about 148% for the same on a per-capita basis. Between 1974 and 1977, family income of FHA buyers increased by 29.2% for new homes and 23.5% for existing homes. In the same period, personal disposable income rose by 33% and, on a per-capita basis, by 30%.

6. News releases of the U.S. Department of Housing and Urban Development, No. 77-261, August 24, 1977, and No. 78-106, March 30, 1978.

7. Starts of new houses under FHA, VA, and Farmers Home Administration programs equalled 21.5% of all private single-family starts in 1974, 24.0% in 1975, and 20.9% in 1976. The underlying figures include a small number of 2- to 4-family structures and of FHA loans under subsidy programs. Financing through the Farmers Home Administration is limited to low- and moderate-income borrowers. The combined FHA-VA transactions for existing homes accounted for 15.9% of the sales of such homes reported by the National Association of Realtors in 1974, 16.6% in 1975, and 14.8% in 1976. For the Farmers Home Administration, the distribution over farm and other dwellings is indicated by the home mortgage pools guaranteed by the agency. At the end of 1976, the amount was $3.4 billion for farm houses and $10.2 billion for other homes (*Federal Reserve Bulletin*, Table on Real Estate Debt).

8. Housing Census of 1970, and Annual Housing Surveys (based on sample surveys) for later years. The annual average for 1970-1973 accounts for 3½ years since the 1970 Census was taken in April, whereas data for the 1973 Housing Survey (and subsequent surveys) were collected from October to December. The definition excludes owner-occupied units in structures with two or more units and mobile homes and trailers.

9. Movers and buyers are not strictly synonymous. For example, an owner-occupant who transfers to another city may rent his property and move back to it later without a purchase transaction. Also the data relate to movers with the same household head in the previous and the present unit. Hence new households acquiring a single-family house are not accounted for. According to special tabulations from the 1973 National Housing Survey, new households represented more than 10% of all single-family house buyers (National Association of Realtors, *Profile of the Single-family Home Buyer*, 1977, p. 12). Nevertheless, the data on recent movers provide valuable and broadly accurate information on first-time buyers.

10. Congressional Budget Office, Budget Issue Paper "Homeownership: The Changing Relationship of Costs and Income, and Possible Federal Roles," Chapter IV. Their data are based on median prices of new homes sold by merchant builders and of existing-home transactions as reported by the National Association of Realtors.

11. Remarks by Henry C. Wallich on "The Business Cycle and The Federal Reserve" at the 1977 Annual Meeting of the National Association of Business Economists, Philadelphia, October 11, 1977.

12. The nominal rates in the text are the "effective rates" reported by the FHLBB for conventional loans by major types of lenders. The 1968 rates were 6.97% for loans on new homes and 7.03% on those for existing property. The 1971 rates were 7.74% and 7.67%, respectively. The 1974 rates were 8.92% and 9.01%, respectively.

13. M. Friedman, "In Defense of Destabilizing Speculation," *Essays in Economics and Econometrics*, edited by Ralph W. Pfouts (Chapel Hill: University of North Carolina Press, 1960).

14. W.J. Baumol, "Speculation, Profitability, and Stability," *Review of Economics and Statistics*, August 1957.

15. Reports of regional underwriters of two mortgage insurance companies covering all major urban areas indicated no speculation except in California. In some cases, speculative purchases were estimated at 1-2% of all purchases, but this seems to be a normal proportion at times of active single-family house markets. However, speculative activity has been observed in some local markets in Arizona and Nevada. For Reno, see David L. Parry, *The Reno Economy and Housing Market*, Special Publications Series of the Federal Home Loan Bank of San Francisco, January 1978, p. 4. The extent of speculation is not indicated in the report.

16. According to a staff report of the FHLB of San Francisco on Orange County, interviews with developers and salespersons in early 1977 revealed that approximately 10 to 20% of the new-home buyers—roughly twice the historical level—would not occupy the homes being purchased. Because speculative intent was concealed by some purchasers, the proportion was probably higher. See Steven W. O'Heron and David L. Parry, *Orange County Housing Markets*, Special Publications Series of the Federal Home Loan Bank of San Francisco, September 1977, p. 26.

17. As an indication of the relative importance of speculators, small sample surveys were made to determine length of ownership by those offering homes for rent. Ownership was one year or less in 56% of the cases in Santa Clara County, 50% in Orange County, 48% in the San Fernando Valley of Los Angeles, and 32% in Contra Costa County. According to the source, length of ownership would be more evenly distributed in the absence of speculation.

18. A similar affidavit has been required by the city of Davis, California. In July 1977 the City Council passed an emergency ordinance under which home purchasers must sign a sworn declaration that they intend to occupy the house for at least one year, with specified exemptions for hardship cases. Violators face criminal penalties of up to six months in jail and a $500 fine. *Sacramento Bee*, July 21, 1977. To our knowledge, this is the only case of municipal regulation of this kind. It may be associated with the city's stringent growth control, which limits the volume of homebuilding.

19. Testimony of Frank E. Hughes, Vice President, Residential Division, The Irvine Company, before the Homeownership Task Force of the U.S. House of Representatives, Long Beach, California, January 17, 1978.

20. Jack Carr and Lawrence B. Smith, "Public Land Banking and the Price of Land," *Land Economics*, November 1975, and Lawrence B. Smith, "The Ontario Land Speculation Tax: An Analysis of an Unearned Increment Land Tax," *Land Economics*, February 1976. These articles include references to extensive general literature on speculation; see also L.G. Telser, "A Theory of Speculation Related Profitability and Stability," *Review of Economics and Statistics*, August 1961, and J.C. Francis, "Speculative Markets: Valuable Institutions or Dens of Inequity?" *Business Review*, Federal Reserve Bank of Philadelphia, July 1972.

21. Following the distinction drawn by Jack Carr and Lawrence B. Smith, arbitrage denotes the purchase of an underpriced asset in anticipation of a sale at the true or full-information price, while speculation involves purchase of an asset at the full-information price in anticipation that this price will rise. See Carr and Smith, "Public Land Banking and the Price of Land."

22. For a more extensive analysis of the effects of speculators' activity on the expectations of nonspeculators in the land market, see Carr and Smith, "Public Land Banking and the Price of Land," pp. 324-326.

23. For a contrary view offered with some qualifications, see James R. Morris, "An Economic Analysis of Real Estate Speculation," Working Paper prepared for the Federal Home Loan Bank of San Francisco, 1978.

4 Characteristics, Motivations, and Expectations of Recent Buyers: Local Surveys

Unfortunately, there are no comprehensive data on the demographic and financial characteristics of recent homebuyers. The FHA statistics, partly reported in chapter 3, relate to a small segment of the market and therefore allow no generalizations. Moreover, information about the buyers' motivations and expectations is totally lacking. At the beginning of the study, the authors hoped that the major mortgage-lending institutions in California would have computerized information that could be used to establish a profile of 1976 home purchasers compared to the profile of buyers in earlier periods. To our astonishment, this expectation turned out to be misplaced. Most institutions had computerized data on property characteristics, but the information on borrower characteristics was buried in the original dockets for each loan, and the dockets for earlier years were often in dead storage. In a few cases, the institutions were just beginning to record and summarize some statistics on borrower characteristics as the surge of homebuying at escalating prices became a matter of concern to management. However, the few data available lacked historical depth.

The paucity of information has been in part alleviated by a survey of 1977 house purchasers, undertaken by the U.S. League of Savings Associations and including over 8,500 borrowers on conventional mortgages at nearly 200 savings-and-loan associations across the country.[1] According to the main findings, 36% of all buyers in the sample had acquired their first home. The median age of all buyers was thirty-two years, and that of first-time homeowners, even less. Unmarried people accounted for 17% of all purchasers and as much as 25% of those who entered homeownership for the first time. Nearly half the buyers had a household of only one or two members, and 45% had households with more than one earner. Median income was $22,700 for all purchasers and $20,000 for first-time purchasers. The median house price was $44,000, but first-time buyers spent a median of only $37,000 partly because they obtained older properties. In other words, price-income multiples were generally within normal ranges. The median net worth of all purchasers was nearly $32,000 although it was much lower for first-time purchasers. The survey report emphasizes the large regional differences in all these characteristics.

To probe more deeply the composition of recent homebuyers and especially their motivations and expectations, a special survey was conducted for this study of homebuyers in Contra Costa and Orange Counties, in the northern and southern parts of California, respectively. The two counties represent suburban growth areas in the San Francisco Bay and Los Angeles urban regions, though each has a significant component of older housing. Between 1970 and 1977, the population grew from 556,116 to 611,621 in Contra Costa County and from 1,421,233 to 1,799,700 in Orange County. Both counties were identified as "hot" housing areas during the past several years. Total and per-capita deed recordings, crude measures of market activity, rose significantly after the 1973-1974 recession, and homebuilding increased considerably (table 4-1).

The limited resources available for the study dictated a mail survey (see appendix H for the questionnaire). From lists of homes purchased in the early months of 1975 and 1977 in the two counties, 1,000 were selected randomly for each of the four cells yielding 4,000 sample points. The two time periods were selected in order to test changes of buyer characteristics and motivations between 1975 and 1977. However, it was anticipated that several factors militated against a definitive test. Mail surveys usually yield a relatively low rate

Table 4-1
Selected Housing Market Indicators, Contra Costa and Orange Counties, California, 1970-1977

		Contra Costa County		*Orange County*
Population				
1970 (April 1)		556,116		1,421,233
1975 (July 1)		586,600		1,713,400
1977 (July 1)		611,621		1,799,700
Annual Percent Change (compounded)				
1970-1977		1.4		3.4
1975-1977		2.1		2.5
Number of Deeds Recorded				
1970		19,787		48,436
1975		28,427		73,550
1977		42,535		108,745
Number of Deeds Recorded per 1,000 Population				
1970		35.6		34.1
1975		48.5		42.9
1977		69.5		60.4
Housing Stock and Home Building				
Total housing units, 1970		178,384		462,803
Percent single-family		77.7%		68.2%

	Total	*Singles*	*Total*	*Singles*
Number of housing units in building permits				
1970	6,736	2,178	23,408	7,234
1975	4,314	3,797	15,438	10,086
1977	10,404	9,059	27,504	15,612

Sources: U.S. Census of Population and Housing, 1970; California State Department of Finance; Security Pacific National Bank; Real Estate Research Council of Southern California; and Real Estate Research Council of Northern California.

of response. Moreover, questionnaires sent to addresses of homes known to have been sold would produce few responses from owners who had purchased property for rent to others. In fact, the response rates turned out to be relatively high, ranging around 43% for the questionnaires delivered (see appendix table H-1), but the number of usable questionnaires was reduced considerably from the number returned. Nearly 10% of the respondents identified themselves as renters of residences known to have been sold. For purposes of analysis, these responses were eliminated from the study. Further, approximately one third of the otherwise usable questionnaires in 1975 involved homes with sale date outside the period encompassed by the survey. In large part, these homes were sold again for owner occupancy after 1975; to maintain comparability, these returns were also eliminated from the analyses.a The number of responses used is indicated in each appendix H table.

Essentially, the survey results reported here pertain to owner-occupants of homes purchased in early 1975 and 1977.[2] As will be shown, the findings for these groups in the two areas are quite consistent, suggesting considerable reliability of the data. Nevertheless, since resource constraints inhibited follow-up surveys of nonrespondents, one must caution against attaching fine precision to the results. The findings must be evaluated in light of other evidence presented in chapter 3.

We examine first the major socioeconomic characteristics of recent home-buyers in the study areas and determine to what extent 1977 purchasers varied from those who bought single-family houses in 1975. This is followed by analysis of the homes acquired in the respective years, including prices paid and other property characteristics. Finally the discussion turns to indicators of motivations and expectations of recent homebuyers, particularly changes in the importance of investment and speculative considerations between 1975 and 1977, and to projections of homebuyers concerning house price versus general inflation.

Characteristics of Homebuyers

Table 4-2 summarizes selected data on 1975 and 1977 homebuyers in Contra Costa and Orange Counties. Detail is provided in appendix tables H-3 to H-13. The age of the household head in the two markets at the time of purchase did not vary significantly, with a median around the mid-thirties. That the 1975 buyers in both areas were somewhat older than the 1977 purchasers is explained by the fact that the surveys were conducted in 1977 when the earlier buyers

---

aSome responses in both 1975 and 1977 reported sales dates well before the periods covered by this study. Some of these homes apparently were sold with very long escrows or not reported as consummated until close of escrow; in other cases, the sales may have fallen through and were incorrectly reported as consummated; in still other cases, questionnaires may have been delivered to the wrong addresses.

Table 4-2
Summary of Major Characteristics of Recent Homebuyers, Contra Costa and Orange Counties, California, 1975 and 1977

Characteristic	Contra Costa County[a]		Orange County[a]	
	1975	1977	1975	1977
Median age[b]	35.0	33.5	37.5	35.6
Median household size	3.2	3.1	3.4	3.3
Median household income	$23,157	$25,828	$23,652	$26,814
Median home price/income ratio	2.15	2.52	2.08	2.79
Percent renters in previous residence	47.7%	38.8%	46.0%	28.4%
Percent purchasing first home	42.2	34.4	36.9	21.0
Percent purchasing existing home	74.6	74.0	65.9	71.2
Percent satisfied with current home[b]	91.1	89.6	90.3	88.0
Percent perceiving home as:				
Too large[b]	16.8	17.8	14.7	19.3
Too small[b]	20.4	7.7	22.3	7.3

[a]For further detail, including frequency distributions and number of responses on each question, see appendix H.
[b]Response as of 1977.

who still occupied their property were presumably two years older. The prime homebuying age group was twenty-five to thirty-four; about 52% of the Contra Costa County respondents in 1977 and 43% in Orange County were in this category.

The household size at time of purchase was typically a little smaller for 1977 than for 1975 buyers in both study areas. The share of one-person households in total home purchasers increased moderately between the two benchmark years and was slightly greater in Orange than in Contra Costa County. In 1977 approximately one out of every eleven buyers in Contra Costa County and one out of eight in Orange County was a single-person household. However, the lion's share in both study areas (and time periods) was captured by the two-person household group. In combination, one- and two-person households in 1977 accounted for 47 and 45% of homebuyers in Contra Costa and Orange Counties, respectively. Their proportion increased slightly between 1975 and 1977. Given the great expansion in total home sales in these areas, the number of small households buying residences increased sharply.

Some measure of the economic status of recent homebuyers is derived from household income before tax. The median income of 1975 buyers in Contra Costa County exceeded $23,000 and was fractionally higher in Orange County. The 1977 median for Contra Costa purchasers approximated $26,000 and was about $1,000 higher in Orange County. The intervening increase of about 12-13% paralleled the rate of general price inflation, suggesting that the typical real income of homebuyers remained about the same in both years. Since home prices rose much more than income and, as will be shown, increased at different rates in the two study areas, the median home price-income ratio moved up significantly, from 2.2 to 2.5 in Contra Costa County and 2.1 to 2.8 in Orange County. These data indicate some "stretching" of the conventional multiples over the two-year period of escalating house prices. The 1975 price-income ratios were within "normal" ranges, but those of 1977 were at or beyond the medians prevailing in the past.

As for the number of breadwinners in households purchasing homes, the share of buyers with more than one breadwinner remained at a stable 35% between 1975 and 1977 in Orange County, but it increased dramatically in Contra Costa County from 26% to 43%. At first glance, the Orange County results appear somewhat suspect when compared to data from other sources, but they become more understandable in light of three pieces of evidence. First the proportion of Orange County homebuyers with more than one breadwinner was already high in 1975 relative to Contra Costa County. Second the share of one-person households in total reported home purchases increased a little more in Orange County between 1975 and 1977 than in Contra Costa County. There can obviously be only one breadwinner in this group. Finally the fraction of buyers who had rented their previous residence decreased much more sharply in the southern than in the northern area, from 46% in 1975 to 28% in 1977 as against 48% to 39%. In view of the surge in house prices, previous homeowners purchasing another residence obtained capital gains that enabled them to make large downpayments reducing the burden of debt amortization. They were in a better position to meet current housing outlays and other expenditures from the earnings of one person. The larger share of owner-buyers in Orange County facilitated purchase by households with only one breadwinner. The contrast between the two areas may also be a function of differences in labor market opportunities or other variables.

The majority of respondents in both areas and periods indicated current housing expenses were "much more" than in the previous residence. In Contra Costa County about two thirds of the 1975 and 1977 survey respondents mentioned paying "much more" on housing, and in Orange County the proportion rose from 57% in 1975 to 67% in 1977. These general returns are consistent with data from surveys in Orange County by a major real-estate firm showing that in 1977 former homeowners increased monthly mortgage payments by 59% from $339 to $538, and previous renters by 88% from $246 to $463.[3] The fraction of gross income going to monthly payments rose from 14 to 22% among former owners and from 13 to 24% among former apartment dwellers. Together with other current outlays on the newly acquired properties, the burden of total housing expenses on the family budget would be still higher. Some buyers may have overextended themselves.

There was a notable decline in the share of first-time buyers among the respondents. In Contra Costa County 42% of all 1975 purchasers, but only 34% of the 1977 purchasers were in this category. The corresponding figures for Orange County were 37% and 21%, respectively. The figures in table 4-2 make it clear that first-time buyers and previous renters are not equivalent. A fraction of the latter had owned a residence some time prior to renting.

As elsewhere, expanded homebuying in Contra Costa and Orange Counties primarily involved the acquisition of existing rather than new homes in both 1975 and 1977. About 70 of every 100 properties purchased were of older vintage. Two additional observations can be drawn from table 4-2. The overwhelming majority of homebuyers in 1975 and 1977 were satisfied with their current homes; the differences between the areas and the periods are not significant. At the same time responses to one criterion for housing satisfaction, the dwelling size, show quite pronounced variations between 1975 and 1977 buyers in both counties. Among the 1975 buyers, about one out of five considered their house too small, and a lower proportion felt it was too large. Among the 1977 buyers, nearly one out of five considered their dwelling too large, and only one out of fourteen thought it was too small. The differences might be attributed to a normal course of events. The feeling of having insufficient space is more likely to surface as people gain experience living in a home. The 1975 purchasers had occupied their property for two years when the survey was taken. A resurvey of 1977 buyers in, say, 1979, might evoke a pattern similar to the response of 1975 buyers in 1977. However, there may be an alternate explanation. The buoyancy of the 1977 single-family house market and the expectations of capital gains may have induced some respondents to acquire a larger home than needed for personal use on the ground that it was a good investment. For example, if the buyer's primary consideration was housing consumption, his family needs might be met by a three-bedroom house with 1½ baths, purchased at $50,000, which in a rising market could be worth $60,000, or 20% more, in a year or so. If the investment motive was dominant, the buyer might be induced to leverage his downpayment a little more and to purchase a residence with four bedrooms and 2 baths for $65,000. With a 20% increase, the home could be worth $78,000 a year later. Ignoring current housing expenses and transaction costs, the "windfall" in the second case would be $3,000 larger than in the first. The question is whether the survey results offer clues suggesting a shift in investment versus consumption considerations between 1975 and 1977. This subject is reserved for later sections.

Features of Houses Purchased in 1975 and 1977

Prices paid by 1977 homebuyers in the two study areas were dramatically higher than those paid by 1975 buyers (table 4-3), confirming the evidence presented in chapter 2. In Contra Costa County the median price was nearly $50,000 in 1975

Table 4-3
Reported Home Purchase Price: Recent Homebuyers, 1975 and 1977

	Contra Costa County		Orange County	
	1975	1977	1975	1977
Less than $30,000	7.1%	3.8%	4.8%	0.4%
30-39,999	22.9	8.9	26.7	2.2
40-49,999	20.4	10.9	20.3	7.2
50-59,999	16.4	16.6	21.9	10.1
60-69,999	16.8	19.2	11.8	18.4
70-79,999	7.5	12.4	7.5	23.5
80-89,999	3.9	11.8	2.1	11.9
90-99,999	2.1	6.2	2.7	8.7
100-109,999	1.4	1.8	0	3.6
110-119,999	1.1	3.0	0.5	4.0
120-129,999	0	2.7	0	1.4
130,000 and more	0.4	2.7	1.6	8.7
	100.0%	100.0%	100.0%	100.0%
N =	280	338	187	277
Median	$49,912	$65,153	$49,079	$75,000
Increase 1975-1977	30.5%		52.8%	
Average annual increase (compounded)	+14.2%		+23.6%	

and more than $65,000 in 1977, an annual compounded increase of 14%. In Orange County the median 1975 price was somewhat below the level reported for the northern area, at $49,000, but rose to $75,000, an annual compounded increase of 24%. Ten percent of the homes in the North and 18% in the South had price tags of $100,000 or more in 1977.

Did the homebuyers of 1977 purchase more substantial homes than those of the earlier year? Also, were the price increases associated with a changing product mix of properties coming onto the market? Because of the limited scope of the surveys, the questions cannot be answered with a high degree of precision, but some clues are available. Table 4-4 shows selected characteristics of homes purchased in the study areas during the two survey periods. In Contra Costa County, the responses indicate that the mix of units bought in the two years was essentially unchanged with respect to two criteria, the number of rooms and baths. The age of existing homes acquired in 1975 and 1977 averaged 16.0 and 15.6 years, respectively. The square footage and neighborhood quality of the houses purchased in 1977 may have been superior, but we have no data on these items. In contrast, the findings for Orange County suggest several notable differences between the homes bought in 1975 and 1977. In the latter year, detached single-family houses represented a somewhat smaller percentage of all purchases than in 1975; yet prices increased at a faster rate than in the northern area. More than a third of the homes bought in 1977 were in attached structures

Table 4-4
Selected Characteristics of Current Residence: Recent
Homebuyers,a 1975 and 1977

Characteristics	Contra Costa County		Orange County	
	1975	1977	1975	1977
Percent three or more bedrooms	84.3%	83.8%	90.8%	83.4%
Percent two or more baths	76.6	74.6	72.7	77.3
Percent separate living room	95.3	93.1	94.7	93.4
Percent separate dining room	66.9	66.9	61.8	69.9
Percent with family room	66.7	67.9	62.7	67.5
Percent with study or den	22.8	21.8	26.1	33.0
Percent single-family detached	81.7	80.1	73.9	63.6

aFor further detail, including frequency distribution and number of responses on
each question, see appendix H.

and presumably included a large number of units in condominiums and planned
unit development projects. The percent of residences with three or more
bedrooms was lower in 1977 than in 1975. However, this statistic of itself may
be misleading since the fraction of both two-or-less and four-or-more-bedroom
houses bought in 1977 exceeded the 1975 percentages (see appendix table
H-14). The change may be attributable to a shift in the composition of
homebuyers. The 1977 buyers included relatively more single-person households
and perhaps married couples with no plans for having children. In any event, the
Orange County homes purchased in 1977 had more bathrooms, separate dining
rooms, family rooms and dens than those bought in 1975. Moreover, the average
age of the used homes in the 1977 sample was only 9.4 years versus 13.8 years in
1975. Since the share of new homes in the total purchases by Orange County
respondents also rose between 1975 and 1977, the buyers in the latter year
occupied more modern residences in younger neighborhoods.

Previous versus Current Residence

The houses bought by the survey respondents represented superior products
compared to their previous dwellings on practically all of seven specified
characteristics (table 4-5 in conjunction with table 4-4). This is true for both
areas and for both the 1975 and 1977 purchasers. The residences acquired by
the respondents had more bedrooms and baths than those they occupied before.
A substantially larger percentage had a separate dining room, a family room, and
a den. Single-family detached units accounted for a greater proportion of the
newly acquired properties than of the previous residences, but this may be
explained by the former renters among the 1975 and 1977 buyers. The only
property characteristic showing no significant change is a separate living room.

Table 4-5
Selected Characteristics of Previous Residence: Recent
Homebuyers,a 1975 and 1977

	Contra Costa County		Orange County	
Characteristics	1975	1977	1975	1977
Percent three or more bedrooms	55.7%	57.5%	59.9%	65.0%
Percent two or more baths	45.0	47.4	45.1	54.9
Percent separate living room	90.2	89.5	90.0	93.3
Percent separate dining room	49.2	53.6	49.1	59.7
Percent with family room	38.8	44.4	39.7	46.8
Percent with study or den	13.3	17.9	12.9	22.3
Percent single-family detached	56.3	60.2	49.7	53.5

aFor further detail, including frequency distribution and number of responses on each question, see appendix H.

Even in the absence of information on square footage of building space and on neighborhood quality, the data suggest considerable upgrading.

To judge from the available criteria, the previous residences of 1977 homebuyers in the sample were on most counts superior to those of the 1975 purchasers. For example, they had more bedrooms, and a larger percentage of the total had family rooms and dens and were in a single-family detached units. This is consistent with the already noted observation that the share of buyers who were already homeowners was considerably greater in 1977 than in 1975.

Concerning the location of previous residences of 1975 and 1977 buyers, the data are presented in table 4-6. A large and apparently growing fraction of Orange County homebuyers already resided in the area when they purchased their homes (60% in 1975 and 64% in 1977). Approximately one fifth of the buyers came from Los Angeles County, and only 4-5% from other California localities. About one out of every nine purchasers in both 1975 and 1977 previously resided in some area of the United States outside California. The somewhat different groupings for Contra Costa County show similar relationships.

Some of the major processes in "upgrading" of housing quality among buyers in any specific area now have been identified. These include (1) intraregional moves from the older parts of urban regions to the new suburbs and interregional migration; (2) shifts from apartment or single-family home rental to homeownership; and (3) shifts from older to newer homes including those newly constructed. In relative terms, it would appear that the contribution of intraregional and interregional moves remained the same in 1975 and 1977. The shift from rental to ownership played a smaller role in 1977 than in 1975 in upgrading housing quality, especially in Orange County (table 4-2). This is apparent from the fact that a smaller fraction of homebuyers in 1977 previously rented compared to the 1975 sample. The influence of acquisitions of new

Table 4-6
Location of Previous Residence of Homebuyers, 1975 and 1977

Orange County Location of Previous Residence	1975	1977
Los Angeles County	21.9%	19.6%
Orange County	60.4	64.1
San Bernardino-Riverside County	0.5	1.1
Other California counties	4.3	3.3
U.S. other than California	10.7	11.2
Abroad	2.1	0.7
	100.0%	100.0%
$N =$	187	276
Contra Costa County Location of Previous Residence	1975	1977
Contra Costa County	55.6%	55.4%
Other California counties	31.4	30.8
U.S. other than California	12.3	13.5
Abroad	0.7	0.3
	100.0%	100.0%
$N =$	278	339

homes on upgrading in Contra Costa County did not change materially between 1975 and 1977 but expanded in Orange County.[b]

The surveys also inquired whether respondents had an "extra bedroom" and if so, what it was being used for. The proportion of respondents reporting an "extra bedroom" was exactly the same in both counties in 1975—60.4%—but was greater in 1977, 63% and 67% in Contra Costa and Orange County, respectively. The lower incidence of extra bedrooms among the 1975 buyers who were surveyed in 1977 may be explained by additions to their families in the intervening years. But it may also reflect greater investment considerations among 1977 buyers. Home purchasers motivated by investment would be more prone to acquire residences that are larger than warranted by current or anticipated household size. As for the use of the "extra bedroom," respondents named a study/office, guest room, sewing room, and space for recreational activities in approximately that order.

[b]The surveys, of course, capture only a segment of the complex interactions between demanders and suppliers in housing markets. The net improvement in aggregate housing consumption in the study areas is probably considerably less than indicated by surveys of buyers. As noted, the majority of recent homebuyers in 1977 previously owned homes in the respective study areas and upgraded their housing with the move. At the same time "downgrading" may have occurred among some sellers of homes who shifted to lower quality rental units or neighborhoods outside the boundaries of the areas surveyed. Given the nature of the study, no inferences can be made on the net effects for aggregate housing consumption among populations in the housing markets. Moreover, nothing is known from surveys on changes in house quality via maintenance and capital improvements among the large number of nonmovers.

Reasons for Purchase

One of the important questions asked the respondents dealt with the express reasons for buying the particular home at the time they did. Answers to this question must be interpreted with caution, especially for the 1975 purchasers. When people are asked to explain past behavior, memories may be somewhat "fuzzy," and respondents may rationalize their actions in the light of subsequent events. Moreover, specified reasons for decisions made in the past (and even the recent past) may conflict with or be modified by behavioral observations, which were not available from the surveys. Nevertheless, some understanding of the motivations of home purchasers may be derived from the relative importance attached by consumers to various factors that play a role in the decision to buy. The findings are conditioned by the 1975-1977 setting. We do not infer a high degree of stability to the responses should a similar question be asked at another time and under different circumstances.

Respondents were asked to rank on a scale comprised of five categories running from "very important" to "not important" 19 factors indicated as reasons for home purchase. They were also provided the opportunity to list and rank factors not mentioned on the survey instrument. The responses for the two counties are summarized in tables 4-7 and 4-8. Generally, they indicate a remarkable degree of consistency between buyers across areas and the two survey periods. We shall concentrate first on the relative importance of expressed reasons for the property acquisition regardless of the time of purchase and then examine some differences between 1975 and 1977 buyers.

The largest single response pertains to the importance of home purchase as "the best investment for my money." Approximately four out of five respondents reported that this reason was important or very important at the time of purchase. Its dominance holds for both counties and for 1975 as well as 1977 buyers. In contrast, only a small fraction of the group surveyed (10% or less) considered "the best investment for my money" to be of little or no importance in their decision.

The responses to this question allow two interpretations. According to one, the purchasers believe that given their decision to buy, the particular property they acquired was the best investment for their money. According to the other, the buyers feel that home purchase as such was the best investment they could make. Responses to another question in the survey instrument lend support to the latter interpretation. Acquisition of a house as a hedge against inflation was given as an important or very important motive by 63 to 70% of the respondents, varying within a narrow margin with area and time of purchase. Inflationary expectations appear also in the item "last chance to buy." This was an important or very important reason for home purchase for about 40-50% of the respondents.

Table 4-7
Reasons for Purchasing Current Home, Contra Costa County Respondents, 1975 and 1977

Reasons	1975				1977			
	Of Little or No Importance	Somewhat Important	Important or Very Important	N	Of Little or No Importance	Somewhat Important	Important or Very Important	N
Neighborhood and location								
Closer to work	61.6%	22.2%	16.1%	261	56.6%	18.3%	25.0%	327
Job transfer	73.9	1.9	24.2	269	75.5	0.9	23.5	323
Better schools	54.3	14.2	31.5	260	56.9	10.2	32.9	325
Better area	21.8	19.1	59.2	262	24.1	17.8	58.0	331
Closer to friends	87.7	7.6	4.5	262	82.1	12.2	5.7	319
Household and shelter								
Larger home	27.4	14.3	58.3	259	27.1	17.6	55.3	329
Newly married, divorced, etc.	80.9	2.7	16.4	256	83.5	4.2	12.3	309
Increased income	57.4	24.7	17.8	263	61.8	16.4	22.0	324
Vacation home	99.6	0	0.4	259	99.0	0.6	0.3	317
Tired of renting	36.9	9.1	54.0	263	47.5	6.8	45.6	322
Financial and investment								
Inflation hedge	18.6	15.2	66.3	264	17.5	12.1	70.4	331
Best investment for money	7.1	14.2	78.7	267	5.4	12.3	82.2	332
Last chance to buy	41.1	20.8	38.1	265	33.3	19.1	47.6	330
Hoped to trade up	76.7	11.9	11.5	261	72.0	13.2	14.8	325
Hoped for capital gain	87.0	7.3	5.7	262	78.7	13.5	7.7	325
Income-tax benefits	15.4	18.4	66.1	266	16.7	17.6	65.8	330
Investment for future rental	95.8	4.2	1.9	261	87.5	7.8	4.7	320
Expected higher interest rate	50.8	22.0	27.2	264	34.9	25.0	30.2	328
Financing available	52.1	16.7	31.2	263	47.1	20.1	32.8	323
Miscellaneous	59.5	0	40.5	84	58.6	1.7	39.7	121

Table 4-8
Reasons for Purchasing Current Home, Orange County Respondents, 1975 and 1977

Reasons	1975				1977			
	Of Little or No Importance	Somewhat Important	Important or Very Important	N	Of Little or No Importance	Somewhat Important	Important or Very Important	N
Neighborhood and Location								
Closer to work	57.4%	16.6%	26.0%	181	54.9%	19.0%	26.1%	268
Job transfer	74.4	1.7	23.8	176	75.3	3.5	21.3	259
Better schools	52.8	15.2	32.0	178	56.0	6.3	37.6	268
Better area	21.4	15.4	63.2	182	22.0	15.2	62.6	270
Closer to friends	82.7	12.8	4.5	179	84.7	8.8	6.5	262
Household and Shelter								
Larger home	23.6	17.6	58.8	182	28.5	15.0	56.6	267
Newly married, divorced, etc.	75.8	4.1	15.1	172	83.9	3.2	12.8	249
Increased income	63.5	23.0	13.5	178	63.6	14.6	21.9	261
Vacation home	100.0	0	0	177	99.2	0	0.8	256
Tired of renting	46.7	7.2	41.1	180	57.7	5.8	36.4	258
Financial and Investment								
Inflation hedge	19.1	17.5	63.4	183	16.4	15.7	67.8	267
Best investment for money	7.0	13.4	79.6	186	10.4	8.9	80.9	271
Last chance to buy	41.0	17.3	41.6	185	36.3	18.0	45.7	267
Hoped to trade up	77.2	12.8	10.0	180	72.5	15.4	12.1	266
Hoped for capital gain	87.1	5.6	7.3	178	80.0	8.8	11.2	260
Income tax benefits	25.1	15.8	59.0	183	18.2	18.2	63.6	269
Investment for future rental	89.0	5.5	5.5	181	90.7	4.6	4.6	259
Expected higher interest rate	49.5	20.3	30.2	187	48.1	27.4	24.4	266
Financing available	56.9	19.3	23.8	181	62.6	15.4	22.0	259
Miscellaneous	45.5	7.3	47.3	55	64.0	1.2	34.9	86

Close to two thirds of the respondents considered the income-tax benefits of homeownership to be important or very important to their decision. Since the buyers of 1975 and 1977 include a large percentage of previous homeowners to whom tax benefits were already available, this finding calls for more extensive discussion. One reason for the importance attached to tax benefits may stem from the much greater amounts of interest and property-tax payments after the respondents acquired a more expensive home, assuming they itemized deductions before and after the move. The buyers were apparently prepared to incur a larger debt and higher property-tax obligations because they viewed the incremental burden at the margin as relatively light—but only because they shared the burden with the federal and state governments. Hence tax benefits assumed considerable significance, particularly for people in higher tax brackets. In other cases, interest and property-tax payments on the previous owner-occupied dwelling may have been so low that respondents had used standard deductions for income-tax purposes but would be better off by itemizing deductions for the newly acquired house. The potential tax benefits for the buyers who were previous renters require no comment. But the importance attached to tax considerations could also involve capital gains. Some respondents who were previous homeowners may have contemplated moving to rental quarters but rejected this alternative and bought instead another house. Among the important reasons for the purchase decision may have been avoidance of the capital-gains tax they would have to pay on sale of their previous residence. The sum total of these and other, more complex circumstances can explain why tax benefits loom so large among the responses.

Most of the buyers indicated that capital-gains expectations ("hoped to resell soon for a capital gain") were of little or no importance in the purchase decision. As might be expected from a survey of owner-occupants, house investment for rental was also unimportant. The same is true for trading-up as a motive for home purchase. Those who "hoped to resell soon and use equity to buy more expensive home" ranked low in the scale of reasons for buying. Interestingly, only one third or less mentioned the availability of financing or anticipations of mortgage interest rate increases as an important or very important factor in their decision.

Among the neighborhood, location, household, and shelter need factors influencing the decision to buy, the desire for a larger home in a better area appeared to be paramount in importance. Other reasons ranking relatively high in importance were the respondents' feeling of being "tired of renting" and their desire to have access to better schools for their children. These findings conform to the results of other studies on moving decisions.[4] All other potential reasons ranked relatively low in importance.

Probably the most significant aspect of the surveys is the great weight given to investment considerations in home purchase as against the consumption components surrounding neighborhood and shelter quality. This emphasis may be partly associated with the fact that respondents on the whole were relatively well housed in their previous residences. True, they achieved some improvement of housing services. As noted, for example, the majority of buyers obtained a somewhat larger house; in Orange County they acquired newer homes probably located in better neighborhoods. Nevertheless, the scale of importance attached to consumption aspects in the decision to buy is low compared to that given to investment aspects. This observation is consistent with two points stressed throughout this volume: The investment component in home purchase has sharply increased in recent years, and this shift is related to inflationary expectations.

What are some of the differences between 1975 and 1977 homebuyers in the importance or unimportance attached to various reasons for home purchase? We concentrate on those factors that evidence consistency among the two study areas and present the results in abbreviated form.

In comparison to their 1975 counterparts, the 1977 homebuyers tended to attribute somewhat greater importance to closeness to work and friends in the purchase decision. The 1977 buyers considered increased income as more important, whereas the need for a larger home and the motive of being "tired of renting" were slightly less important. None of these shifts were large. Somewhat greater response differences were found between 1977 and 1975 buyers with respect to investment and financial considerations. Home purchase as a hedge against inflation and the desperate belief that this was the last chance to buy were still more prevalent as important or very important reasons for the purchase decision in 1977 than in 1975. The 1977 buyers show also greater hopes of "trading up" or making capital gains. However, these two items rank relatively low in importance among both 1977 and 1975 buyers.

Homebuyers' Expectations

The surveys went on to inquire whether respondents agreed or disagreed with the statement "I purchased my home at the time I did because I expected prices to increase further." This item evoked an astonishingly strong agreement. Seven out of ten of the 1975 respondents endorsed the statement in both study areas, with the remainder disagreeing or responding "don't know." Among 1977 homebuyers, agreement with the statement rose to 80% and 84% in Contra Costa and Orange Counties, respectively (table 4-9).

The results may reflect different types of motivations. Presumably, respondents who anticipated continuing inflation in the housing market and the general level of prices would be prone to agree with the statement. Included in this group would be those who consider house purchase an attractive hedge against inflation. Additionally, many respondents may have been induced to purchase homes at the time they did because they anticipated paying a great deal more by

Table 4-9
Percent of Respondents Agreeing or Disagreeing with Statement
that Home Was Purchased Because of Further Expected Price
Increases, 1975 and 1977

Home Purchased Because of	Contra Costa County		Orange County	
Further Expected Price Increases	1975	1977	1975	1977
Agree	69.7%	79.9%	70.4%	84.1%
Disagree	24.5	14.7	21.5	10.5
Don't know	5.8	5.3	8.1	5.4
	100.0%	100.0%	100.0%	100.0%
N =	277	339	186	277

delaying the decision. This reasoning would be reflected among first-time buyers as well as the majority of owner-buyers in our surveys who desired to upgrade their housing quality. The homeowner who shifts from a $50,000 to an $80,000 home pays $30,000 more. If both the old and the new property experienced price increases of 20%, the difference would become $36,000. Moreover, some sophisticated owner-buyers may respond to differential increases in past home prices even within the same urban region. In the face of rising prices, they would sell their residence if it was located in an area with relatively low value enhancements and buy a house in an area where they expect greater appreciation.[5] Finally, the respondents who agreed that their home purchases were predicated on further expected price increases include a group anticipating the realization of windfall gains. Some of these may be people who purchased homes for resale at an early opportunity and expected to occupy the units only briefly.

The expected annual rate of home value appreciation at the time the properties were purchased varied enormously, from 2 to 70%. However, the mean appreciation per year anticipated by 1975 buyers was 11.8% and 13.5% in Contra Costa and Orange Counties, respectively; the figures were 14.3 and 17.2% for the 1977 buyers. The latter on average had significantly higher expectations, probably because they acquired their homes some time after the house price inflation began.[c]

The expectations on home value appreciation may be juxtaposed to the respondents' projections of general price increases for 1978. The latter range narrowly between 6.3 and 6.8%, depending on the area and time of purchase. In other words, the anticipated general price inflation is far below the anticipated house price increase. This finding must be interpreted with caution. For one thing, consumers adjust expectations rapidly in the face of changing conditions. Second, the survey question on home appreciation probed into expectations at

---

[c]At this point one must reiterate that some 1975 buyers had sold their homes by 1977. These are not included in the responses to the questionnaire. If those selling versus those holding consistently have higher expectations, this alone could explain some of the differences in anticipated value appreciation between 1975 and 1977 buyers.

the time of purchase for an unspecified period, whereas the responses on consumer prices were requested to indicate expectations for the coming year. Even with these limitations, it would appear that homebuyers in 1977 anticipated the rate of home price increases to exceed the rate of general price advances by a considerable margin—more than twice as large. Generally, differential price changes of such magnitude do not persist for very long. Forces on both the demand and the supply side come into operation to reduce or eliminate the differentials.

Despite the expected value appreciation, the majority of respondents in both study areas indicated that they would not sell their homes immediately irrespective of the rate of home price increases. This may not mean they would be unwilling to sell at *any* price, but probably expresses an awareness that sale would necessitate finding an alternative residence at prices or rents that may leave them no better off than before, especially when transaction costs were considered. As was reported earlier, the majority of buyers were satisfied with their homes. It is one thing to anticipate value increases and quite a different thing to act on them by immediate sale. As might be expected, the higher the rate of home price increase, the larger the proportion of recent homebuyers who would be prepared to sell, but the pattern is not smooth. Among 1977 purchasers, 35% in Contra Costa County and 40% in Orange County mentioned that they would consider selling their homes immediately if the values increased by 30% or more. What kinds of adjustments in housing accommodations the potential sellers might be prepared to make after a sale cannot be ascertained from the surveys.

Summary

Leaving aside fine detail and interarea variations, some of the important threads in the survey responses can now be tied together. Features that distinguished homebuyers in 1977, a year of hectic demand, from those of the more "normal" 1975 period when the economy was just emerging from a deep recession include the following. The incomes of 1977 buyers were moderately higher than those of their 1975 counterparts, but they paid a great deal more for the residences they acquired. The result was a significantly less favorable home price-income ratio and a more severe burden of current housing expenses on family budgets. The burden was partly relieved by the fact that the 1977 buyers comprised a larger share of previous homeowners. These buyers were presumably in a position to make higher downpayments derived from capital gains on the sale of their previous residences and could therefore hold down increases in mortgage payments. Equally important is the finding from industry surveys in Orange County covering the same period that, in general, monthly loan payments as a share of income among 1977 buyers were not severely out of line with historical relationships, although other current ownership expenses must have risen. The 1977 buyers included a somewhat larger contingent of one-person households and of two-person households with more than one breadwinner.

The evidence is quite strong that both 1975 and 1977 homebuyers upgraded housing and neighborhood quality, but the upgrading was much greater in 1975 than in 1977. On the other hand, the evidence is mixed on the question whether households purchased larger and presumably more expensive houses than needed for use (measured by the presence of an extra bedroom).

One of the clearest and most significant results pertains to the great role of investment and related financial considerations in the purchase decisions of the 1975 and especially the 1977 buyers. Home purchase as (1) an inflation hedge, (2) an opportunity to capture larger income-tax benefits, and (3) the "best" investment for my money" ranked very high among the responses. To what extent this marked a departure from previous motives for homebuying cannot be determined since past studies of single-family house purchasers concentrated on location, neighborhood, and shelter attributes.

Investment decisions, generally, consider the actual or imputed returns during the holding period as well as the proceeds from the sale of the investment adjusted for risk. Some literature specifically refers to assumptions and beliefs that single-family houses for rent perform poorly compared to investment alternatives. Seldin and Swesnik, for example, suggest that among real-estate investment market alternatives, rental houses present the fewest obstacles to entry and exit, but are believed to be the least profitable.[6] Beaton indicates that single-family homes are considered to be an undesirable type of investment, although selective investors have enjoyed a modicum of success.[7] The implicit assumption is that owner-occupancy—that is, renting to oneself—yields attractive consumption benefits and imparts better control of the residential environment but, aside from income-tax benefits, does not produce financial returns commensurate with alternate investments. Assertions of this type were based on evidence in noninflationary periods and may have been supported by observations in selected cities and neighborhoods where single-family homes at times depreciated rapidly and showed high vacancies. As price increases began to accelerate in the past several years and spread from suburban growth areas to older sections of cities, the earlier statements no longer held. The surveys in northern and southern California suburban areas, together with other findings of this study, indicate indeed that previous notions about the investment merits of the single-family house have been thoroughly revised in the marketplace, at least for a while.

According to the surveys, recent homebuyers tend to hold high expectations of future capital appreciation of their properties. Their anticipations are probably greatly influenced by the house price inflation of 1975-1977, the period of their purchases. Whether they will be validated is open to serious question. Even in the absence of average house price decreases, the capital gains expected by recent buyers are in all likelihood unsustainable. This matter is reserved for discussion in chapter 7, which deals with the market adjustments following the escalation of home prices.

Notes

1. U.S. League of Savings Associations, *Homeownership: Realizing the American Dream* (Chicago, 1978). The data refer to loan applications between April and June 1977. See the source for the metropolitan and nonmetropolitan areas included in the survey.

2. In Orange County 86 and 82% of eligible responses were for sales between January and May in 1975 and 1977, respectively. In Contra Costa County the respective proportions are 91 and 92%. Appendix table H-2 presents the distribution of responses by date of sale.

3. Walker and Lee Real Estate, *Housing Insights* (Anaheim, Calif.: The authors, July 29, 1977). This report mentions that "new" monthly payments cover principal, interest, taxes, and insurance. Whether "old" monthly payments for previous homeowners cover the same items is not clear.

4. See, for example, E.W. Butler, et al., *Moving Behavior and Residential Choice: A National Survey* (Washington, D.C.: National Academy of Sciences, Highway Research Board, 1969), National Cooperative Highway Research Program Report 81; also Elizabeth Roistacher, "Residential Mobility"; Greg J. Duncan and Sandra Newman, "People as Planners: The Fulfillment of Residential Mobility Expectations"; and Elizabeth Roistacher, "Residential Mobility: Planners, Movers and Multiple Movers" In Greg J. Duncan and James N. Morgan, *Five Thousand American Families—Patterns of Economic Progress* (Ann Arbor, Mich.: Survey Research Center, University of Michigan, 1975), Volumes II and III.

5. Considerable mystery surrounds the issue of relative changes in home prices. In Orange County, for example, home prices for a constant sample of properties rose more rapidly than in Los Angeles County in the period 1975-1977. During 1977, price increases in Orange County lagged behind those in Los Angeles County.

6. Maury Seldin and Richard H. Swesnik, *Real Estate Investment Strategy* (New York: Wiley-Interscience, 1970), p. 138.

7. William R. Beaton, *Real Estate Investment* (Englewood Cliffs, N.J.: Prentice-Hall, 1971), p. 270.

5

Factors Associated with the Price Escalation

This chapter examines the factors that may have a bearing on the price surge for single-family houses. The discussion focuses on two hypotheses: (1) the presence of excess demand for homes over available supply that is attributable to normal market forces considered in conventional analysis, and (2) the emergence of inflationary expectations among homebuyers as a cause of excess demand. Both hypotheses imply short-term market disequilibrium. Their treatment here will be supplemented by the exploratory model of house prices in chapter 6.

Manifestations of Excess Demand

The presence of excess demand regardless of its sources would manifest itself in a rapid decline of inventories of unsold houses held by builders and falling vacancies in the existing housing stock. Just as merchandise inventories are apt to be drawn down in response to unanticipated increases in demand before new orders are placed by retailers or other business firms, idle housing units represent the buffer for absorbing an incipient expansion of housing demand before builders proceed to step up their production. The question is whether unused housing inventories declined markedly in 1975-1976, the initial period of the surge in house prices. The answer is affirmative for southern California and the San Francisco-Bay area, the state's major urban regions for which data are available. The fall of inventories in the United States as a whole lagged behind the decline in California. This finding suggests an uneven geographic distribution of excess demand at the beginning of the house price escalation, reflecting the familiar differences in local housing market conditions.

Builders' Inventories: California

We turn first to builders' inventories. Table 5-1 shows biannual data on inventories of unsold new houses in the seven-county area of southern California. The grand total of unsold inventories decreased moderately as early as 1974 from the peak of 30,000 units in December 1973, and the decline accelerated after December 1974. By June 1976, the overhang of unsold new units was at a lower level than any recorded since late 1970, and its volume kept on falling to June 1977. Among the components of the inventory, unsold

Table 5-1
Unsold Inventories of New Homes in Seven-county Area of
Southern California,[a] 1970-1977

Period	Completed	Under Construction	Total
Tract Homes			
1970 Dec.	8,740	5,639	14,379
1971 June	3,868	6,468	10,366
Dec.	3,773	6,598	10,371
1972 June	3,130	7,288	10,418
Dec.	3,203	6,771	9,374
1973 June	2,168	9,274	11,442
Dec.	4,104	5,608	9,712
1974 June	3,465	4,442	7,907
Dec.	3,235	3,756	6,992
1975 June	2,256	3,260	5,516
Dec.	1,705	4,724	6,429
1976 June	896	5,080	5,976
Dec.	675	6,017	6,692
1977 June	145	6,078	6,223
Dec.	726	11,359	12,085
Homes in Planned Unit Developments			
1970 Dec.	968	1,138	2,106
1971 June	909	1,922	2,831
Dec.	1,475	4,205	5,680
1972 June	2,455	5,589	8,044
Dec.	3,919	6,800	10,719
1973 June	3,856	10,895	14,751
Dec.	5,741	14,579	20,320
1974 June	8,935	10,558	19,493
Dec.	12,116	8,678	20,794
1975 June	11,513	5,316	16,830
Dec.	7,793	4,275	12,068
1976 June	3,795	706	6,465
Dec.	1,729	3,131	4,860
1977 June	493	2,194	2,687
Dec.	1,416	4,055	5,471
Grand Totals			
1970 Dec.	9,708	6,777	16,485
1971 June	4,777	8,390	13,167
Dec.	5,248	10,803	16,051
1972 June	5,585	12,877	18,462
Dec.	7,122	13,571	20,693
1973 June	6,024	20,169	26,193
Dec.	9,845	20,187	30,032
1974 June	12,400	15,000	27,400
Dec.	15,351	12,434	27,785

Table 5-1 continued

Period	Completed	Under Construction	Total
1975 June	13,769	8,576	22,345
Dec.	9,498	8,999	18,497
1976 June	4,691	7,786	12,477
Dec.	2,404	9,148	11,552
1977 June	638	8,272	8,910
Dec.	2,142	15,414	17,556

Source: Real Estate Research Council of Southern California, *Residential Research Reports*. Based on surveys of all new projects of five or more homes, with data obtained from the developer, the Tract office, and visual inspection. Smaller projects such as houses constructed by builders on scattered lots are excluded. Projects are covered by the surveys for the first time when construction starts and remain in the surveys until completed and sold out. The volume of inventories is slightly understated, particularly in recent periods, since sales include "reservations" as well as actual sales contracts.

aIncludes the following counties: Los Angeles, Orange, Riverside, San Bernardino, Ventura, Santa Barbara, and San Diego.

residences in tract developments are probably more revealing than those in planned unit developments (PUDs), which are mostly attached houses and include a larger proportion of resort and senior-citizen communities. And changes in the number of *completed* houses remaining unsold are more revealing than those in the number of unsold units under construction, which are highly sensitive to cyclical fluctuations of single-family house starts. Inventories of completed houses in tract developments began to decline as early as the first half of 1974 and were virtually disappearing in 1976-1977. Those in PUDs, which had accumulated in an unusually large volume through 1973-1974 after an extraordinary boom in this type of development, began to recede in the first half of 1975, and they dropped rapidly thereafter. Unsold tract houses under construction started to increase in the second half of 1975 as homebuilding recovered. Unsold PUD units under construction remained on a downward trend through mid-1977. Overall inventories rose in the second half of 1977. Although the reversal was most pronounced for residences under construction, it is significant because it indicates some weakness in precompletion sales.

The evidence in table 5-1 is consistent with the notion that growing demand manifests itself first in sharp reductions of the number of unsold new homes. Even the great increase in homebuilding in the seven-county area, from a low of 33,152 building permits in 1974 to 47,747 in 1976 and about the same volume in the first half of 1977 alone, did not serve to halt the decline in inventories. This was partly due, of course, to a lag between permits and house completions. Nevertheless, the persistent drop of inventories together with the highly positive response of builders to a favorable market allows the inference of *excess* demand.

Figure 5-1 expresses the inventory of completed units as a percent of all completed new houses in the seven-county area. Because the sales experience in tracts and PUDs has varied considerably, the data for the two types of development are portrayed separately. Completed tract units yet unsold declined from 25% of all completed units in December 1974 to 7% in June 1977. In PUDs, the unsold inventories of completed houses have also decreased relative to all completed units, but they tend to be larger than in tract developments throughout the period studied. More comprehensive data in appendix table I-1 show the relative inventory changes for units under construction as well as completed dwellings, plus statistics for each of the seven counties. As one would expect, conditions in the individual counties differed a great deal. For completed homes, for example, Orange County shows the greatest relative fall of inven-

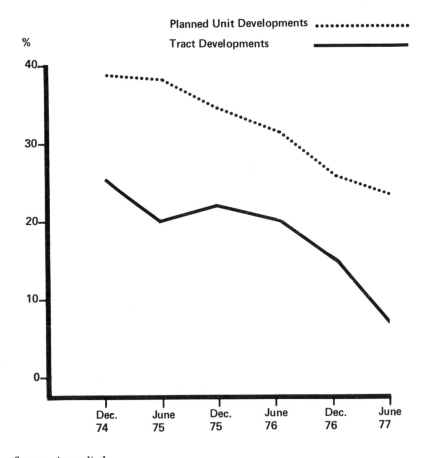

Source: Appendix I.

Figure 5-1. Unsold Completed Houses as a Percentage of All Completed New Single-Family Houses in Seven-County Area of Southern California, December 1974 to June 1977

tories, San Bernardino County the smallest, and Ventura and Santa Barbara Counties exhibit no consistent decline. The county data serve as a reminder of the local nature of housing markets. Notable differences would also be found for intracounty areas.

Corresponding reports for the San Francisco-Bay area (table 5-2) are less frequent and less complete than those for southern California. The broad movement of unsold house inventories as of January of each year parallels the trends in the southern part of the state, increasing greatly in the 1971-1974 period and dropping sharply between early 1974 and early 1977. The decline began during 1974 for both completed homes and units under construction. Here again, the unsold inventory of completed dwellings had virtually disappeared by January 1977. The table also shows that the inventory as a percent of all new houses that were completed or under construction was dropping sharply between early 1975 and early 1977. Data for individual counties would merely reiterate the point of area variations, already made for southern California, and are therefore omitted.

Builders' Inventories: United States

Inventory changes in the nation as a whole have differed from those recorded in the two principal California areas. Figure 5-2 presents seasonally adjusted monthly data for sales of new single-family houses, houses for sale (the

Table 5-2
Unsold Inventories of New Homes in Nine-County San Francisco Bay Area, 1971-1977[a]

January of Each Year	Completed Units		Units under Construction		Total Inventory
	Number	Percent[b]	Number	Percent[c]	
1971	2,300	13.0	2,453	55.0	4,753
1972	2,422	10.0	3,244	44.0	5,666
1973	4,698	19.0	3,634	45.0	8,332
1974	6,105	26.0	7,386	66.0	13,491
1975	4,843	26.0	3,010	65.0	7,853
1977[d]	590	5.0	1,777	22.5	2,367

Source: Real Estate Research Council of Northern California, *Real Estate Research Report,* seriatim.

[a]Includes the following counties: Alameda, Contra Costa, Marin, Napa, San Francisco, San Mateo, Santa Clara, Solano, and Sonoma. The data are for all developments including planned unit developments. According to the source, "efforts were made to survey all existing tracts in the Bay area which qualified for survey; however, it is possible that additional tracts exist in the region that were not surveyed."

[b]Unsold units in January as a percent of completions in the preceding year.

[c]Unsold units at end of month as a percent of units under construction at end of month.

[d]No report available for 1976.

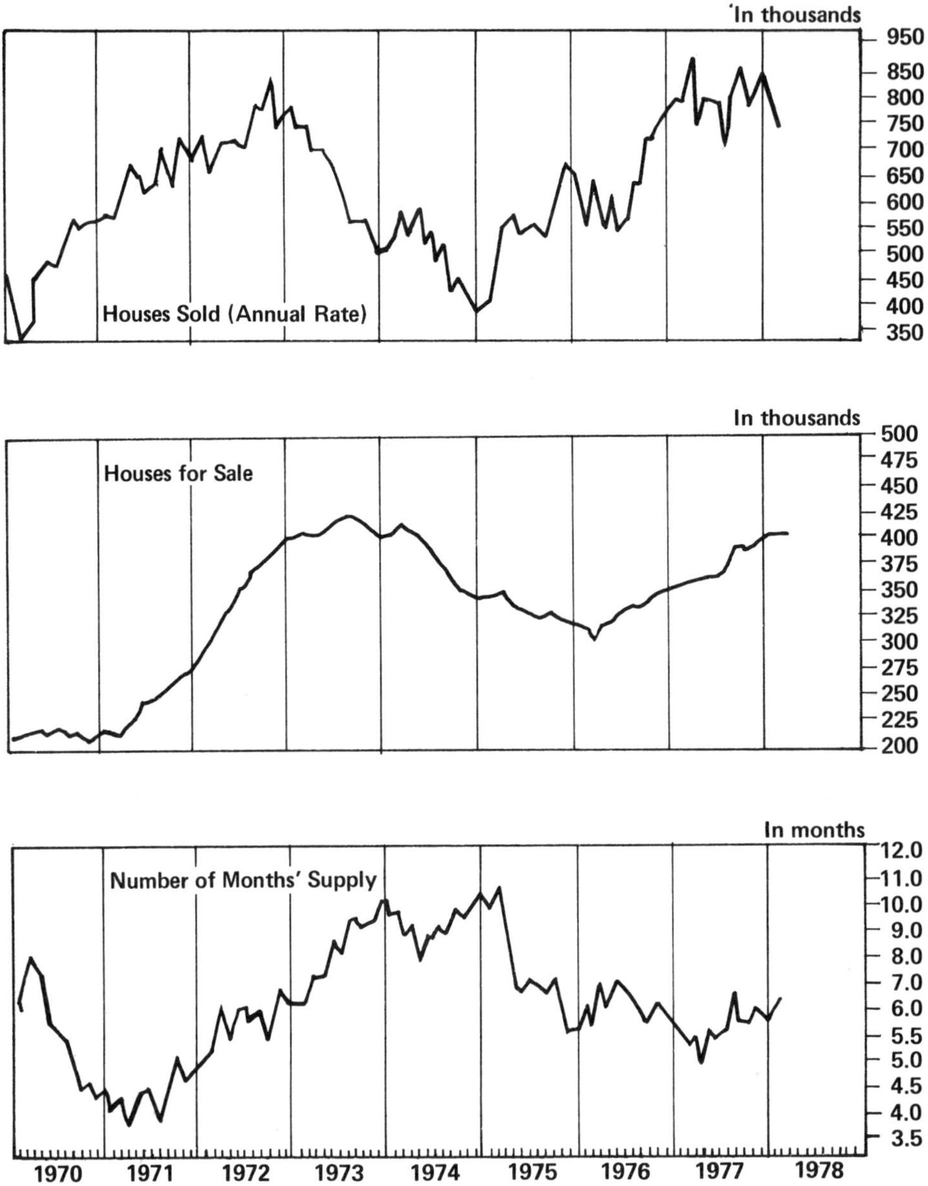
In thousands
950
850
800
750
700
650
600
550
500
450
400
350
Houses Sold (Annual Rate)
In thousands
500
475
450
425
400
375
350
325
300
275
250
225
200
Houses for Sale
In months
12.0
11.0
10.0
9.0
8.0
7.0
6.0
5.5
5.0
4.5
4.0
3.5
Number of Months' Supply
1970
1971
1972
1973
1974
1975
1976
1977
1978

Source: Bureau of the Census. For the underlying data and pre-1970 statistics, see appendix table I-2.

Figure 5-2. New One-Family Houses Sold, for Sale, and Number of Months' Supply at Current Sales Rate (seasonally adjusted)

inventory of unsold homes), and the inventory ratio expressed as the number of months' supply represented by unsold units at current sales rates. The volume of sales exhibits a pronounced cyclical pattern akin to that for single-family house starts and requires no further comment. Inventories show rapid accumulation during the housing boom of 1971-1972, mainly because they include the large number of units under construction, and a high level throughout 1974. The subsequent decline to early 1975 was moderate, from an annual rate of more than 400,000 homes to some 300,000, a volume substantially exceeding the inventories prevailing in the 1963-1970 period. The inventory-sales ratio, increasing sharply since 1972, reached an unprecedented 10 months' supply in early 1975, and the 1976 ratios of six to seven were still high in light of historical experience. Between June 1973 and June 1976, total inventories in the seven-county area of southern California dropped by over 50%. Inventories in the United States during a similar period based on figures for the month of May declined by 21%. Thus the absorption of available new homes was far slower in the nation than in the California region. This helps explain why California led the escalation of house prices.

Changes in the nationwide sales performance for new residences can also be observed from data on the median number of months elapsing between start and sale (figure 5-3 and appendix table I-2). The marketing period lengthened from 1973 to early 1975 for both sold houses and units yet to be sold, reflecting the severe business recession intervening during this period and the overhang of homes remaining unsold after the housing boom of 1971-1972. After early 1975, the marketing period for sold homes was quickly reduced to "normal," but much was made in 1975 and 1976 of an alleged persistence of abnormally long periods for the disposition of new units yet to be sold. A "two-tier" market was said to have developed: the "old-new" houses, which were moving slowly, and the "new-new" dwellings with more normal selling periods.[1] This segmentation was held to be so serious that it gave rise to federal legislation. Because of apprehension that a large overhang of unsold homes left from the housing slump of 1973-1974 impeded new construction, the federal government adopted a housing tax credit for purchasers of new unsold units started before March 26, 1975. The buyer could deduct 5% of the sales price from his taxable income, up to $2,000.

As it turned out, the concern over the two-tier market and the federal intervention were largely based on faulty statistics. The revised data on marketing periods for 1973-1977, issued in early 1978 and used here, show far more moderate differences between houses sold and still for sale than did the original figures, varying by one to two months in the critical period from late 1974 to early 1976. Such differences were well within the range of previous experience. While a two-tier market existed for a while, it was not of extraordinary magnitude.

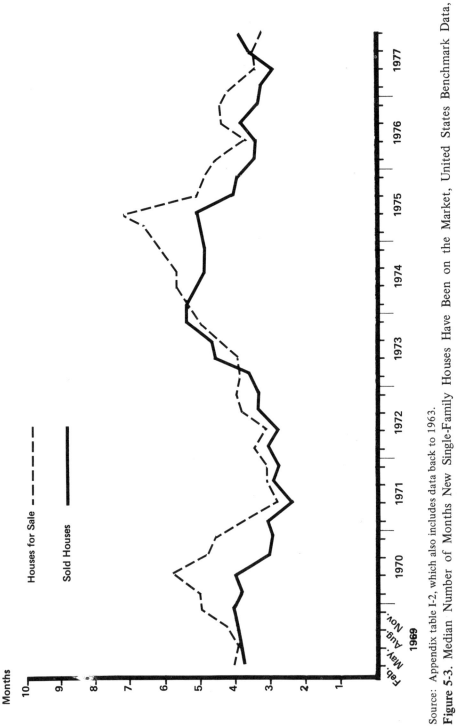

Source: Appendix table I-2, which also includes data back to 1963.

Figure 5-3. Median Number of Months New Single-Family Houses Have Been on the Market, United States Benchmark Data, 1969-1977

Housing Vacancies

Builders' inventories indicate changing market conditions for *new* houses. The question remains whether vacancy data for the entire housing stock are consistent with the movement of unsold new homes. To answer this question, we examine vacancy changes in both the single-family house and the multiple housing segments. For one thing, statistics in some local areas are available only for the whole market. Second the owner-occupancy and rental sectors are interrelated through the price-rent mechanism. The role of single-family houses in the rental supply constitutes the most direct link. One third of the rented year-round housing units were in single-family structures in 1975, and 36.7% in 1970. Of all occupied single-family houses, 16.2% were rented in 1975 and 18.2% in 1970.[2] The importance of the price-rent relationship was vividly illustrated by tenure shifts in the 1940-1950 period when rent levels were held down through war and postwar controls while house prices remained unregulated. Between the two benchmark dates, the number of rented single-family structures declined from 9.9 million to less than 7.7 million, or from 50.6% of the total occupied rental supply to less than 40%. Many owners of single-family houses chose to sell at market prices rather than lease them at controlled rents. Of all occupied single-family houses, 43% were rented in 1940 and only 28% in 1950.[3] The current growth of local rent regulations could have similar effects.

As for *local* vacancy changes, one must unfortunately resort to a proxy: the count of idle electric meters as a percent of total residential meters. The proxy indicates the direction of changes in vacancies but not vacancy rates.[4] Data for two California areas are presented in table 5-3. In southern California, the percent of idle meters in the single-family house market declined sharply between late 1973 and early 1977, reaching a low level unprecedented since 1970 and corroborating the evidence obtained from the movement of builders' inventories. Changes in vacancies as well as builders' inventories are consistent with the presumption of excess demand. Vacancies in multifamily dwellings began a sustained decrease somewhat later, during 1975. In the San Francisco-Bay area, on the other hand, the less reliable idle-meter data for all types of housing units reveal a more erratic pattern—a low level fluctuating within the range of 1.5 to 2.0% followed by a fall in late 1976.

The earlier analysis of builders' *nationwide* inventories showed a relatively slow decline in 1974 and 1975. Official vacancy statistics based on sample surveys for the United States and four major census regions conform to this finding (table 5-4). Between 1974 and II-1977, quarterly homeowner vacancy rates in the United States varied around the historical 1.2 and 1.3% level without any sustained change, and they decreased only in the second half of 1977. Among the regions, the West shows a fairly sharp and continuous drop beginning as early as IV-1975. No other region exhibits a comparable movement. Because of the low level of homeowner vacancy rates, their changes over time are subject to considerable sampling variability. Hence rental vacancy rates, which are larger and involve relatively lower sampling errors, are more revealing. The U.S. rental

Table 5-3
Idle Electric Meters as a Percentage of Total Residential Meters in
Selected Areas of California, 1970-1977[a]

Year and Month	Southern California[b]			San Francisco Bay Area[e]
	Single-family Houses[c]	Multifamily Structures[c]	All Types[d]	All Types of Housing
1970 March	1.6%	3.1%	2.1%	1.3%
June	1.8	3.7	2.2	1.4
Sept.	1.8	3.9	2.5	n.a.
Dec.	1.8	4.2	2.4	1.3
1971 March	1.9	4.2	2.4	1.3
June	1.9	4.8	2.6	1.6
Sept.	1.9	4.8	3.0	n.a.
Dec.	1.7	4.9	2.9	n.a.
1972 March	1.8	5.1	3.0	1.7
June	1.8	5.3	3.1	2.0
Sept.	1.9	5.1	3.2	n.a.
Dec.	1.9	5.2	3.2	n.a.
1973 March	1.8	4.6	3.0	n.a.
June	1.9	4.8	3.1	n.a.
Sept.	1.9	4.9	3.2	2.3
Dec.	2.0	4.9	3.1	1.9
1974 March	2.0	4.7	3.0	1.9
June	1.9	4.9	3.0	2.0
Sept.	1.9	4.7	3.1	1.9
Dec.	1.8	4.7	2.9	1.6
1975 March	1.8	4.7	2.8	1.7
June	1.7	4.4	2.7	1.9
Sept.	1.5	3.9	2.6	1.9
Dec.	1.4	3.6	2.3	1.5
1976 March	1.3	3.2	2.1	1.5
June	1.3	3.3	2.1	1.7
Sept.	1.2	3.1	2.0	1.6
Dec.	1.2	2.9	1.9	1.2
1977 March	1.1	2.6	1.7	1.4
June	1.2	2.6	1.7	

Sources: For southern California, see table 5-1. For San Francisco Bay area, see table 5-2.

[a]For the procedures in the count of "idle" meters, see Residential Research Committee of Southern California, Residential Research Report, Third Quarter 1975. "The net effect of the system is to produce a complete and extremely accurate count of meters not assigned to a customer on 42 days every two months on a continuing basis." However, idle meter counts are useful in indicating the direction of changes in vacancies but do not measure vacancy rates. On the whole, they understate vacancy rates since meters may be left on after the premises have been vacated or before new housing is occupied. The data for apartment buildings are deficient to the extent that some such buildings have a "master" meter for all units.

[b]Includes the following six counties: Los Angeles, Orange, Riverside, San Bernardino, Ventura, and Santa Barbara.

[c]Units in Southern California Edison Co. territory only.

[d]Includes single and multiple units in territories of all reporting utility companies.

[e]Includes the following counties: Alameda, Contra Costa, Marin, Napa, San Francisco, San Mateo, Santa Clara, Solano, and Sonoma. No separate data are reported for single and multiple units.

Table 5-4
Residential Vacancy Rates in the United States and Four Major Census Regions, Quarterly, 1974-1977[a]
(not seasonally adjusted)

Period		Homeowner Vacancy Rates					Rental Vacancy Rates				
		U.S.	N.E.	N.C.	South	West	U.S.	N.E.	N.C.	South	West
1974	I	1.2	0.8	1.0	1.4	1.5	6.2	4.1	6.4	7.9	6.2
	II	1.1	0.6	1.0	1.4	1.3	6.3	4.0	6.4	7.9	6.8
	III	1.2	0.8	1.0	1.6	1.5	6.2	4.7	6.1	7.8	6.0
	IV	1.3	0.8	1.1	1.6	1.7	6.0	3.8	5.4	8.4	5.7
1975	I	1.2	0.9	1.0	1.5	1.6	6.1	4.3	5.1	8.4	6.0
	II	1.2	1.1	0.9	1.4	1.3	6.3	4.0	6.3	8.1	6.7
	III	1.4	1.0	1.0	1.7	1.8	6.2	4.2	6.1	7.5	6.9
	IV	1.2	1.0	0.9	1.5	1.3	5.4	3.9	5.3	6.8	5.3
1976	I	1.2	1.1	0.8	1.6	1.2	5.5	4.1	5.8	6.5	5.5
	II	1.2	0.9	1.1	1.6	1.2	5.8	5.0	6.0	6.6	5.5
	III	1.3	1.0	1.2	1.6	1.1	5.7	5.0	5.5	6.7	5.4
	IV	1.2	0.9	1.0	1.6	1.0	5.3	4.7	5.3	5.8	5.1
1977	I	1.3	0.9	0.9	2.0	1.0	5.1	4.8	5.3	5.8	4.4
	II	1.3	0.8	1.2	1.8	0.9	5.3	5.2	4.7	5.5	5.7
	III	1.1	1.0	0.9	1.4	0.9	5.4	5.4	5.1	5.7	5.5
	IV	1.0	0.9	0.8	1.5	0.8	5.1	4.9	5.2	5.6	4.4

Source: Bureau of the Census, Current Housing Reports, Housing Vacancies.
[a]Includes housing units available for sale or rent for year-round occupancy. Excludes units rented or sold awaiting occupancy, units held off the market, and seasonally vacant housing. Recent changes in the excluded categories were well within the margins recorded for earlier years.

rates tended downward in 1976 and 1977, falling to little over 5%, but their decline in the West was greater—from 6.9% in III-1975 to 4.4% in early 1977. Since California dominates the statistics for the West, the data lend some support to the point that excess demand manifested itself in California before it appeared elsewhere. It should be noted, however, that counts of overall vacancies and unsold new houses do not represent entirely independent statistics. The Bureau of the Census classifies unoccupied new units as vacant if construction has reached a point where all exterior windows and doors are installed and final usable floors are in place.

Reasons for Excess Demand—The Conventional Approach

According to conventional analysis, demand may at least temporarily outpace the available supply of single-family dwellings if it is bolstered by major demographic changes, by substantial gains in consumer income, or by greater availability and reduced costs of mortgage loans such as lower interest rates and/or lower downpayment requirements and longer maturities. Excess demand may also develop if builders are greatly constrained in supplying newly constructed houses. Each of these possible reasons for demand-supply disequilibrium warrants investigation. In a later section, inflationary expectations are discussed as a force inducing excess demand for homes.

Demographic Changes

It has long since been established that nationwide population changes affect the demand for housing or for single-family dwellings mostly in the long run but not over short periods of time. This observation makes it highly improbable that the sharp price increase for single-family houses in 1975-1977 was caused by demographic factors. The case is quite different for subareas of the nation. There are numerous examples of severe pressures on the local housing supply when a county or city becomes the site of a new industrial plant or a military installation of great size or when large defense contracts serve to expand local employment opportunities. Internal migrations associated with such forces or similar circumstances can create excess demand for housing in some places and excess supply in others.

Whether one considers net household formation, the large share of non-family households in the total, the decline of both the average family size and household size, marriage and divorce statistics, the increasing number of persons in typical homebuying age groups, the growing importance of women in the employed labor force, or the fall in births and birth rates,[a] changes in recent years represent trends initiated in earlier periods. One finds "more of the same." For example, divorces that often result in two households instead of one and that may under favorable economic conditions raise the demand for single-family houses, have been increasing in 1974-1976, but they have been on an upward trend for a long time.[5] At best, one may speculate that the demographic forces favoring the long-run demand for residences were subdued in the severe recession of 1973-1974 and became reactivated in the subsequent business expansion. As a result, the pent-up and the current demand combined in 1975-1977 to generate such pressures on the inelastic short-run supply that house prices increased sharply.

In the context of this study, the increasing number of married women in the employed labor force warrants special attention. The growth as such is also a long-run phenomenon, but public regulation becoming effective in 1975 transformed it into a new force of major consequence to the demand for owner-occupied homes. Previously home mortgage lenders tended to disregard or discount wives' income for loan qualification purposes, although their practices

---

[a]The decline in births and the concomitant decrease in the number of children per family affects the housing market in various ways. It allows families to shift their expenditures from child-raising and education to other things, including a better dwelling or earlier purchase of a house. Another possible effect is a reduction in the size and a modified design of housing units demanded.

varied a great deal. Lenders inclined to the expectation that wives may be employed intermittently or part-time even if they held a full-time job at the time of loan application, or that married women of child-bearing age may become pregnant and turn to their traditional role in the family. For similar reasons, many lenders used special caution for home purchase loans to single women with or without children. Under the Fair Housing Act of 1974 and the more comprehensive Equal Credit Opportunity Act of 1975, mortgagees were required to extend credit without sex discrimination. Among other things, this meant full recognition of wives' earnings in qualifying applicants for a mortgage loan.[6]

Thus even if the effects of the antidiscrimination rules were somewhat diluted in the marketplace,[b] the new legislation served to raise the demand for single-family houses precisely in the period on which this study is focused. First, they qualified families or single women for home purchase who were previously excluded from the market. Second, and particularly important in the case of working wives, they qualified households with two earners for a larger mortgage loan; a larger loan amount available to home shoppers in many cases induces them to buy a higher priced property. Lenders in southern California report that one third to half of recent home loans were made to families with more than one breadwinner, with wives accounting for the vast majority of extra earners. This was a much higher percentage than ever recorded in previous years. Some married women may go to work to offset the husband's income decline or the impact of inflation on family budgets. In the main, however, their larger representation in the employed labor force reflects long-term social trends. This is also true for unmarried females whose employment gain can have an impact on the house market. Single persons have become more frequent housebuyers than before, accounting for up to 15% of all home loans made by some California institutions. This group unquestionably includes unmarried women in higher income brackets, although it is difficult to distinguish between non-working widows and divorcees and employed females. Single people or two unrelated people establishing their own households is a time-honored trend. In the past few years, however, a rather new dimension has been added: an increasing number of such persons have become home purchasers. This remarkable change seems to reflect new lifestyles, growing consumer taste for the single-family house, and investment motivations. In any event, it reinforced the demand for homes and contributed to the price escalation.

---

[b]The prohibition of discrimination against females did not entail a complete dichotomy of conditions before and after the regulations took effect. First some homebuyers in the preregulation period resorted to junior financing when lenders disregarded or discounted wives' earnings in determining the amount of the first mortgage, or purchasers may have accumulated the second earner's income to make a larger downpayment, which reduced monthly payments but may have involved some delay in home acquisition. Second as pointed out in the text, some lenders had been more lenient than others in recognizing wives' earnings for loan qualification, so the transition from the preregulation to the postregulation period was not as abrupt as it may appear. Third given the many variables in determining mortgage amounts in each case, the interpretation of the new rules by lenders may have varied.

In the case of California, moreover, recent changes in net migration to the state have given fresh impetus to the demand for housing generally and, by inference, to the demand for single-family homes (table 5-5). Net migration, a substantial source of demographic growth in the postwar period and exceeding the natural increase of population until 1966, was declining sharply in the next few years. This movement has been reversed since 1973, and inmigrants have again contributed increasingly to total population growth. As a result, the state's share in the national increase of population, falling precipitously between 1965 and 1970, has been restored to its position in the mid-1960s.

The recent turnaround in the movement of people to California must have had a considerable impact on net household formation. In the absence of specific data, let us assume that the 172,000 inmigrants of 1976 formed households averaging two persons, which accounts for individuals not establishing a household and those representing single-person households as well as families with children. If so, the 86,000 households resulting from inmigration would equal half the total 1976 increase of households, estimated at 174,000. One must add that the data on inmigration and households are estimates

Table 5-5
Estimated Increase in California Civilian Population, Its Main Components, and Its Relation to U.S. Civilian Population Increase, 1964-1977
(numbers in thousands)

Year[a]	Total Increase	Natural Increase[b]	Net In-Migration[c]	Migration as % of Total	California Total Increase as % of U.S. Increase
1964	550	245	336	61.1%	20.8%
1965	462	214	260	56.3	18.8
1966	380	222	216	56.8	20.9
1967	321	159	201	62.6	17.4
1968	272	173	126	46.3	14.7
1969	261	155	102	39.1	12.8
1970	243	186	27	11.1	9.4
1971	247	166	50	20.2	9.7
1972	204	144	35	17.2	9.3
1973	243	130	111	45.7	14.8
1974	238	131	104	43.7	15.1
1975	330	145	182	55.2	19.7
1976	325	150	172	52.9	19.4
1977	364	174	190	52.2	21.1

Source: California Statistical Abstract for 1964-1976. For 1977, Advance Report 77 E-2 of the Population Research Unit of the California Department of Finance.

[a]Fiscal years beginning July 1.

[b]Excess of births over deaths in the resident population.

[c]Obtained by subtracting the natural increase from the estimated total population increase.

showing broad directions and magnitudes of change rather than precise numbers. Nevertheless, it is noteworthy that net household formation in California since 1970, measured for overlapping three-year periods to eliminate sometimes erratic annual changes, has increased steadily. In contrast, net household formation in the United States rose in 1972-1974 over 1970-1972 but declined in 1974-1976.[7]

Consumer Income

Although there is reason to believe that consumers' propensity to buy residences responds strongly to long-term and sustained cyclical changes in their real income, aggregate income gains during the economic expansion beginning in the spring of 1975 have hardly been sufficient to provide a major explanation of the rush into home purchase at sharply rising prices. The U.S. data for 1975-1977 in table 5-6 show rates of real income increases comparable to those experienced in

Table 5-6
Percent Changes in Consumer Income in the United States and California, 1966-1977
(based on incomes in 1972 dollars)

Period	United States		California	
	DPI[a]	PCDPI[b]	DPI[a]	PCDPI[b]
1966	5.1%	3.5%	4.6%	2.6%
1967	4.1	2.9	4.4	2.5
1968	3.8	2.8	4.6	3.2
1969	2.4	1.5	2.2	0.1
1970	4.1	3.0	3.9	2.4
1971	3.7	2.6	2.7	1.3
1972	4.2	3.3	1.9	1.1
1973	6.7	5.9	5.6	4.4
1974	−1.5	−2.2	0.1	−0.4
1975	1.8	1.0	2.5	1.1
1976	3.8	3.1	4.3	2.7
1977	4.6	3.8	5.9	4.2
Compound Rates of Change per Year				
1965-1968	4.4%	3.2%	4.5%	2.8%
1968-1970	3.2	2.2	3.0	1.5
1970-1972	3.9	3.0	2.3	1.2
1972-1974	2.4	1.7	3.1	2.0
1974-1976	2.9	2.1	3.4	1.9
1975-1977	4.2	3.4	5.1	3.5

Sources: Edmund G. Brown, Jr., *Economic Report of the Governor, 1978* (Sacramento: California State Printing Office, 1978). For California, total and per-capita disposable income derived by using implicit price deflator for personal consumption expenditures from U.S. Department of Commerce.

[a]Disposable personal income.

[b]Per-capita disposable personal income.

previous periods of business recovery. Disposable personal income (DPI) rose by less than 2% in 1975, following a decline in the previous year (a rare occurrence in the annals of consumer earnings since the Great Depression), by 3.8% in 1976, and 4.6% in 1977. According to the average annual compound rates shown at the bottom of the table for groups of years, real DPI rose by 2.9% per year in 1974-1976 and 4.2% in 1975-1977. The latter was at or below the rate for two of the three previous cyclical upswings since 1950, as measured by major fluctuations in GNP.[8]

It would have taken an unusual spurt of real income in recent years to attribute much of the homebuying spree at escalating prices to greater spending power. No such spurt has occurred. However, a highly specific income effect was noted in the section on demographic changes: The long-term growth in the number of families or households with two breadwinners and in female employment generally began to influence home purchases in 1974-1975 as discriminatory credit practices of mortgage lenders were outlawed.

Real income in California moved up faster than in the nation during the 1975-1977 period. Together with increasing inmigration, income gains exerted a more positive influence on the propensity to buy homes. Because of California's population growth, however, per-capita DPI in 1975-1977 rose at about the same rate as in the United States. On this reckoning, the income effects on homebuying in the state and the nation were not materially different.

Availability and Cost of Mortgage Loans

The mortgage-financing system provided ample funds to accommodate the recent growth of homebuying at rising prices (table 5-7). Net lending on 1- to 4-family houses by all suppliers of funds increased from $41.4 billion in 1975 to $67.6 billion in 1976, or by 63%, and again to $95.8 billion in 1977, another 42%. The amounts were at all-time peaks. The series as a whole shows typical cyclical changes—large additions to debt accompanying the 1971-1972 expansion in new construction, a sharply reduced volume during the subsequent housing recession, and the renewed surge after 1974. When net lending is related to outstanding balances at the beginning of each period (bottom of the table), it reveals growth throughout the 1972-1977 period, but that growth was especially marked between 1975 and 1977.

According to the underlying data for the four major financial institutions,[9] the large net increases in home mortgage holdings are mostly accounted for by savings-and-loan associations and commercial banks. The former, experiencing huge inflows of savings, stepped up their net lending from less than $14 billion in 1974 to nearly $37 billion in 1976 and 50 billion in 1977. Banks, drawn into the mortgage market by anemic demand for business loans, raised their net home loan investment from $2.3 billion in 1975 to as much as $10.9 billion in 1976

Table 5-7
Net Increase in Mortgage Debt on One- to Four-Family Houses,
United States, 1971-1977

Period	All Holders[a]	Four Financial Institutions[b]	Federal and Related Agencies[c]	Mortgage Pools or Trusts[d]
		Billions of Dollars		
1971	$27.0	$22.3	$1.7	$4.2
1972	43.2	34.2	1.2	4.0
1973	44.0	32.3	2.7	2.9
1974	33.2	19.7	6.3	5.0
1975	41.4	24.5	4.4	9.4
1976	67.6	49.6	−2.3	14.0
1977	95.8	68.1	0.2	18.5
Percent Changes per Year, Compound Rates[e]				
1972-1974	12.5%	11.2%	10.6%	65.0%
1974-1976	11.4	10.2	3.1	50.3
1975-1977	14.3	12.9	2.8	59.7

Sources: *Federal Reserve Bulletin.* The revised debt estimates of the Federal Reserve Board begin at the end of 1970.

[a]Includes "individuals and others" not shown separately.

[b]Commercial banks, mutual savings banks, savings-and-loan associations, and life insurance companies.

[c]Includes FNMA, FHLMC, GNMA, Farmers Home Administration, Federal Land Banks for nonfarm mortgages, and FHA and VA.

[d]Includes mortgage balances backing securities insured or guaranteed by GNMA, FHLMC, and the Farmers Home Administration. Only partial data available for 1971 and 1972. Excludes mortgage-backed securities issued by savings-and-loan associations and a few commercial banks, but the underlying loans are accounted for in the data on net lending by the institutions.

[e]Based on outstanding balances at beginning of each period, that is, the averages pertain to three years for each period.

and $15.1 billion in 1977. Mutual savings banks contributed only moderately to the availability of home loans. Life insurance companies continued to reduce their portfolios. Their holdings of home mortgages shrank by $2.9 billion between 1975 and 1977 (and by $12 billion since 1970).

The greatest expansionary force in net lending during recent years have been the mortgage pools or trusts, the novel financing device that draws on the securities market for mortgage investment and that was pioneered by the Government National Mortgage Association and the Farmers Home Administration and later adopted by the Federal Home Loan Mortgage Corporation. The net funds provided by mortgage pools or trusts rose from $5 billion in 1974 to $14 billion in 1976 and over $18 billion in 1977, exceeding by far the net home mortgage lending by all commercial banks. The average annual portfolio additions expressed as a percent of outstanding balances show spectacular increments in comparison to those of the traditional lenders. In 1973, mortgage pools or trusts accounted for 3.3% of total home loan holdings. Their market share at the end of 1977 approximated 10%. In contrast, the portfolio of federal and related agencies themselves represented 6.5% of the total in 1973 and only 5.5% in 1977.

Apart from their role in the issuance of mortgage-backed securities, federal and related agencies have played a minor part in net acquisitions of home loans since 1974. Pursuing a countercyclical policy, as they should, they dropped the volume of net lending from $6.3 billion in the recession of 1974 to $4.4 billion in 1975, became net sellers in 1976 as ample funds were available from private lenders, and made a negligible net investment in 1977. The decline in the agencies' net lending was in small part caused by a drop in FHA and VA holdings of loans they had taken over in lieu of foreclosure. In late 1977, however, the agencies began to step up their mortgage acquisitions as credit tightened.

Some analysts have been concerned over an excess of net lending on homes in recent years over the value of net purchases of new and existing homes by households. This implies net liquidation of house equities that presumably became available for nonhousing purposes. At a time of large property price increases when sellers of homes obtained substantial amounts of cash over and above their mortgage loan balances and did not necessarily reinvest all of the proceeds in downpayments on other homes, liquidation of housing equities was apt to increase. Another possible cause of liquidation was the apparently growing tendency of homeowners to incur additional mortgage debt for uses not related to property transactions or improvements. But the magnitudes involved are difficult to estimate and seem to have been overstated. This matter is discussed in appendix J.

Turning to California, the absence of home mortgage data corresponding to table 5-7 compels resort to a proxy: the net lending by savings-and-loan associations in the state. In the 1970s about 80% of the associations' total mortgage loans were on 1- to 4-family houses, so the periodic changes are acceptable approximations to home lending. The data in table 5-8 again show the familiar cyclical fluctuations, but the expansionary trend over the 1970-1977 period was far greater than for S&Ls in the nation as a whole. Net lending by California associations in 1977 was 8.3 times the amount recorded for 1970. Net lending by associations in the United States was only 5.8 times the 1970 volume. The average annual percent changes at the bottom of table 5-8 exceed those for "all holders" in the United States (table 5-7) since 1974, and by an especially great margin between 1975 and 1977. The growth rate in the latter period was 17% for California savings associations and only 14% for all holders of home mortgages in the nation. The differential may be largely explained by the fact that savings-and-loan associations have raised their share in total California real-estate financing substantially in the past few years.[10]

As for the cost of mortgage loans to borrowers, a composite terms-of-credit

Table 5-8
Net Increase in Mortgage Loan Holdings of FSLIC-Insured
California Savings-and-Loan Associations, 1970-1977

Period	Million $	Period	Million $
1970	1,470	1974	2,686
1971	3,657	1975	5,298
1972	5,292	1976	9,453
1973	3,916	1977	12,219

Percent Changes per Year, Compound Rates[a]

Period	Change
1970-1972	11.6%
1972-1974	11.1
1974-1976	12.5
1975-1977	17.3

Source: Outstanding balances reported in California Savings and Loan League, Data Book 1977.
[a]Based on outstanding balance at beginning of each period.

index was prepared for this study from the FHLBB data on average effective interest rates, loan maturities, and loan-price ratios for conventional home loans made by major types of lenders. The common procedure of analyzing changes in interest rates alone is unsatisfactory since they may be modified by changes in the noninterest terms of loans. An extension of average maturities, for example, may wholly or partially offset the effect of rising interest rates on monthly payments. An increase in the loan-price ratio reduces the downpayment requirement but raises monthly payments because of the larger amount of the mortgage even if the interest rate and loan maturity remain unchanged. The cost of borrowing is measured most adequately if changes in each of the three terms are weighted in accordance with their monetary impact on monthly payments.[11]

The composite terms-of-credit index disregards changes in house prices and is best considered a measure of monthly payments per dollar of house price. (Since one of the three terms is the loan-price ratio, which affects the amount of loan, it would be erroneous to designate the composite index as a measure of borrowing costs per dollar of loan.) At a later point, the composite index is applied to changing house prices; the results will show borrowing costs actually incurred by home buyers in terms of monthly loan payments. Throughout, the underlying figures have been converted to indexes to facilitate comparison. The formula for the composite index per dollar of house price is specified in appendix K.

Table 5-9 shows the composite index and its three components for conventional home loans in the United States, separately for new and existing

Table 5-9
Terms-of-Credit Composite Index for Conventional Home Loans Made by Major Types of Lenders in the United States, 1968-1977
(per dollar of house price; 1970 = 100)

Period	Newly Built Homes				Existing Homes			
	Effective Interest Rate	*Maturity (Years)*	*Loan/ Price Ratio*	*Monthly Payment*	*Effective Interest Rate*	*Maturity (Years)*	*Loan/ Price Ratio*	*Monthly Payment*
1968	83	102	103	91	84	100	103	95
1969	92	102	102	96	94	100	101	97
1970	100	100	100	100	100	100	100	100
1971	92	104	104	94	92	106	104	96
1972	90	108	107	97	90	113	107	96
1973	94	105	108	102	96	102	106	98
1974	106	105	106	108	108	101	102	107
1975	107	107	106	109	110	105	103	108
1976	106	108	106	108	109	107	104	107
1977 I	106	111	107	108	107	112	105	107
II	106	110	106	108	107	114	107	107
III	107	112	106	108	108	114	105	106

Source: Federal Home Loan Bank Board, releases on "Terms of Conventional Home Mortgages." See technical notes attached to each FHLBB release. It should be noted that the data for each of the three terms are weighted averages. A 1973 revision of the series may affect the 1972-1973 changes.

homes. Since periodic changes for the two categories of houses are quite similar, the analysis is confined to terms of credit for existing property. As one would expect, the composite exhibits some cyclical characteristics. Between 1968 and 1970, terms of credit tightened, mainly because interest rates were rising and loan-price ratios declining (which required a larger loan per dollar of house price), while maturities remained unchanged. In the two subsequent years, terms were more favorable to borrowers, and this was indeed a period of expanding sales of existing and new homes. Interest rates dropped by 10% and maturities lengthened considerably. The effects of these changes on the cost of borrowing were partially offset by increased loan-price ratios. Between 1972 and 1974, the composite index shows a substantial increase of borrowing costs, but the index remained at about the same level throughout the 1974-1977 period, the focus of our study.

Among the components of the index, interest rates rose sharply between 1972 and 1974 and remained quite stable until late 1977. Loan maturities were cut back during the recession of 1973-1974 but were extended later, especially in the first three quarters of 1977. The longer maturities served to soften the impact of high interest rates. The loan-price ratio inched up after 1974 for loans on existing homes though not for those on new houses. For the former, the higher ratio meant larger monthly payments per dollar of house price while reducing downpayment requirements. Thus the stability of the composite index in 1974-1977 was the net result of largely offsetting changes in the components of the index.

The composite index makes it clear that the cost of home mortgage borrowing as such has increased moderately. In 1976 and the first three quarters of 1977, it exceeded the 1971 cost, the lowest level of the decade to-date, by little more than 11% for loans on existing property and by about 15% for those on new homes. During the same period the CPI rose by 51%. If 1968 is taken as a benchmark year, the 1977 borrowing costs on existing houses were about 13% higher, those on new houses, a little over 18%. In this span of time, the CPI increased by 76%. The moderate advance relative to other prices and the stability of borrowing costs in 1974-1977, when general inflation reached new heights followed by diminishing increments, helps explain the growing volume of home purchases despite near-record levels of mortgage interest rates.

This perspective is modified when the upward thrust of house prices is taken into account. Table 5-10 presents an index of actual monthly payments by applying changes in the composite cost of borrowing to the changing house prices reported by the FHLBB in the releases on terms of home mortgages. In other words, the loan terms and house prices are based on the same transactions. For convenience, the indexes per dollar of house price and those for actual borrowing costs are placed side by side. Both sets of data relate to home loans made in each reported year.

In contrast to the cyclical movements of the "pure" cost of borrowing,

Table 5-10
Index of Monthly Payments on Conventional Home Loans Made by Major
Types of Lenders in the United States Compared with Composite Index
of Cost of Borrowing, 1970-1977
(1970 = 100)

	Newly Built Homes			Existing Homes		
Period	Monthly Payments[a]	Cost of Borrowing[b]	Difference	Monthly Payments[a]	Cost of Borrowing[b]	Difference
1970	100	100	—	100	100	—
1971	96	94	2	102	96	6
1972	102	97	5	107	96	11
1973	107	102	5	107	98	9
1974	122	108	14	123	107	16
1975	137	109	28	138	108	30
1976	147	108	39	148	107	41
1977 I	162	108	54	164	107	57
II	162	108	54	166	107	59
III	167	108	59	172	106	66

Source: See table 5-9.

[a]Composite cost of borrowing per dollar of house price multiplied by house prices shown in table A-1, column "Federal Home Loan Bank Board."

[b]From table 5-9.

actual costs or monthly payments have kept increasing throughout 1970-1977 (with a minor exception for new houses in 1971), a result of rising property prices. Between 1974 and 1977, when the composite index of borrowing cost was nearly stable, all of the rise in actual monthly payments was caused by the advance of house prices. Actual payments increased at an average annual (compound) rate of 9.4% for new houses and 7.2% for existing property between 1972 and 1974, slightly less than 10% between 1974 and 1976 for both categories, and by 10.3% and nearly 12%, respectively, between the third quarters of 1976 and 1977. The rise in actual payments between 1970 and the third quarter of 1977 exceeded the rise in overall consumer prices.

Calculations corresponding to those in tables 5-9 and 5-10 have been performed for the two major metropolitan areas of California, drawn from the same source. The results are shown in table 5-11, while the underlying detail for the composite index of terms of credit is placed in appendix table L-1. The findings for the Los Angeles and San Francisco Bay areas in the crucial 1975-1977 period differ markedly from those for the United States. Actual mortgage payments increased as a much faster rate than in the nation as a whole, particularly for buyers of existing homes. In III-1977 they exceeded twice the amount paid by 1970 purchasers. At the same time the pure cost of borrowing (per dollar of house price) declined after 1974-1975 in contrast to its stability in the United States. In other words, some "stretching" of loan terms did occur in

Table 5-11
Index of Monthly Payments on Conventional Home Loans Made by Major
Types of Lenders in Two California Areas Compared with Composite
Cost of Borrowing, 1970-1977
(1970 = 100)

	Newly Built Homes			Existing Homes		
Period	Monthly Payments	Cost of Borrowing	Difference	Monthly Payments	Cost of Borrowing	Difference
Los Angeles-Long-Beach-Anaheim						
1970	100	100	–	100	100	–
1971	87	97	–10	97	94	3
1972	90	95	5	97	92	5
1973	104	101	3	111	100	1
1974	128	108	20	138	108	30
1975	141	109	32	154	107	47
1976	175	106	69	175	104	71
1977 I	177	106	71	190	103	87
II	187	105	82	202	102	100
III	203	107	96	215	104	111
San Francisco-Oakland-San Jose						
1970	100	100	–	100	100	–
1971	80	94	–14	89	91	–2
1972	92	95	–3	94	92	2
1973	107	96	11	111	98	13
1974	127	105	22	137	107	30
1975	154	104	50	150	105	45
1976	165	101	64	169	104	65
1977 I	176	101	75	178	104	74
II	184	100	83	191	103	89
III	205	101	104	208	103	105

Source: See table 5-9; for house prices, table A-3.

California. Hence the difference between the indexes of actual payments and of borrowing costs as such became increasingly larger than those in the nation. The evidence indicates that the relatively greater price rise in California was accompanied by moderate easing of loan terms, probably in response to the huge flows of deposits received by savings-and-loan associations in the state and the resulting pressure to invest the funds.

For the FHA segment of the market, debt service data are available directly. The reported dollar amounts were converted into an index comparable to the index of monthly payments in table 5-10. The results for the United States and California are given in table 5-12. By-passing detail for the earlier periods, the data for the United States clearly indicate that monthly payments on FHA loans in recent years have also increased at a fast pace but not as sharply as those on conventional mortgages. In California, debt service on new homes rose more than in the nation, but that on existing homes slightly less. The extraordinary

Table 5-12
Index of Debt Service on Single-Family Houses Financed
with FHA-Insured Loans,[a] United States, 1970-1977

	United States		California	
Period	New Homes[b]	Existing Homes	New Homes[b]	Existing Homes
1970	100	100	100	100
1971	95	97	100	97
1972	96	96	100	97
1973	96	98	119	98
1974	115	123	136	117
1975	135	148	139	146
1976	149	153	156	151
1977 I	153	155	162	151
II	155	154	167	151
III	158	161	170	158

Source: Federal Housing Administration.

[a]Insured under Section 203b. Debt service includes interest, amortization, and the mortgage insurance premium. Since the latter is paid by the borrower, the U.S. data are comparable to the monthly payments shown in table 5-10.
[b]"Proposed homes."

increases in the Los Angeles and San Francisco Bay areas for conventional mortgages are not observed for FHA loans in the state as a whole.[12]

Restraints on New Homebuilding

As was pointed out at the beginning of our discussion of excess demand, restraints on homebuilding may be one of the causes of temporary market disequilibrium. According to a widely held view, such restraints contributed measurably to demand-supply imbalances in recent years, as well as to cost and therefore price escalation. There is ample documentation of the inhibiting effects on home construction of municipal moratoriums on sewer and water hookups, other local growth management ordinances, environmental reviews, and similar requirements that took effect mainly in the past few years. Their frequency and severity have varied from area to area. Among their general effects are shortages of buildable lots, costly delays, and greater land development expenses to builders.[13] Hence it is alleged that the supply of new single-family houses in the housing recovery since 1975 could not catch up with the rapidly growing demand. Whether the attendant price escalation is viewed as a result of deficient supply or excess demand makes a difference in semantics but not in substance so long as the source of market imbalance is identified.

Without denying an inhibiting impact of additional or stricter regulations in

Table 5-13
Cumulative Percent Increase of Starts of Single-Family Houses
in the United States during Four Expansion Periods
(based on quarterly data for seasonally adjusted annual rates)

	Number of Calendar Quarters[b]			
Expansion Period[a]	*First Three*	*First Six*	*First Nine*	*First Twelve*
IV-1960-III-1963	11.7%	11.0%	1.3%	17.7%[c]
IV-1966-III-1968	38.6	32.6	41.7[d]	—
I-1970-I-1973	41.5	68.7	83.7	96.1
I-1975-IV-1977	38.1	59.4	89.5	106.9

Source: U.S. Bureau of the Census, *Housing Starts*.
[a]Starts of single-family houses were first reported in I-1959 and show a decrease to IV-1960. The table omits the short miniexpansion from I-1965 to IV-1965, with an increase of 13.2%, which was followed by a sharp decline through IV-1966.
[b]Calendar quarters of recovery from trough.
[c]The percent increase relates to 11 quarters, the duration of this expansion period.
[d]The percent increase is for 8 quarters, the duration of this expansion period.

the course of time, one must raise the question whether it was of sufficient magnitude to affect materially the cyclical expansion of homebuilding in 1975-1977. As a pragmatic test, table 5-13 compares the percent increase of single-family house starts during the recent expansion with that of earlier expansion phases, measured in each case for the first three, six, nine, and twelve calendar quarters of the upswing. The comparison extends back to the recovery of homebuilding starting in late 1960; data on single-family starts were first reported in 1959 and the years 1959-1960 were marked by a recession of house construction. In fact, the expansion of IV-1960 to III-1963 can also be omitted from the analysis; it was indistinct, sometimes halting, and of minor magnitude.

The rate of recovery in the first three quarters of the current expansion equaled that of the same period of the IV-1966 to III-1968 expansion and was only a little below that of the boom of I-1970 to I-1973. Considering the first six quarters, the current expansion was somewhat weaker than the preceding upswing. As the time period is extended, the current expansion shows a higher rate of increase than was ever registered before. In the first twelve quarters of the present boom, starts of single-family homes rose by 107% as against 96% in the comparable period of the preceding boom.

That the rate of gain in the first six quarters of the present expansion was somewhat below the rate recorded for the first six quarters of the 1970-1972 boom *may* be the result of supply constraints. It may have taken longer for builders to obtain lots ready for development and comply with stricter regulations. However, the difference may also be explained by the duration and severity of the contractions preceding the two expansions. The slump of homebuilding in 1973-1974 was the worst on record since World War II. It lasted two years and curtailed the volume of starts by more than 44%. The recession from IV-1968 to I-1970 lasted only five quarters and resulted in a 25% decline. (The peak quarters are not counted in the length of either recession.) The long duration and great severity of the 1973-1974 slump made it more difficult for builders to gear up for volume construction. This view is reinforced by the impressive rate of expansion after the first six quarters. As for land, many homes started in the early recovery phase of the current boom were probably constructed on parcels acquired by builders and subdividers in previous periods. Starts in the later expansion phase probably required greater inputs of newly acquired land and of site preparation. That this phase showed such a great rate of increase in starts would indicate that buildable lots were obtainable despite the restrictions, though at high prices. Hence the claim that new public regulations impeded homebuilding materially seems exaggerated, but it may well apply to individual localities. The real impact of the regulations will be felt in the future. At this writing, reports of shortages of developed or developable land are appearing with alarming frequency.

Recent increases in California homebuilding, based on seasonally adjusted permit authorizations for single-family houses, also show rates that are well in line with those for the two preceding expansions (table 5-14). In fact, the cumulative increase in the nine quarters of the boom—from IV-1974 to I-1977—was over twice as large as in the same period of the 1970-1972 expansion. But it should be noted that California permits reached their peak quite early, with 195,000 units. The data after I-1977 show substantially lower though fluctuating levels. The decrease is in contrast with continued gains in the *sale* of both new and existing houses and with continued expansion of single-family house starts in the nation as a whole.

Does the decline in permits indicate that supply constraints in the form of

Table 5-14
Cumulative Percent Increase of Building-Permit Authorizations for Single-Family Houses in California during Three Expansion Periods
(based on quarterly data for seasonally adjusted annual rates)

	Number of Calendar Quarters[a]			
Expansion Period	*First Three*	*First Six*	*First Nine*	*First Eleven*
I-1967-IV-1968	56.3%	71.1%	86.1%[b]	—
I-1970-IV-1972	37.8	86.0	92.3	126.6%[c]
IV-1974-I-1977	51.1	80.4	201.7[c]	—

Source: Security Pacific National Bank, "California Construction Trends."

[a]Calendar quarters of recovery from trough.

[b]Percent increase is for seven quarters, the duration of this expansion period.

[c]Percent increase for total duration of this expansion period.

lot shortages and environmental regulations caught up with the California homebuilding boom after it had lasted only nine quarters? Possibly, but not necessarily. The extraordinary rise in permits from 120,700 in I-1976 to 201,567 in I-1977 was probably anticipatory and unsustainable even in the face of hectic sales activity. An unusually large proportion of sales had been of the prestart variety, and builders were hard-pressed to get construction underway or completed for the many units sold under previous contracts. Also mortgage lenders report that uncertainty over the continuance of the sales boom caused them to approve construction loans for relatively small segments of projects, with additional financing contingent on sales experience. Altogether, the decline of permits may have been a symptom of leveling off in the California market. In any case, the speed of the recent expansion of home construction, compared to the speed of the two preceding expansions, precludes the hypothesis of severe statewide supply constraints, but there are local exceptions. The most important of these seems to be the control of building activity under the California Coastal Zone Act.[14]

The outcome of our pragmatic test of supply constraints for both California and the nation may provoke the argument that homebuilding would have expanded even faster in the absence of additional restrictions. This point can be neither proved nor disproved. The fact remains that the rate at which builders increased the supply was well in line with previous experience.

As a final point, recent controls of residential development may have contributed to higher costs of construction, sites, and site preparation even if they did not constrain the quantity of homebuilding materially. For example, environmental restrictions in many cases reduced the number of houses that could be built on a given parcel, increasing the unit cost of land and development. Within our national data framework, we can examine whether average prices of new homes have risen relative to those of existing homes, both types being subject to the same broad demand forces. Between 1974 and 1976, the excess of prices for new units over those for old units financed with conventional mortgage loans increased from 15.6% to 17.2%, but it declined to 14.3% in 1977. The average excess of 1971-1973 when homebuilding was also booming in terms of completions and sales was of about the same magnitude (15%). The recent excess of prices for new homes sold by merchant builders over prices for existing homes reported by the National Association of Realtors rose more sharply from 8.6% in 1974 to 13.7% in 1976 and was 13.1% in 1977. In this case, the price differentials were much larger than in 1971-1973 when they averaged only 3.6%. Thus the evidence on the impact of regulatory constraints on prices for new units relative to those for old property is unclear. Besides, an increase in the price spread may reflect a host of variables not related to building restrictions, including the tendency of owner-buyers to favor high-quality products when they purchased new houses.

The Role of Inflationary Expectations

The analysis so far suggests, although it does not prove, that the conventional variables—population changes, income gains, variations in the availability and cost of home mortgage loans, or recent constraints on homebuilding—are not sufficient for full explanation of the price escalation of single-family houses since 1975. Demographic factors raising the demand for homes have been operative for some time before the price surge and merely continued cumulatively during the critical period under review. Income gains were at best normal for a period of general business expansion. The only identifiable change impinging directly on demand and prices since 1975 was legislation removing credit discrimination against women. As a result, lenders had to recognize fully the earnings of females for purposes of home loan qualification. In combination with the growing share of working women in the employed labor force, this increased the loan amounts available to households with two earners. Home sales to single females likewise benefited from the new regulation. The availability of mortgage funds through 1977 favored homebuying, but there was no decline in the cost of borrowing that might explain a burst of demand and an attendant price surge. The regulatory constraints on homebuilding probably had a moderate impact on market imbalances in the 1975-1977 period, although they may become a more serious handicap in the future.

Some exceptions were noted for California. The renewed wave of inmigration in recent years added significantly to the demand for houses. Noninterest terms of home loans were somewhat eased, so the composite index of borrowing costs declined slightly while it remained stable in the nation as a whole. The slow recovery of homebuilding in 1975 indicates that environmental and other regulations may have been more effective in constraining new construction in the state than in other parts of the country. Thus the *initial* price escalation in California was probably in large measure a function of forces endogenous to the house market: unanticipated demand for homes relative to supply. This conclusion is consistent with the rapid decline in builders' inventories and vacancies in California (but not in the United States as a whole) during the early phase of the 1975-1977 period.

On the whole, however, one is hard put to attribute the escalation of house prices to variables incorporated in conventional analysis. Hence we now turn to an unconventional variable: inflationary expectations of a broad segment of the population. The hypothesis of inflationary expectations implies that even though the initial price surge in California owed its origin to "normal" market forces, its persistence and intensity were based on fears of further price increases and that such fears spread to many other areas. As causes of house price escalation, conventional demand variables and inflationary expectations may well have been operating in sequence or simultaneously, depending on local conditions. The geographic diffusion of high rates of price increase was probably aided and abetted by the wide publicity given to the California market, but one need not assume any specific mechanism for the transmission of information on house prices ("as California goes, so goes the nation") to explain the rapid spread of inflationary expectations. It is enough to recall the general inflation since 1973, the growing consciousness of inflation among the public, the consequent search for investments believed to provide reasonable protection against it, and the increasing recognition that the single-family house was an asset with considerable appreciation potentials.

As for general inflation, the sharp increases in consumer prices during 1973-1974 represented a novel, jolting experience. The CPI rose by 8.8% between December 1972 and 1973 and again by 12.2% between December 1973 and 1974. Only in the two immediate postwar years and in one year of the Korean hostilities had prices increased at similar rates.[15] The general inflation of 1973-1974 was not immediately accompanied by an unusual price surge for single-family houses, for it coincided largely with a severe economic recession and a decline in housing demand. The combination of recession and inflation caused consumers to save rather than to spend more.[16] Nevertheless, the experience of 1973-1974 had lasting effects on consumers' concern over inflation. Although the price rise moderated substantially after 1974, the CPI increase averaged more than 6% in the next two years—far above the "tolerable" norm of 2-3% that does not seem to induce significant changes in the pattern of household expenditures and savings. The persistence of rates of price rise considered high by the public, as well as the shock of the 1973-1974 experience, has contributed to the widespread apprehensions over inflation potentials. As Arthur M. Okun has put it,

> This country has not adapted, and is not adapting, to 6-percent inflation. The tolerable rate of inflation in this society is considerably below 6-percent. In the early sixties, 1.5 percent inflation was generally regarded as tolerable; in the early seventies, a 3-percent rate was widely accepted. If we were now to label 6-percent inflation as acceptable, who could believe that such a decision was the final turn of the ratchet?[17]

[Inflationary expectations are, of course, nationwide phenomena although they may vary among different people at any one time as well as from one period to the next. When they are introduced as a variable contributing to the escalation of house prices, one encounters the fact of locally segmented residential markets. As shown in chapter 2, the price surge for homes began at different times in different regions and localities and proceeded at diverse rates of change. This observation is entirely consistent with the hypothesis that inflationary expectations played a significant role in the price increase for single-family dwellings. In each area, that role is modified by the great variety of housing market conditions and, in some cases, general business conditions as well. Thus the relatively slow rise of house prices in the northeast region during the 1975-1977 period reflects the retarded growth in population and economic development of many parts of the region. Outmigration, dearth of employment opportunities, and diminished confidence in the future can prevent inflationary expectations from being transformed into a strong expansion of home purchase and the concomitant price increase. More generally, local demographic variables, differences in housing vacancies and builders' inventories, the structure of the economic base and its sensitivity to cyclical swings, and diverse rates of employment and income gains in recent years are among the reasons why the effects of inflationary expectations on the timing and extent of house price increases have varied so much from area to area. While fear of inflation has become a pervasive force, one would expect the localism of housing markets to result in an uneven response to it.

[Alternatively, one may assume that consumers' actions in the single-family house market have been conditioned by their observation of local price increases for residences. If so, inflationary expectations were related to the movement of home prices rather than the general price level. This hypothesis would explain directly why house prices have shown such diverse rates of change in different areas.] There is no theoretical or empirical basis for accepting this version in preference to the previously offered interpretation that nationwide inflationary expectations interact with local conditions in such fashion as to generate substantially different rates of house price increases in various places.

The next section documents consumers' expectations of general price movements and their opinions on the timeliness of home purchase at the national level.

Findings of Consumer Surveys

The Michigan consumer surveys show continuous though fluctuating expectations of rising general prices (table 5-15). Especially noteworthy is the increase between 1976 and 1977 in the proportion of respondents anticipating a price advance of at least 5%. In 1977, the proportion reached or exceeded one half of all respondents and approximated two thirds of those with incomes of $15,000 or more, who represent the vast majority of homebuyers. There was a similar 1976-1977 increase in anticipations of a price rise of 10% or more, but only one-fifth to one quarter of the respondents expected inflation of this magnitude at the latest survey dates. Also the average expected price increase was greater in 1977 than in the preceding year. Altogether, the recent surveys show inflationary expectations at a higher level than at any previous date included in the table, except for the fall of 1974 when consumers had experienced about a year of price advances at double-digit rates, partly as a result of skyrocketing oil prices.

Table 5-15
Consumers' General Price Expectations, United States, 1973-1977[a]

Survey Dates		5-9%	10% or More	Combined	Same or Go Down	Mean Increase (%)[b]
			Expected Price Increase During Next 12 Months			
All Respondent Families						
Oct.-Nov.	1973	19%	20%	39%	31%	6.4
October	1974	20	38	58	15	10.7
Oct.-Nov.	1975	23	21	44	22	7.2
February	1976	26	16	42	27	5.8
May	1976	24	15	39	22	5.8
Aug.-Sept.	1976	26	17	43	20	5.4
Nov.-Dec.	1976	24	13	37	32	4.8
February	1977	26	24	50	18	7.4
May	1977	34	21	55	18	6.9
Aug.-Sept.	1977	27	23	50	19	7.2
Nov.-Dec.	1977	32	22	54	16	6.9
Families with Incomes of $15,000 or More						
Oct.-Nov.	1973	28%	22%	50%	29%	6.4
October	1974	24	43	67	15	11.1
Oct.-Nov.	1975	29	30	59	19	8.2
February	1976	32	15	47	24	5.4
May	1976	32	18	50	16	6.4
Aug.-Sept.	1976	35	11	46	21	5.0
Nov.-Dec.	1976	35	11	46	26	5.3
February	1977	36	22	58	16	7.5
May	1977	45	22	67	11	7.2
Aug.-Sept.	1977	40	23	63	13	7.0
Nov.-Dec.	1977	44	20	64	11	6.5

Source: "November-December 1977 Survey of Consumer Attitudes," Survey Research Center of the University of Michigan, table 16.

[a]Omits respondents expecting price increases of less than 5%, those who said prices will rise but did not know how much, and the relatively few who stated "don't know" what price changes to expect.

[b]Mean calculated by treating the respondents who expected prices to go down as if they said that prices would decline by 3%, those who responded "same" = 0, and by taking the midpoint for the "up" category of respondents.

In light of consumers' price expectations, it is not astonishing to find that they developed more favorable attitudes to home purchase (table 5-16). Here the responses of families with income of $15,000 or more are especially relevant. In this group, the proportion of respondents who considered it a "good time to buy" rose sharply though irregularly in 1976 and 1977, reaching a peak of 72% at the May 1977 survey date. After the spring of 1976, "good time" responses increasingly exceeded "bad time" responses. More important from the viewpoint of price expectations, the proportion of respondents who believed it was a good time to buy because prices would go higher doubled between late 1975 and May 1977 when it reached 56%. Although it declined at the two latest survey dates,

Table 5-16
Consumers' Opinions on House Purchase, United States, 1973-1977[a]

Survey Dates	Good Time To Buy	Reasons		Bad Time to Buy	Reasons	
		Prices Going Higher[b]	Favorable Interest Rates[c]		Prices High[d]	Interest Rates High[e]
All Respondent Families						
OctNov. 1973	21%	*	*	65%	*	*
October 1974	15	12	3	71	30	67
OctNov. 1975	33	23	8	50	26	29
February 1976	41	27	13	38	23	25
May 1976	39	25	11	43	25	23
Aug.-Sept. 1976	47	31	10	36	26	14
Nov.-Dec. 1976	44	32	7	45	28	20
February 1977	48	34	10	42	24	17
May 1977	62	50	6	29	22	10
Aug.-Sept. 1977	56	39	7	37	28	13
Nov.-Dec. 1977	55	42	7	35	30	8
Respondent Families with Income of $15,000 or More						
OctNov. 1973	26%	*	*	68%	*	*
October 1974	17	14	4	70	25	73
OctNov. 1975	40	28	13	45	26	33
February 1976	46	29	19	36	22	27
May 1976	51	30	17	36	22	23
Aug.-Sept. 1976	61	38	16	29	19	15
Nov.-Dec. 1976	56	38	12	35	21	22
February 1977	60	43	17	34	19	19
May 1977	72	56	9	21	18	8
Aug.-Sept. 1977	68	50	10	25	21	9
Nov.-Dec. 1977	66	48	10	27	22	10

Source: "November-December 1977 Survey of Consumer Attitudes," Survey Research Center of the University of Michigan, tables 23 and 24.

[a]Omits the rather large percentage of respondents stating "uncertain, depends."

[b]Combines: "Prices won't come down; are going higher" and "Prices are low; good buys available." Although responses to these items could represent different perceptions, their combination introduces no distortions. Since early 1975 "Prices won't come down; are going higher" (statement I) has evoked far greater response than "Prices are low; good buys available" (statement II), and a sharply increasing response as well. For families with income of $15,000 or more, statement I responses rose from 14% in May 1975 to 51% in May 1977, with minor interim fluctuations. Statement II responses in the same period ranged irregularly between 5% and 10%. The figures relate to families who felt it was a good time to buy.

[c]Combines: "Credit tighter later; interest rates up" and "Interest rates are low." These items could also represent somewhat different perceptions. Responses to "Interest rates are low" between May 1975 and May 1977 exceed those to the alternative statement in seven of nine survey periods, at times by substantial margins, for families who felt it was a good time to buy. Again, the combination of the two responses involves no significant distortion.

[d]Full response: "Prices are high; may fall later."

[e]Combines: "Credit is tight; interest rates high" and "Interest rates down later."

*Questions not asked.

about one half of the respondents still anticipated prices to move up. That price expectations rather than credit conditions played the dominant role in consumer attitudes can be inferred from the low and decreasing percentage of respondents who gave the level of interest rates as a reason for saying it was a good time to buy homes.

The consumer attitudes captured in the Michigan surveys appear even more distinctly in our own surveys of actual homebuyers in two California counties (see chapter 4 and appendix H). One need only recall the large percentage of 1975 and especially 1977 purchasers who considered "hedge against inflation" or expected further increases in house prices as important or very important factors in their decision to buy.

Investment and Consumption Components in
Home Purchase

On the whole, the consumer surveys confirm the persistence of public apprehension over general inflation, and they are consistent with the hypothesis that anticipation of higher house prices was a significant factor in the recent price escalation.[18] Home purchase for owner-occupancy has always been motivated by two considerations: the consumption of housing services and the investment in real property. Under conditions of reasonably stable prices, consumers' housing decisions are for the most part based on expected flows of residential services from owned or rented units, tenure and neighborhood preferences, and simple comparisons between the cost of renting and periodic homeownership expenses involving at best a calculation of the opportunity costs of the equity invested in a house. In the recent years of sharply rising house prices, however, the investment aspect seems to have gained in importance for a large part of the homebuying public.

Conceptually, one can view the demand for residential services as distinct from the decision to invest in housing. The demand for residential services is substantially a function of current income and their prices relative to those of other goods and services. To take an extreme case, if all consumers occupied rental units (and assuming costs of moving were low) upward or downward adjustments in housing consumption would vary rapidly as incomes or relative prices changed in the short run. Investors, however, have a longer time horizon and base their decision on the present value of anticipated future returns including the expected price of the asset when the investment is terminated. The investment decision invariably projects demand into the future and compares the return on a given asset to alternatives. Hence the investor's asset demand based on expectations may depart from the current demand for housing services.

In home purchase for occupancy, the investment and consumption decisions are combined, and the components of the joint demand for houses as assets and as suppliers of services are difficult to separate. As investors, for example, middle-income households may be induced to purchase large and expensive homes because they expect to sell the property at favorable prices in the future. However, as occupants they will raise the level and periodic expense of the housing services they obtain. Through relative depreciation and obsolescence, they will also consume some of the capital investment, although they can slow this process by careful maintenance and capital improvements.

The growing importance of investment considerations in home purchase has paralleled the general search for assets believed to be "inflation-proof." As a result of increased public consciousness of inflation and its consequences for personal income and wealth, individuals have for years sought investments considered to be promising hedges against the erosion of the dollar's purchasing power. The more affluent have shifted some of their funds into vacant land or income property, real estate or cattle and other syndicates, gold and silver, precious coins or stones, rare books and art objects, or they have ventured into commodity speculation. In some of these cases, tax shelter loomed large along with expectations of capital appreciation. In others, the investors had to forego income or even incur negative returns if storage and insurance and other costs for gold, silver, coins, and so on, were considered. However, all these investments remained fringe activities although the total amounts involved many billions. For the less affluent or less venturesome, the single-family house has in recent years emerged as a favorite hedge against inflation, easily accessible, highly leveraged, yielding returns in housing services as well as expected capital gains, and with an impressive record of steady price appreciation in comparison with alternative investments.[19] Such a comparison is shown in table 5-17 for selected variable-price assets. Conceptually, the comparisons indicate the experience of persons investing in the various assets at average prices of the initial year and selling the assets at average prices of the terminal year in each of the specified periods. The two series of house prices used in the table are intended to minimize the problem of changing product mix. Even so, the new house bought in 1967 was no longer new in 1976. Since prices for existing and new homes have largely increased at similar rates, this is no serious flaw.

In the 1968-1977 and 1970-1977 periods, investment in houses compares very favorably with investment in common stock and, by implication, in mutual funds. House prices throughout show capital appreciation. Common stock prices were exposed to large periodic fluctuations; over the longer periods, they indicate losses (1968-1977) or moderate advances (1970-1977) far below those for single-family homes.[20] The value increase per acre of farm real estate exceeded the appreciation of houses since 1972 and for the longer periods in the United States but not in California. Gold and silver show superior long-run appreciation, but their prices have been subject to short-run fluctuations.

Table 5-17
Price Changes for Selected Variable-Price Assets, 1968-1976[a]
(percent changes for specified periods)

Asset	1968- 1970	1970- 1972	1972- 1974	1974- 1976	1968- 1977	1970- 1977
Single-family houses						
Existing[b]	15.2%	17.1%	18.9%	17.9%	114.8%	86.4%
New 1967 house[c]	11.6	11.4	20.8	21.1	104.6	83.4
Common stock[d]						
Dow Jones	−24.5	30.9	−14.4	11.2	−6.4	23.7
Standard & Poor's	−15.7	31.2	−24.1	23.1	−0.5	18.0
NYSE	−17.4	31.9	−27.3	24.2	−3.1	17.4
Farm real estate[e]						
U.S.	9.3	12.8	41.7	29.4	164.5	141.9
California	4.8	1.8	8.9	11.5	30.5	24.5
Gold[f]						
Handy & Harman	–	–	173.1	−21.7	–	153.7[g]
Engelhard Ind.	–	–	172.5	−19.9	–	152.3[g]
Silver[h]	−17.4	−4.9	179.5	−7.5	115.5	161.0

[a]The listed price changes relate only to capital market values and ignore dividends or other returns on capital. The assets vary greatly in their capacity to yield income. For single-family houses they may be viewed as owner-benefits perhaps measured by imputed rent or as net yields from rental units. Common stock may or may not pay dividends. The same is true for returns on farm real estate. Holdings of gold and silver yield negative income because of storage and insurance costs.

[b]Average sales prices from National Association of Realtors.

[c]Average sales prices of a near-standard house built in 1967; see table A-1 for data and chapter 2, note 6, for detail.

[d]Composite indexes.

[e]U.S. Department of Agriculture, Economic Research Service, Farm Real Estate Developments, seriatim. Indexes (1967 = 100) for average value per acre. Rates of change based on February or March indexes.

[f]Derived from dollar prices per troy ounce (spot prices). Data begin in 1971, before gold ownership by U.S. citizens became legal.

[g]Average for 1972-1976.

[h]Derived from Handy & Harman spot prices per troy ounce.

Unfortunately, no information is available on investments in real-estate and other syndicates, but no supporting data are required for the assertion that investors in most real estate investment trusts have sustained heavy losses. To complete the comparisons, we add illustrations of the experience for fixed-price assets, which may be bonds or savings accounts or other dollar claims. Investors in such assets in 1968 and holding them through 1977 suffered a loss of principal value of 74%, or 8.2% per year, if the CPI is used to convert nominal into real dollar values. The loss for those investing in 1972 and holding the assets through 1977 was 44.8%, or nearly 9% per year. In other words, the annual returns on investment would have had to average 8% and 9% respectively, in order to preserve the real value of the assets without yielding income to the owner. Such returns have been barely approximated for the composite of corporate bonds (disregarding quality ratings) and were unobtainable on savings deposits in the period under review.[c] In contrast, the appreciation of house prices has kept pace with or has exceeded consumer price increases.

Of course, the data used here cover a limited span of time. The results would differ for earlier periods, but they would have no bearing on the explanation of the recent surge in house prices. Besides, house prices have generally shown an upward trend since World War II, though at more moderate rates than those recorded in the 1970s and with (usually short) interruptions. Among the exceptions are properties in deteriorating neighborhoods or in cities and towns with diminishing population and a weakening economic base. One can assume that the prevailing long-term increase of house prices did not go unnoticed as the experience of earlier generations of homebuyers was transmitted to later generations, and it may have contributed to the public's confidence in the investment merits of homeownership in recent years when general inflationary expectations gathered momentum.

The foregoing analysis of the role of inflationary expectations in the recent surge of house prices is descriptive and suggestive but does not attempt to quantify their importance relative to other market forces. The model of house prices in the next chapter is intended to explore the significance of the many variables determining the prices of single-family homes.

Notes

1. This pattern may have been partly associated with regional variations in builders' inventories and in the construction and sale of new homes. Regional variations in building seasons are likely to influence the ratio of unsold to sold homes. Data for the four main census regions on new homes sold and unsold, available from the C-25 series of the Bureau of the Census and HUD, are not used here because the reported quarterly figures are not seasonally adjusted.

2. Bureau of the Census and HUD, *Annual Housing Survey: 1975*, p. 1. The data refer to detached and attached single-family houses exclusive of mobile homes and trailers.

3. 1940 and 1950 *Census of Housing*. The comparison does not imply that the entire tenure shift was due to changing price-rent relationships, but one can safely assume that most of it was.

4. For detail, see footnote a to table 5-3. The results of the periodic local vacancy surveys conducted by the Postal Service are held to be unreliable and are therefore not used here.

[c]Reinvestment of interest receipts is excluded from the calculation since the data for variable-price assets in table 5-17 relate only to capital values.

5. Some of the demographic trends favoring housing demand may be briefly specified. The number of persons in the twenty-five to thirty-four age group increased from 22.2 million in 1965 to 32.9 million in 1976, or from 11.5% of the total population to nearly 15%. However, recent short-term changes were less pronounced. The number of people in this age class rose by nearly 2.2 million in 1970-1972, about 2.4 million in 1972-1974, and approximately 2.3 million in 1974-1976. Divorces more than doubled between 1965 (479,000) and 1976 (1,077,000), or from 2.5% of total population to 5.0%. In this case, short-term changes show some decline, from 137,000 in 1970-1972 to 132,000 in 1972-1974 and 100,000 in 1974-1976. The marriage rate per 1,000 population increased from 9.3% in 1965 to 11.0% in 1972 and fell thereafter to 9.9% in 1976. However, the number of unmarried mixed-sex couples living together, the "twosomes," has risen so fast that marriage statistics have become an increasingly unreliable indicator of demand for separate dwelling units.

6. Some states have also amended their legislation so as to prohibit discrimination against women by state-chartered financial institutions. For California, see CCH California Regular Session, 1973, New Laws, p. 2779, which is an amendment approved October 2, 1973. We are not aware of any systematic record of enforcement. A consent decree following a suit by the U.S. Department of Justice was reported in February 1978 as the first of its kind. Under the decree, the Prudential Federal Savings and Loan Association of Salt Lake City, the largest association in Utah, was required to consider alimony and child-supporting payments in income qualification for loans, to cease its practice of differentiating between male and female income for loan qualification, and to set identical interest rates on loans to male and female borrowers. *The Wall Street Journal,* February 1, 1978.

7. The figures for net household formation are as follows:

	California	United States
1970-72	460,000	4,462,000
1972-74	571,000	5,081,000
1974-76	604,000	4,616,000

8. Personal disposable income in real terms rose by 1.8% a year during the 1950-1953 expansion, by 4.3% between 1954 and 1957, and by 4.8% in the 1961-1969 period (compound rates). While troughs and peaks of real GNP occurred in different calendar quarters of the specified or adjoining years, the annual data are sufficient for our purpose.

9. The detailed data for types of financial institutions are readily available in the table on real estate debt in the *Federal Reserve Bulletin* and are therefore not reproduced in this volume.

10. The associations accounted for 59.6% of the estimated mortgage debt secured by California real property in 1976 compared with 53.8% in 1974. This

increase has been fairly steady over the years. The market share was less than 50% in 1967. (California Savings and Loan League, Data Book 1977.) No data are available for the home mortgage debt separately, but a similar increase seems most likely.

11. For an earlier effort to construct a composite of terms of home mortgage loans, see George F. Break, *The Economic Impact of Federal Loan Insurance* Washington, D.C.: National Planning Association, 1961, pp. 229-230. Break's data relate to 1925-1947. His statistical formula is as follows:

$$\text{Composite terms of credit} = \frac{\text{WAIR}}{\text{WAM} \times \text{WALVR}}$$

where WAIR denotes weighted average interest rates, WAM weighted average maturities in years, and WALVR weighted average loan-to-value ratios. The formula's weakness is the implied equal weight given to each of the three loan terms, when in fact changes in each term may have unequal effect on monthly payments.

12. FHA data are available for metropolitan areas, but the number of transactions in most of these is relatively small, and analysis for metropolitan areas would introduce a mass of statistics yielding little insight because of the low share of FHA in total markets.

13. For a recent discussion of these restraints, see several papers in *The Cost of Housing,* Proceedings of the Third Annual Conference of the Federal Home Loan Bank of San Francisco, December 6-7, 1977. The increased development expenses result in part from the practice to shift outlays once financed by local governments to builders or to impose fees on builders to cover such outlays. Among the facilities involved are water and sewerage, storm drainage, and land for schools and parks. Some localities impose a construction tax, a bedroom tax, or a school fee. See *Hearings of the Homeownership Task Force of the U.S. House of Representatives,* Long Beach, California, January 17, 1978, especially the testimony of Assemblyman Dennis Mangers. The shift of infrastructure expenses from local governments to private developers means that the burden is borne by purchasers of new homes. In contrast, the burden of municipal financing is borne by all local taxpayers, particularly property taxpayers including the industrial and commercial as well as the household sectors.

14. For detail, see Fred E. Case, "The Impact of Land Use and Environmental Controls on Housing Costs," in *The Cost of Housing,* Proceedings of the Third Annual Conference of the Federal Home Loan Bank of San Francisco.

15. The CPI rose by 11.4% in 1947 and by 10.8% in 1948 as wartime controls were dismantled. The index rose also by 10.8% in 1951 when the Korean war created pressures on the supply of goods while price regulation was tardy and incomplete.

16. Personal saving increased from 6.2% of disposable income in 1972 to 7.8% in 1973 and remained above 7% in the next two years, subsiding to 5.6% in 1976 and 5.1% in 1977.

17. Arthur M. Okun, "The Great Stagflation Swamp," *Challenge,* November-December 1977. The quoted portion of his article appears on pp. 10-11.

18. This does not imply that price expectations were the only cause. The economic recovery since 1975 contributed to the growing demand for single-family homes. For the multiplicity of factors that influence consumer attitudes, see George Katona, "The Theory of Expectations," in B. Strumpel, J.N. Morgan, and E. Zahn, *Human Behavior* (Amsterdam, N.Y.: Elsevier Scientific Publishing Co., 1972).

19. According to unverifiable reports, there has been some recent increase in purchases of single-family houses intended as pure investment, that is, for rental. Overall, no tendency toward growing investment for rental can be observed between 1970 and 1976. The number of renter-occupied single-family houses (detached and attached) kept fairly stable at about 8.5 million, while owner-occupied structures of this type increased from 46.8 million to 53.6 million. (Housing Census of 1970 and 1976 Annual Housing Survey, General Housing Characteristics).

20. These results are consistent with a more comprehensive study by Eugene F. Fama and G. William Schwert, "Asset Returns and Inflation," *Journal of Financial Economics,* November 1977. Among other things, the authors find that private residential real estate in 1953-1971 was the only one of several assets they investigated that provided a complete hedge against both expected and unexpected inflation. Treasury bills and U.S. government bonds were a complete hedge against expected but not against unexpected inflation. Common stock returns were negatively related to the expected component of the inflation rate, and probably also to the unexpected component. The authors measure the return to private residential real estate as the rate of increase in the home purchase price component of the CPI.

An Exploratory Model
of House Prices

Previous chapters examined the potential impact on house prices of a large number of variables. Precisely how these variables combined in shaping prices and price movements could not be specified. The goal of this chapter is to correct this limitation by quantitative analysis. In attempts to develop and test a house price model for the United States covering the period 1968-1977. In the process, selected housing demand and supply variables are studied in interaction. This approach, of course, has limitations of its own. Some of the forces impacting on the market for single-family dwellings are captured in broad quantitative measures, which may only weakly express the complexities of recent experience.

First the conceptual underpinnings of the model are presented. This will be followed by an exposition of the model structure. Finally the model is tested, and the results are examined in light of other evidence presented earlier.

General Framework

The theoretical foundations for the development and testing of housing models have expanded considerably in recent years. Agreement exists on certain fundamental factors determining housing production, consumption, price formation and the movement of prices. Nevertheless, the complexities of housing markets and submarkets and the difficulty of measuring precisely the influence of certain forces have invariably necessitated the introduction of simplifying assumptions. The nature of these assumptions, whether explicit or implicit, in part derive from the particular aspects of housing markets observers want to highlight, as well as some real differences in views on the role of selected variables in shaping housing demand and supply. Concerning the latter, for example, disagreement over the impact of credit on housing markets has occasionally been at a high pitch. Some theoretical constructs have incorporated the notion of credit rationing and credit availability as a centerpiece. Others have at best conceded that changes in the supply of funds and credit terms have a temporary impact but reject the proposition that they affect long-term housing demand.

In the context of this study the choice of constructs is substantially guided by the goal of explaining the short-run levels and changes in house prices that have characterized the past few years and, in particular, the inordinate increases in the period from 1974 to 1977. In the process, one cannot ignore the possibility that housing markets have been in a severe state of disequilibrium, with corrections in the offing but not observed during the period under consideration. One implication is that certain variables, which in light of other evidence might be expected to assert themselves over longer periods, could prove to be insignificant in short-run quantitative analysis or behave in a perverse fashion.

One of the first problems to be resolved in housing market analysis is to give more precise meaning to the term *price*. Home purchase for owner-occupancy essentially involves two types of decisions that are jointly determined.[1] One of these is the purchase of an asset and the other is the purchase of housing services. The purchase price of the asset is substantially influenced by the discounted present value of the anticipated returns from the investment adjusted for risk. In turn, the price investors are willing to pay is related to the returns available on alternative investments subject to a wealth constraint. The anticipated return is also an outgrowth of the interaction between the demand for and the supply of housing services. The price demanders are prepared to pay for housing services in owner-occupied units is a function of expected income and the characteristics of households that desire to consume such services, plus the prices of alternatives including both nonhousing goods and services and rentals. The supply of housing services is functionally related to costs of capital inputs plus depreciation and operating costs.

Two difficulties immediately present themselves. First prices observed in the market over time may embody different quantities or qualities of services in housing units. The fact that transactions prices are on an upward trajectory might mean more services are being purchased rather than that prices per unit of service are rising. One recent study in Lexington, Kentucky, for the period 1965-1975, observed that the recorded market price changes are substantially larger than those calculated after adjustments for housing attributes using a hedonic price approach.[2] For the period studied in Lexington, the mean price index rose by 86%, whereas the hedonic price index showed an increase of only 59%. Most of the divergences occurred after 1970. Hence price movements over time may in part reflect changes in the composition of the bundle of services. The discussion in chapter 2 of alterations in the "product mix" of single-family residences coming on the market was related to this subject.

The second difficulty stems from the fact that the joint purchase of assets and housing services cannot easily be separated in the case of owner-occupancy. Home purchasers may, of course, adjust the utilization of the capital they have purchased for owner occupancy, but only within limits. Struyk, for example, proposes that the amount of housing stock demanded for investment would at least be large enough to facilitate the consumption of housing services to meet a family's minimum living requirements. The converse of this proposition according to Struyk, namely, that the demand for housing services places a maximum constraint on housing investment, is less likely to hold because families could always leave rooms unused or, more generally, utilize at a low rate the stock purchased.[3]

An important consideration is that market prices for homes incorporate per unit investment and service demands and, over time, possibly changing attributes—that is, quantities of service or investment units. Owner-occupants may be quite willing to pay a high price per unit of housing service because they anticipate that the long-term investment return each will receive is high. Several reasons may explain such behavior. For example, owner-occupants may expect to utilize units more intensively over time. Young couples without children purchasing homes may plan to raise families eventually and increase the utilization of their dwellings. Rooms formerly closed off are then furnished, and such actions in a sense function like a reduction in vacancies, which cannot be observed directly. There are numerous other reasons why the utilization of housing units may change over time. Also prospective homebuyers may advance or delay their decisions to purchase depending on assumptions they make concerning future income, prices, credit conditions, and so on. Only in perfect markets may it be assumed that current prices for housing services are rapidly transformed into capital values. The failure of rent and house price movements to correspond closely suggests that markets are by no means perfect. Related to this is that "inflationary expectations" influence the demand for homes by shifting future demand into the present. If people anticipate rising prices with increased downpayment requirements, they may opt for house purchase today rather than delay the transaction and incur the risk that downpayment requirements will increase faster than their savings, or that their income will not support higher mortgage payments.

Stock-Flow Relationships

One of the distinctive features of housing markets is that the existing stock plays a dominant role in influencing prices and rents in the short run. Since the period required to plan and produce additions to the housing stock is relatively long, the short-run supply schedule is relatively inelastic. With the short-run demand for housing more elastic than the supply, a sudden and unanticipated shift in demand may be expected to have quite pronounced effects on prices and rents. Moreover, as a consequence of the lag in supply adjustments, prices and rents may remain above or below equilibrium levels for considerable periods. Such periods may be prolonged by weaknesses in the information flow systems and the attendant failure to provide timely signals to housing producers on whether they should expand or contract output and, if so, by how much. Among the implications are a characteristic tendency to overcompensate. Limited information on competitors' plans and actions in an industry with large numbers of relatively small producers generates a "bandwagon" effect. Producers expand or curtail output in concert without proper regard for the actions of competitors. The effects are sharp fluctuations in new housing production with fairly long periods of excess demand being followed by excess supply.

The perennial issue of fluctuations in production around some normal demand may have become particularly acute in recent years. The very strong expansion in residential construction in 1970-1972 was followed by an extremely severe contraction in 1973-1974. Since both the expansion and contraction were significantly associated with assisted housing programs, the sequence of rapid growth and subsequent collapse of firms active in this sector was especially pronounced. In the process, the condition where current prices and rents and changes therein offer reasonably good information on projected levels and changes may have been disturbed because of the unexpected severity of the amplitude in fluctuations on both the upswing and the downswing. According to this reasoning, recent home price increases could be viewed largely as the outcome of a longer lag in the response of builders to demand. While the rate of expansion in homebuilding in 1975-1977 was broadly in line with previous upswings (chapter 5), it may have been less than the rate of increase in the demand for single-family houses, with the result that excess demand pushed up the level of house prices.

Realization of equilibrium conditions is further complicated by fluctuations in the spatial demand for housing. These fluctuations are especially important at the local level, and are also associated with variations in regional and interregional developments and migration.

The interactions between regional and local housing markets are sketched out here only in broad terms. Changes in aggregate demand for all goods and services have differential effects on economic development of regions and localities. These in turn produce differences in the rate of growth or decline in labor market opportunities and income. In the process, regional in- or outmigration is induced from low to high income areas and from areas with high to low unemployment. Accompanying this process is the possibility that growth areas may experience excess housing demand with declining areas facing an excess supply. Particularly if interregional migration rates change and are unanticipated, the problems of excess housing demand and supply are aggravated. Some evidence suggests that interregional migration in the United States between 1970-1975 accelerated compared to 1965-1970 with the West and the South being the prime targets of destination for migrants from the Northeast and North Central regions of the nation.[5] Conditions of excess demand in high versus low or no-growth regions, when combined with pervasive inflationary expectations throughout the nation therefore may have contributed to influence the timing and speed of the home price movements. The findings in chapter 2 that most, but not all, metropolitan areas with relatively high rates of home price increases and none with low rates of increases are in the South and West may provide some confirmation on this point.

The dominant role of the existing housing stock is well illustrated by the fact that of the approximately 81 million units in the United States in October, 1976, only about 13 million units—16% of the total stock—were built between April 1970 and October 1976.[6] The implications of the dominance in stock-flow relationships have been examined by L.B. Smith, among others, and may be summarized as follows.[7] Abstracting from the complex structure of the housing market, it can be shown that short-run house prices and rents in the existing housing stock are formed by the interaction of an approximately unitary elastic demand and relatively inelastic supply. These prices/rents may be considered as the obtainable price for new housing units. Homebuilders take the obtainable price and adjust their production to a level where the upwardly sloping construction cost curve intersects the price line.

Since additions to the housing stock through new construction in the short run represent only a very small fraction of the total stock, house prices are nearly independent of the volume of homebuilding. Moreover, under normal market conditions, housing demand changes relatively slowly. Major reasons are that the demand is determined substantially by permanent as contrasted to current income, household formation, and the real rate of interest, and all of these change slowly. Additional reasons include (1) the large role of housing expenditures in consumer budgets and wealth, which tend to induce inertia in residential mobility; (2) high search and transaction costs—brokers' commissions, escrow fees, moving costs, and so on; and (3) the existence of contractual commitments—prepayment penalties on mortgage loans or long-term leases in renting. Especially when consumer decisions involve home purchase, the costs, commitments and risks are of a magnitude not to be taken lightly.

Expansion or contraction in housing demand, again under normal conditions, not only moves slowly but to some extent is anticipated by housing producers. Over the very long run, for example, it has been observed that "demand for residential housing is influenced by the growth of population, or at least by the growth of population in those age groups in which marriage rates and rates of household formation are especially high. . . ."[8]

Since investors, be they landlords or owner-occupants renting to themselves, are sensitive to the long life of residential structures, it may be assumed that they are not blind to factors surrounding demand for their properties when their investment is terminated. Taking a shorter time horizon, investors will also consider recent and anticipated movements in income and relative prices. These enter the demand function and are incorporated by producers and investors in their decisions. It seems reasonable, therefore, to concur with Smith that " . . . decisions concerning the profitability of new construction are based not directly upon existing prices, rents and vacancies, but rather on projected equilibrium prices, rents, and vacancies, where current prices, rents and vacancies serve to indicate future equilibrium levels."[9] However, this statement may require modification when examined in the perspective of single-family house markets during the past few years.

Inflationary expectations, of course, are one element that inhibits smooth adjustment in the market between the short and long run. Such expectations are reflected in an upward shift of the demand for the housing stock as the public advances purchases from the future to the present. The public's behavior cannot be equated with an increase in the demand for housing services. But for reasons cited earlier, the demand for housing services cannot be clearly distinguished from the demand for the stock when dwellings for owner-occupancy are involved. One would expect that inflationary expectations are reflected more in asset prices paid for housing than in actual or imputed rent movements, at least initially.

Assuming for the moment that Smith's analysis is correct and that "current prices, rents and vacancies serve to indicate future equilibrium levels," the sharp increase in house prices associated with inflationary expectations will stimulate new construction since initially builders' profits are high. Eventually, expansion of supply and other forces such as income or wealth constraints on consumers come into operation to dampen price increases or reverse them unless the expected rate of inflation is continually expanding. If the increased demand for the capital stock is not accompanied by similar increases in the demand for housing services, eventually the short-run return on investment in the form of the present value of actual or imputed net rents will be incommensurate with other investments. The growth of supply, higher actual or imputed vacancies, and a reduced investment return will reestablish the long-run equilibrium.

The tendency toward longer-run equilibrium may be delayed in several ways. The initial upward shift in the demand schedule due to inflationary expectations may create a momentum where the single-family house market for a while assumes a life of its own. Information on actual or anticipated profits is rapidly disseminated without check of its accuracy, and the rush of speculators into the market further increases demand. With an inelastic stock supply and adjustment lags in the production of new housing, the speculative expectations for some time are supported by actual experience.

The lags in supply adjustments of new housing not only result from the relatively long planning and production period but may be associated with financial markets and governmental regulations. If the availability of funds is effectively constrained, builders produce fewer units than without the constraint. In this case price will be above marginal costs, pure profits are earned, and excess demand persists. Of course, a constraint on the availability of finance need not be binding if the level of output where price equals marginal cost of builders is below the financial constraint level.[10]

Governmental regulations can influence housing supply schedules in a variety of ways. As the demand for ownership housing grows, for example, regulations that inhibit conversion of rental to ownership types of units—for example, condominium conversions—may restrict supply even in the existing stock. However, such regulations probably are not as pervasive as those that apply to new construction. Three types of effects may be distinguished in the new construction sector. The first effect bears on time of construction and influences the shape of the long-term supply schedule; the second, having to do with building and environmental regulations, shifts the supply schedule; and the third effect, related to growth management and controls, may occasion non-market rationing.

Let us assume again that builders take as given the prices determined in the standing stock and suddenly face new planning requirements. For the sake of simplicity, it is further assumed that the requirements do not affect the level of builders' production cost schedules but delay initiation of construction. The immediate effect of delays will be to change the slope of the long-run supply curves at each point in time. We can visualize a family of supply schedules running from inelastic in the very short run to elastic schedules in the very long run. The delays will postpone delivery of newly constructed units. When demand is at a high level, the delays will contribute to excess demand in intermediate periods but increase the supply in later periods. However, this is likely to be a one-time effect because eventually builders change their production schedules and initiate projects earlier. The first-order effect then will be for prices to rise in the short run and to remain at higher levels for longer periods before they adjust to the long-run equilibrium as new output expands.

The role of building and environmental controls impacts directly on the level of builders' cost schedules at all levels of output but not uniformly because such controls may affect the production of low-priced units more severely than that of high-priced dwellings. With the cost schedules shifted upward, long-run prices will be higher. In part, increases in costs may be dampened by innovation.

The third type of effect of regulations would be associated with an absolute constraint on output. Sewer moratoria and building-permit restrictions are illustrations. If the constraint is binding and comes into operation at an output below the quantity where price is equal to the marginal cost of builders, pure profits may be earned by builders. Eventually it will have a feedback effect on the price of housing in the existing stock. An alternative outcome is for builders' profits to be captured by landowners of parcels with permission to develop. Or builders eager to bend the rules may seek ways of influencing public officials and forego some part of their profits.

In local or regional analyses where public regulations and constraints are identifiable, they may be introduced in a model to measure the quantitative impact on prices and supply. In a multiregional or national model, this is difficult to do. Nevertheless, the potential effects of regulatory constraints on the delivery and cost of new housing units cannot be ignored.

The Model

The model of house prices we shall test for the United States is essentially a component of a larger model developed and tested for Canada by Smith.[11]

Variations on the model are introduced to determine specifically whether inflationary expectations were significant in influencing house price movements in the period under consideration—1968-1977. The reduced form equation of the model is indicated in 6.1:

$$P = p(\frac{Y}{H}, G, \frac{OS}{H}, \frac{VS}{H}, C, Ex)$$ (6.1)

where

P = the stock price of homes
Y/H = permanent income per household (adjusted for price level changes)
G = prices of goods and services other than housing
OS/H = the stock of occupied homes per household
VS/H = the stock of vacant homes per household
C = the cost of home mortgage credit relative to other credit
Ex = a measure of consumer inflationary expectations

The reduced form equation generally follows from the structural model. However, since the structural model is not tested here, the possibility exists that estimated parameters will be biased.

Leaving aside for the moment specific operational definitions of variables, the a priori postulate is that home prices are positively related to permanent income per household. Similarly, house prices should be positively associated with prices of other goods and services. In turn, the two stock variables, OS/H and VS/H, should have an inverse relation to house prices. Expansion of the housing supply relative to households might be expected to exert downward pressure on prices, holding other variables constant.

Variable C, the relative cost of home mortgage credit, is a little more difficult to interpret. If cost and availability of credit are assumed to affect the demand for single-family houses in the short run, one would expect credit costs to be negatively related to prices. Less stringent credit conditions represented by lower interest and more attractive terms should increase demand for the stock of homes and raise prices in the short run, and vice versa when credit conditions become more stringent. Operationally, cost and availability of credit might be disentangled and dealt with separately. We shall come back to this point in the test of the model. A negative relationship between relative mortgage credit costs and house prices may also be subject to an alternative interpretation. As credit becomes less stringent, the flow of funds into mortgage-lending institutions increases largely because the returns to savers on accounts with controlled interest or dividends become more competitive with credit market instruments. In the process the pool of mortgage credit expands, loan terms become more attractive to borrowers, and home purchases increase. In the face of an inelastic supply of housing, prices are pushed up in the short run. When credit becomes more stringent, the flow of funds to mortgage lenders diminishes (as it does at this writing), the supply of home loans declines, and the escalation of house prices moderates. The effects on the market are the same under either interpretation. Finally, it may be postulated that high costs of mortgage funds have no significant impact on the demand for homes when potential buyers expect financing to be still more difficult in the future and/or anticipate further substantial increases of house prices.

Since inflationary expectations are partly built into interest rates and we desire to extract such expectations, the cost of mortgage credit in the generalized model is specified as relative to the cost of other credit. Inflationary expectations thus enter directly into the model as a separate variable.

Inflationary expectations can have diverse impacts on home purchase. If prospective homebuyers anticipate the future rate of inflation to exceed the current rate, they will advance their purchase to an earlier date. Current prices appear favorable relative to expected future prices. In the process, demand for the standing stock increases and home prices rise. The price increases themselves now raise expectations and bring more demanders into the market. Under these conditions the rate of price increase will accelerate over time. This situation has prevailed in the past few years, to judge from the attitudes expressed by the American public. According to consumer surveys, a high and rising proportion of the public agreed it was a good time to buy for the reason that home prices were high but going higher (chapter 5). On the other hand, should potential homebuyers expect the future rate of inflation to be lower than the current rate, they would be more inclined to postpone purchase, especially if they anticipate their income gains to exceed the relative increase in housing prices. If consumer surveys are reliable indicators, however, this condition did not obtain in recent years.

The question must be resolved as to how inflationary expectations concerning single-family houses might be revised downward through forces operating within the housing market. The high and rising prices have already brought a response on the supply side in recent years. They may be expected to stimulate producers to continue adding to the supply for some time. Since the demand for housing services does not grow at the same rate as the demand for the stock, utilization of the stock is decreased. This will be reflected in a rising stock per household and higher vacancies. The longer the production period, the more elastic the supply schedule. Therefore, even if the short-run price increases associated with a demand shift raise expectations and induce demanders to enter the market, the greater elasticity of the supply schedule over time should eventually curb the rate of price increase. As the rate of price increase slows down, expectations are also revised downward, and the cycle is reversed. Constraints on the supply side may, of course, delay the adjustment process. In any event, however, market equilibrium may not be achieved for some considerable time. The supply may be expanding sharply, and prices may yet continue to rise. This situation would apply particularly if factors exogenous to the housing sector reinforce inflationary expectations. An increase in the general rate of inflation would be a case in point.

Alternatively, revisions in inflationary expectations might come about directly through the actions of housing investors. Drawing on Struyk, one might postulate that the demand for housing as an investment is a function of the demand for housing services, the rate of return on a housing unit, the rate of return on other investments, and a household's wealth. The rate of return (r_o) on housing investment is related to the price of housing services and of the stock through the following identity:

$$r_o \equiv \frac{P_{so} - P_o}{P_k} - d$$

where

P_{so} = price of housing services
P_o = price of operating inputs
P_k = price of stock per unit
d = depreciation

It is quite obvious that, holding other factors constant, an increase in the price of the capital stock (P_k) will reduce the rate of return and decrease the stock demand. An increase in the rate of return on alternative investments, a decline in the price of housing services, or escalating costs of operating inputs would have similar results in reducing the demand for the capital stock and, in a roundabout way, eventually the price (P_k). Such effects may be incorporated into an equilibrium framework. How does the system operate under inflationary expectations when for a period of time demand for the housing stock is expanding and the relative price of the stock increasing?

The rate of return on housing investments might be viewed as a discounted rate of all future incomes. Decomposing the rate for individual time periods in the future might indicate that, if investors anticipate the demand for housing services to increase over time (or operating costs to fall), they are willing to pay high prices and to earn low returns in early versus later periods. However, given the discounting process, as prices rise and expected high rates of future incomes are pushed further into the future, their present value is lowered. Equally important, expectations are revised in the face of experience. If the demand for housing services does not expand (or operating costs do not fall) in accordance with expectations, the actual rate of return is less than anticipated. Eventually, expectations are revised downward to conform to experience, and prices will level off or fall.

In the model, the expectations of investors in single-family houses are incorporated in several ways: (1) direct measures of consumer expectations concerning the rate of general inflation; (2) indirect measures of expectations on the rate of general inflation, and (3) the movement of past house prices. No attempt is made to specify the actual and expected rates of returns accruing to housing investors from operations and value changes combined. The measures used, however, may serve as partial surrogates for investment behavior. The expectations variables essentially argue that homebuying decisions are based on actual and expected rates of inflation. The actual rate of inflation may exceed or be less than the expected rate. Particularly during periods when the expected rate of inflation exceeds the actual rate of inflation consumers will have a strong incentive to shift into variable price assets that offer the possibility of a hedge. Homes, as an example of a variable price asset, might be particularly attractive under these conditions.

The rate of inflation embodies both expected and unexpected components. It has been suggested that housing prices respond rapidly to both expected and unexpected inflation and that home purchase represents a superior hedge.[12] compared to many other alternatives. This proposition implies that the housing market is comparatively efficient and adjusts quickly to expected and unexpected inflation. However, since the results based on this assumption leave a considerable amount of unexplained variance, an alternative proposition might be that consumers' decisions to purchase or not to purchase homes are determined substantially by experience specific to the single-family home market. At any level of prices, consumers observe past prices and price changes and form their views on the future by reference to these. The time horizon of past prices considered by current buyers may be short or long, and tests of the model will provide some insights on this point. Neither formulation, of course, identifies the reasons for shifts in the expected rate of inflation or in changes in past home prices that influence current decisions. However, one can infer that these shifts are embodied in the factors that enter into the rate-of-return calculations.

Methods

The general model developed in the previous section was tested for the United States using quarterly data for the period from the first quarter 1968 through the second quarter 1977. The variables used and the sources are indicated in appendix 6A at the end of this chapter. The aggregate model attempts to explain the level and rates of change in the weighted quarterly average of home sales prices. The weighted quarterly average was derived from the number and value of existing and new-home sales as reported by the National Association of Realtors and the U.S. Department of Commerce, respectively. This variable was not adjusted for potential changes in the quality of homes for the reason that no national data were available on this point for existing-home sales. Therefore, the variable does not express the price for some standardized unit of housing purchased. This may seem to be a flaw, but its significance should not be overestimated, for the measure of house prices used is dominated by existing-home sales. Qualitative improvements in the existing stock will occur as new units become part of the stock while old units of poorer quality are removed. At the same time, however, the standing stock ages and may depreciate rapidly if it is utilized at a high rate. Capital improvements of existing dwellings modify this process only to a limited extent. Moreover, qualitative changes in the admixture of new and existing homes coming onto the market are influenced by their relative shares in total transactions. If new homes, where qualitative changes over time are more likely, were to represent a growing share of transactions, our price variable might incorporate a significant bias. During the period studied, the very opposite was found; for every new home sold at the end of the period, 4.3 existing homes were bought or sold compared to 2.8 at the beginning.

An alternative measure of new home prices, the price index for the 1974 type house, was introduced into the model as a dependent variable. The model runs, with few exceptions, showed little or no significant effect on the explanatory variables, however, and analysis of this measure of price was not pursued extensively.

The independent variables in the model include measures of income, the price of alternative goods and services, the cost and availability of credit, the housing stock, consumers' expectations of general inflation, distributed lags of past house prices, and seasonal dummies. Two alternative measures of income are introduced: permanent disposable income per household or per capita, and current income per household or per capita in constant dollars. Permanent income is held to be a better predictor of house prices than current income.

Concerning costs for alternative goods and services, we tried the implicit GNP price deflator and also the CPI for all items less the shelter component. The CPI evidenced a better relationship to home prices than the GNP price deflator. Therefore, the former was used unless otherwise indicated.

Two forms of the cost-of-credit variable were included in the tests. One of these is the yield spread between conventional mortgages and new issues of utility bonds. This variable takes account of the interdependence of money and credit markets. A high positive yield spread would indicate that mortgage investments are relatively attractive to lenders and results in expanding supply of mortgage funds, and vice versa if the yield spread is low or negative. The supply side argument in this reasoning, of course, must be juxtaposed to the demand side, which would suggest the very opposite. The sign on this variable, therefore, cannot be determined in advance. The other credit variable is the yield spread between conventional mortgages and three-months' Treasury Bills. If the contention is correct that Treasury Bills accurately reflect the expected rate of inflation, the spread can be viewed as a surrogate for the real rate of interest on mortgages.

Several alternatives of the housing stock variable entered into the model. One of these is the number of owner-occupied plus "vacant for sale" homes per household, per capita or per population thirty years of age or older. Since a great many single-family homes in the United States are rented, we also examined the performance of an alternate measure, namely, the total occupied plus vacant stock per household or per capita. Finally, we disaggregated the stock into occupied and vacant units per household or per capita and studied their influence separately. The directionality of this variable, regardless of how defined in relation to house prices, should clearly be negative. A high and rising stock per household or per capita would be expected to exert a negative influence on prices and price change. As will be evident, this variable with few exceptions shows a relationship contrary to that postulated, and in some cases it is significant. Hence a note on its construction is appropriate.

No quarterly data on the housing stock are available and no annual data for the period 1970 to 1973 have been developed by official sources. As a result, a completely new series had to be designed. The series was derived from data reported in the 1970 Census, the subsequent *Annual Housing Surveys,* quarterly reports on housing vacancies, and data on housing completions. After recordation of the housing stock in the United States as reported in the U.S. Census and *Annual Housing Surveys,* quarterly estimates of the total housing stock were calculated by reference to housing completions plus mobile home deliveries. For the period April 1970 through October 1976, this involved allocation of the net additions to the stock in accordance with housing completions between the benchmarks for which the stock data were available. The respective benchmarks are April 1, 1970, and October 1 in the years 1973, 1974, 1975, and 1976. Projections were then prepared back to the beginning of 1968 and forward through the second quarter of 1977, using relationships between housing completions and removal rates for periods in which the relationships are reported. One of the implications of the procedure is that additions to and removals from the stock are assumed to be in phase from quarter to quarter.

Given the total housing stock, the next step was to allocate the stock between occupied and vacant units. Quarterly reports on vacancies were the primary means for making this allocation. The total occupied stock was then distributed between ownership and rental units drawing on the 1970 Census and the later *Annual Housing Surveys* and on vacancy data. In the process, several data revisions for earlier periods by the U.S. Bureau of the Census were taken into account.

Because the model expresses the housing stock variable per household per capita, or per population thirty years of age or older, we also prepared quarterly estimates of the number of households in the United States and the population thirty years or older. Household data are available annually from current population reports. The additions to households in each year were allocated to each quarter using data on marriages. Quarterly estimates of the population thirty years and older were interpolated using annual data on the age distribution in census reports. Quarterly data on the total population in the United States were readily available from the same source.

Series on the expected rate of inflation were obtained from reports of the Survey Research Center at the University of Michigan. These surveys are taken semiannually and provide comparisons between the mean price expectations of consumer and changes in the CPI. The semiannual data were converted to quarterly data through interpolations. The analysis introduces expectations expressed by consumers in alternative ways. One involves substituting the expected rate of inflation for the increase in the CPI. Another takes the difference between the actual and the expected rate of change in the price level and incorporates this variable in the model. The relationships between the actual or expected rates of inflation and home prices should be direct. In the second formulation the a priori directionality is less clear and would depend on the behavior of home prices in response to unexpected inflation—that is, the difference between the actual and the expected rate. The subjectivity of consumer expressions on the anticipated rate of inflation suggests the introduction of an alternate, less subjective indicator. The three-months' Treasury Bill rate was adopted as a surrogate.

Consumer behavior in house purchase may, of course, be associated either with actual and anticipated movements of general prices or with those in the single-family house market. Hence the model uses also distributed lags of past home prices as a variable measuring the expected rate of inflation. Although information flows concerning transactions and prices in the market are normally weak, prospective homebuyers acquire some knowledge through advertisements, "shopping tours," and contacts with friends, neighbors, colleagues, and real-estate agents. Market observation by consumers became more acute in recent years when the growing volume of house purchases at escalating prices received widespread public attention. On this ground, one can postulate that information on the state of the market became an important factor in forming consumers' expectations and their decisions to buy. If so, current purchases and prices would be largely influenced by some distribution of past purchases and prices. To examine this question, second-degree polynomial distributed lags of past prices were introduced into the model. The length of the lags was assumed to be four or five quarters.

Given the consistent increase in home prices during the period studied, the introduction of distributed lags of past prices is fraught with statistical problems when levels of home prices are examined. However, the rates of change in house prices show considerable variation over time. Therefore the model relates current rates of price changes to distributed lags of past price changes.

The method used to test the model is regression analysis. It was anticipated that serial correlation would present problems common to all time-series studies. Therefore whenever the Durbin-Watson statistics suggested serial correlation or was in the region of indeterminacy, the Cochrane-Orcutt procedure was followed to reestimate the equations from the residuals. Since the procedure involves a series of iterations, these were stopped when rho (the correlation coefficient associated with errors of adjacent time periods) changed by less than .005. This decision may affect the "optimal" estimate of rho.[13]

Results

We begin the discussion of results with a straightforward test of the model developed by Smith for Canada. In light of serial correlation found in the OLS (ordinary least square) estimates, we present results obtained via the Cochrane-Orcutt (CORC) procedure. T-statistics are shown in brackets.

$$PCOMB = -21,281.2 + 633.5 \; Q'1 + 1143.9 \; Q'2$$
$$\qquad\qquad (.90) \qquad (3.93) \qquad\quad (6.12)$$

$$+ \quad 897.7 \; Q'3 + 1.19 \; IPER1$$
$$\qquad (5.30) \qquad (1.90)$$

$$- \; 4,804.9 \; NPER1 + 309.4 \; CPILAG$$
$$\qquad (0.14) \qquad\qquad\quad (16.45) \qquad\qquad\qquad\qquad (6.2)$$

$$R^2 = .996 \qquad\qquad DW = 1.72$$
$$SEE = 509.2 \qquad\quad \rho = .83$$
$$3Q'68 - 2Q'77$$

Equation 6.2 indicates that the combined price of new and existing homes (PCOMB) is related directly to the CPI (minus shelter) lagged by one quarter (CPILAG). Home prices are also directly related to the lagged permanent income per household (IPER), but this variable is only marginally significant. Current income (in constant dollars) turned out to be even less significant. The sign on the owner-occupied plus "for sale" housing stock per household (NPER1) variable is negative, but the coefficient is not significant. This variable proved to be most troublesome in the analysis. In the OLS estimates the relationship between prices and the per-capita stock was direct. Other versions of the stock variable were tried but yielded no major improvement in the estimates. The equation also indicates considerable significance of the seasonal variables. A fairly consistent pattern in home prices during the period studied is for prices to rise during the first three quarters of the year and to drop or level off in the fourth quarter.

The Durbin-Watson statistic is large enough to reject the null hypothesis of serial correlation. In only one quarter did the estimated values of home prices differ from actual values by more than $1,000. For the most part, the values as shown by the standard error of the regression were within $509 (see figure 6-1).

Equation 6.3 introduces a credit variable (BNDRTE) and a measure of inflationary expectations (RINFL). The variable BNDRTE reflects the difference between yields on conventional mortgages and newly issued AAA utility bonds. The variable RINFL is the difference between the actual and anticipated increases in the consumer price level. In this equation, both permanent income (IPER2) and the housing stock (NPER2) are calculated on a per-capita basis.

$$PCOMB = - 36,468.3 + 613.0 \ Q'1 + 1065.7 \ Q'2$$
$$ (2.26) \quad (3.82) \qquad (5.18)$$

$$+ 827.5 \ Q'3 + 3.54 \ IPER2 + 85,042.3 \ NPER2$$
$$(4.82) \qquad (2.02) \qquad (0.93)$$

$$+ 266.01 \ CPILAG + 6.61 \ RINFL - 0.92 \ BNDRTE$$
$$(8.03) \qquad (0.98) \qquad (0.30) \qquad\qquad (6.3)$$

$$R^2 = .996 \qquad DW = 1.71$$
$$SEE = 503.6 \qquad \rho = .81$$
$$2Q'68 - 2Q'77$$

The results shown again are for CORC rather than OLS. Per-capita permanent income lagged by one quarter, the lagged consumer price level and the seasonal variables are all significant. The housing stock, credit, and inflationary expectations variables are not significant. Moreover, the credit and stock variables have the "wrong" sign.

A large number of alternative formulations of the above two equations were attempted. The RINFL variable, it will be recalled, reflects the difference between the actual and anticipated price level changes. Removal of the RINFL and CPILAG variables and substituting them with the price increases anticipated by consumers (EINFL) produced no improvement in the fits. Similarly, the substitution of a credit variable expressed as the difference between the mortgage yield and the three-months' Treasury Bill rate (MYBR) yielded no significantly different results.

One alternative procedure was to redefine the dependent home price variable as an index (IPCOMB) and to express it as a ratio of the CPI (CPINOR). This new variable (IPCOMNOR) fluctuated fairly narrowly around 1.0 from early 1968 until the first quarter of 1971. Beginning in 1971 until the third quarter of 1973, the index rose to 1.15 and then began to drop to 1.06 in the last quarter of 1974. Starting in 1975 the index rose again, but unevenly, reaching 1.20 in the second quarter of 1977.

Equation 6.4 illustrates the introduction of the redefined dependent variable.

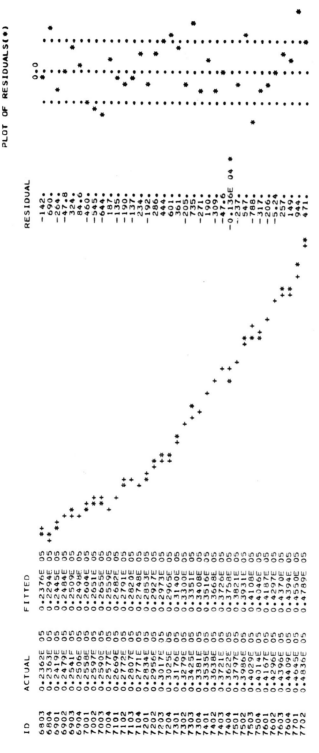

Figure 6-1. Plot of Actual (*) and Fitted (+) Values of Home Prices, 1968-1977

[a]Decimal should be moved five spaces to the right to obtain correct prices.

$$IPCOMNOR = -0.34 + .016\,Q'1 + .025\,Q'2$$
$$\; (0.88)\;\;(3.65)\quad\;\; (4.53)$$

$$+ .021\,Q'3 + .00012\,IPER\,2$$
$$(4.48)\qquad (2.47)$$

$$+ 2.19\,ONPER3 - 8.55\,VNPER3 + .000081\,MYBR \qquad (6.4)$$
$$(2.40)\qquad\quad (-1.37)\qquad\;\; (2.21)$$

$$R^2 = .96 \qquad\qquad DW = 1.52$$
$$SEE = 0.013 \qquad \rho = .84$$
$$3Q'68 - 2Q'77$$

The results conform to most of the tests on this variable. The income and seasonal variables are significant and have the correct signs. One of the Stock variables (ONPER3), which is the ratio of the owner-occupied stock per population thirty years of age and above is significant, but the sign is wrong. In the other stock variable (VNPER3), the vacant stock available for sale per population thirty years old or more, the sign is correct, but the coefficient is insignificant. The credit variable (MYBR) is significant, and the sign suggests that upward movement in home prices relative to the general price level are positively related to the yield spread between mortgages and other credit instruments. On the alternative credit variable (BNDRTE), the sign of the coefficient also was positive but less significant. Generally, with redefinition of the house price variable as a ratio of the general price level, the credit variables asserted a stronger influence than formerly. The persistent positive sign on the credit variable would argue that the relative attractiveness of mortgages compared to other credit instruments was associated with the ratio of home prices relative to the general price level.

Explorations were also directed to meeting the possible objection that the dependent variable incorporates a bias over time by including not only higher prices but also higher quality homes. To this end, equations were run on the average sales price for the kinds of new houses sold in 1974. The results, however, generally were disappointing and produced no substantially different findings. The current income variable and the price level or the price of existing homes were significant, but not consistently in some of the runs. The stock variables (ONPER3 and VNPER3) assumed the correct sign but were not significant.

So far the analysis suggests permanent income and the general price level as having significant influence on the price of homes in the model. Lower utilization of the stock as measured by owner-occupied or "vacant for sale" stock per household, per capita, or per population thirty years of age and older, did not exert significant downward pressures on home prices. The last finding is clearly contrary to that of Smith in Canada who, however, dealt with a longer time period.

The strong association between the general price level and house prices led to an alternate formulation of the dependent variable as a ratio of IPCOMB/ CPINOR. Tests on the redefined dependent variable were indicative of the potential influence of one of the credit variables on home prices, but produced anomalous and statistically significant results on one of the stock variables. Taken at face value, this finding might be interpreted as showing that monetary stringency that traditionally has produced narrowing (or negative) yield spreads between mortgages and other instruments acted to curb exuberance in the housing market, while monetary ease expressed in widening yield spreads added to the upward pressure on prices. This interpretation may be juxtaposed to the alternative position that fundamental forces of housing supply and demand including rates of stock utilization, vacancies, permanent income and relative prices determine house prices. The model runs do not reject the demand variables but offer little explanatory power on the effect of the fundamental supply forces on prices for the years studied. Moreover, consumer expectations on the general price level, as defined here, also appeared not to have a significant influence on home prices.

We now turn to the question whether the price developments internal to the house market influenced expectations and increased demand pressures. When distributed lags of past home prices were introduced into preceding equations, the results suggested some potential influence of previous prices on current prices. However, this outcome was to be expected in a period during which prices (with the exception of seasonal variations and other minor disturbances) advanced consistently. Hence we took an alternative approach by using first differences in prices and examining how well the model would perform in explaining rates of price change.

Along the lines of earlier equations, the dependent variable was first defined as the rate of change in estimated home prices and regressed on the independent variables including the rate of change in the general price level (CPILGX). A representative result is shown in equation 6.5, which is based on ordinary least squared (OLS).

Aside from the seasonal variable, none of the variables found significant in the earlier analysis of the level of prices had much explanatory power. As may be noted in equation 6.5, the T-statistics, apart from the seasonal dummies, suggest little explanation on the other variables.

$$PCOMBX^* = \quad - 15.8 + 45.9\,Q'1 + 40.8\,Q'2 + 21.31\,Q'3$$
$$\qquad\qquad (2.14)\quad (7.91)\qquad (6.98)\qquad (3.26)$$

$$+ 1.69\,DSPERX^* + .13\,NPERIX^* + .031\,CPILGX^*$$
$$(1.12)\qquad\qquad (.27)\qquad\qquad (.09)\qquad\qquad\qquad (6.5)$$

$$R^2 = .73 \qquad\qquad DW = 1.80$$
$$SEE = 12.08$$
$$2Q'68 - 2Q'77$$

*These variables were all scaled by 1,000 since the frequently low value of rates of change presented computer capacity problems.

The dependent variable was then redefined as the rate of change in the ratio of the index of house prices relative to the CPI (IPCOMNORX). Essentially we tried to explain the rate at which the gap between indexes of house prices and the general price level widened or narrowed. The results were somewhat more positive. Equation 6.6 exemplifies the OLS results obtained from equations using this approach.

$$IPCOMNORX^* = -74.98 + 41.25Q'1 + 37.56Q'2$$
$$\quad\quad\quad\quad\;\;(1.93)\quad(7.23)\quad\quad(6.54)$$

$$\quad\quad + 23.18\;Q'3 + .000047\;DSPERX^*$$
$$\quad\quad\quad(4.02)\quad\quad\quad(1.34)$$

$$\quad\quad + \quad.55\;ONPER3X^* - .046\;VNPER3X^* \quad\quad\quad\quad (6.6)$$
$$\quad\quad\quad(1.23)\quad\quad\quad\quad\quad(1.92)$$

$$\quad\quad + \quad.11\;BNDRTE$$
$$\quad\quad\quad(2.11)$$

$R^2 = .75 \quad\quad\quad\quad DW = 1.98$
$SEE = 11.78$
$3Q'68 - 2Q'77$

*These variables were all scaled by 1,000 since the frequently low value of rates of change presented computer capacity problems.

The seasonal dummy variables and the spread between the mortgage and utility bond yields are significant. The vacancy variable is marginally significant, but neither income nor the other stock variable provides explanatory power. Results did not change markedly when alternate series of income or the stock were introduced into the equations. The credit variable continued to be significant, and the vacancy variable at best was marginally significant in other computer runs.

We then introduced polynomial distributed lags of the dependent variable into the model. Given the relatively short period studied, a severe constraint was placed on the length of the lags. A four- or five-period lag with a second-degree polynomial was specified. Generally, the results did not vary significantly between these lag periods.

Incorporating the behavioral variables with lagged dependent variables in the model created severe statistical problems; the procedure left few degrees of freedom. Nevertheless, it is noteworthy that the positive influence of past rates of change on current price changes is so strong that it swamps the significance of the other variables in the model except for the seasonal dummy variables. But the significant positive influence is of relatively short duration exceeding no more than two quarters. Significantly negative coefficients for the fourth and fifth quarters suggest a persistent short-run disequilibrium in house prices in the period under study. Current prices may "overshoot" their mark perhaps because buyers and sellers are strongly influenced by price changes in periods just preceding their decisions.

Removal of the behavioral variables from the price change equation and retention of the distributed lag of past prices and seasonal variables hardly changes the coefficients of determination. This suggests that seasonal factors and recent price changes had a very significant influence on current rates of price changes in the period analyzed. Confirmation is found in equation 6.7, which regresses home price changes using CORC on a five-quarter distributed lag of past price changes (with a zero end-point restriction) and seasonal variables.

$$PCOMBX^* = \quad -7.16 + 26.83 \, Q'1 + 9.95 \, Q'2$$
$$\qquad\qquad (2.34) \quad (7.63) \qquad\quad (2.84)$$

$$+ \quad .73 \, Q'3 + \quad .74 \, PCOMBX^*_{t-1}$$
$$\quad (0.19) \qquad (13.35)$$

$$+ \quad .32 \, PCOMBX^*_{t-2} + \quad .045 \, PCOMBX^*_{t-3}$$
$$\quad (12.79) \qquad\qquad\quad (1.51)$$

$$- \quad .10 \, PCOMBX^*_{t-4} - \quad .12 \, PCOMBX^*_{t-5}$$
$$\quad (3.00) \qquad\qquad\quad (4.69) \qquad\qquad\qquad\qquad (6.7)$$

$R^2 = .96$ $DW = 2.06$
$SEE = 4.55$ $\rho = .38$
Mean lag $= -.41$.   Sum of lag coefficients $= .88$
$1Q'70 - 2Q'77$

*These variables were all scaled by 1,000 since the frequently low value of rates of change presented computer capacity problems.

The results with PCOMBX as the dependent variable lend qualified support to the hypothesis that past price changes for a relatively brief period do exert a positive influence on current price changes and indirectly to the inflationary expectations hypothesis based on the movement of house prices. The pattern of lag weights is fairly similar for four- and five-period lags. No surprises emerged when the alternate price change variable IPCOMNORX was tested.

One of the interesting results of equation 6-7 is shown in figure 6-2, which plots actual versus fitted values. The rates of home price change (as distinguished from dollar increases) in some periods of 1976 and 1977 were not unusually high when contrasted to those in some quarters of earlier years. For example, rates of price change in the second quarter of 1977 were exceeded in the second quarter of 1972 and 1975. Similarly, the first-quarter change of 5.3% in 1977 exceeded only slightly the 5.0, 4.5, and 4.8% recorded in 1973, 1974, and 1975. It seems that price increases of the magnitude that became headline news in 1976 and 1977 in retrospect were not so extraordinary in the context of the

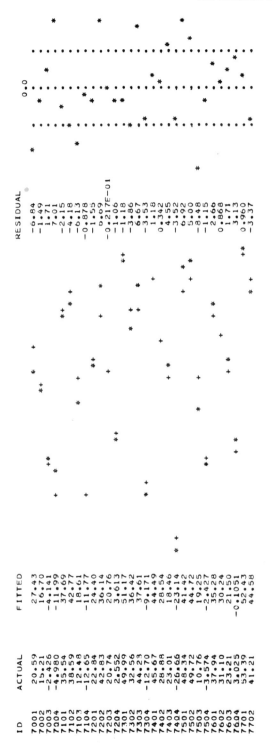

Figure 6-2. Plot of Actual (*) and Fitted (+) Values of Quarterly Rates of Change in Home Prices, 1970-1977

United States as a whole. Yet the fact remains that in the period 1968-1970 only one quarter evidenced a price rise of more than 3%. After 1970 increases of 3% or more per quarter became common. This observation is consistent with the acceleration of price movements shown in table 2-1 for groups of years. It seems that a structural change may have been initiated in the 1970s when past price increases indeed began to raise expectations on their continuation, especially since they persisted throughout the 1973-1974 recession. The model does not capture this situation directly, but it is indicated in the attitudes of consumers reported by the Survey Research Center at the University of Michigan.

Also, the quarter-by-quarter changes in the sale of existing homes (table 6-1) show significant increases in activity after 1970, with relatively modest downturns during the severe recession starting late in 1973. Well over twice as many existing homes were sold in the second and third quarters of 1977 as in the same periods in 1970. Since the stock of owner-occupied and for-sale properties grew by only about 17%, the rate of home sales relative to the stock increased substantially. In the respective quarters, 2.0 to 2.1% of existing homes were sold in 1977 as against about 1.3 to 1.4 in 1970. The figures illustrate the classic problem in analysis of an economic sector where the stock is large relative to the flows. Major movements in flow demand are associated with minor shifts in the total stock. This discrepancy would explain in part why the explanatory power of the behavioral variables in the model is modest. All homeowners or renters are affected by changes in income, relative prices, and so on; at the margin, only a very small fraction of the public acts by entering the market. Minor shifts in variables difficult to quantify may occasion large changes in transactions and prices.

Not the least of the components in the model whose quantification proved to be difficult is the supply of homes. According to conventional theory, relative home price increases of the magnitude characteristic during the middle 1970s eventually induce a supply response, though it may be delayed because in the

Table 6-1
Number of Existing Homes Sold per Quarter, United States, 1968-1977
(1,000 units)

	1st Quarter	2nd Quarter	3rd Quarter	4th Quarter
1968	344	425	448	353
1969	375	460	435	324
1970	335	441	473	365
1971	451	575	558	435
1972	521	620	626	485
1973	584	676	619	455
1974	562	677	610	422
1975	505	692	685	568
1976	657	833	837	674
1977	762	988	1009	

Source: National Association of Realtors.

short run the schedule is inelastic. The results of the model show little or no significance of the occupied-housing stock variable and, in some tests, suggest that variable to operate perversely—that is, a growth in the occupied stock relative to households or population was significantly associated with price increases. Only when the house price change variable was redefined as a ratio relative to the CPI did supply factors assert themselves directly, but weakly, through vacancies and indirectly through the credit variable.

The poor explanatory power of the supply variables in the model may simply reflect the relatively short time span covered. The supply adjustments considered in theory relate to a longer period. Another reason for the weak performance of the supply variables may be their poor specification in the model. Measures of the effective housing supply are difficult to obtain. The assumptions we made to quantify removals from the housing stock may call for revision. Also the model does not include inter- and intraregional shifts in population and economic activities, which may leave a residue of "vacant available" or underutilized housing in one area combined with temporary shortages in others. The longer run supply schedule in recent years may have become less elastic because of environmental and related control measures. Further work is called for on these and other issues.

Lacking further evidence, the exploratory housing model provides at best tentative conclusions that need further study before they can be fully accepted or rejected. The results generally suggest that levels and changes in house prices between 1968 and mid-1977 were significantly related to permanent income, the general price level, seasonal factors, and distributed lags of past house prices. Adjusting house price changes for the general price level indicated that relative ease of mortgage credit, that is, the yield difference between the mortgage and other credit instruments, contributed significantly to the rate at which the gap between indexes of house and consumer prices was narrowing or expanding. Moreover, the vacancy variable was also marginally significant in explaining the rate of change in this gap. Direct measures of consumer expectations on the general price level had low explanatory power in all the versions of the model. But the strong influence of recent rates of home price changes on current rates suggests that substantial and broadly sustained price increases began to raise expectations of prospective homebuyers. The notion of home purchase as a profitable investment gained strength in the process and expressed itself in great expansion of demand during the period under study. In the absence of any strong moderating effect of supply in the short run, factors on the demand side, including rising price expectations, were the prime forces in moving house prices sharply forward during most of the 1970s.

Notes

1. R.J. Struyk, *Urban Homeownership*, (Lexington, Mass: Lexington Books, 1976), pp. 27-43.

2. M.G. Ferri, "An Application of Hedonic Indexing Methods to Monthly Changes in Housing Prices, 1965-1975," *Journal of the American Real Estate and Urban Economics Association,* Winter 1977, pp. 455-462.

3. R.J. Struyk, *Urban Homeownership* p. 28.

4. L.B. Smith, *The Postwar Canadian Housing and Residential Mortgage Markets* (Toronto: University of Toronto Press, 1974), p. 39.

5. The President's Urban and Regional Policy Group Report, *A New Partnership to Conserve America's Communities—A National Urban Policy* (Washington, D.C.: U.S. Department of Housing and Urban Development, April 1978), HUD-S-297.

6. See U.S. Department of Commerce, *Annual Housing Survey: 1976* (Washington, D.C.: U.S. Government Printing Office, 1978), Current Housing Reports H-150-76, General Housing Characteristics, Part A.

7. L.B. Smith, *Postwar Canadian Housing,* p. 18-22.

8. Moses Abramovitz, *Evidences of Long Swings in Aggregate Construction Since the Civil War* (New York: National Bureau of Economic Research, 1964), Occasional Paper 90, pp. 131-32.

9. L.B. Smith, *Postwar Canadian Housing,* p. 20.

10. See L.B. Smith, ibid., p. 19.

11. L.B. Smith, ibid., pp. 27-69.

12. Eugene F. Fama and G. William Schwert, "Asset Returns and Inflation," *Journal of Financial Economics,* November 1977, pp. 115-146.

13. The iterative techniques may produce a local rather than global minimum. For discussion, see Robert S. Pindyck and Daniel L. Rubinfeld, *Econometric Models and Economic Forecasts* (New York: McGraw-Hill, 1976), p. 112.

Appendix 6A

Table 6A-1
Variables in U.S. Housing Price Model, 1968-1977

(1) PEXIST = Sales price of existing homes; Source: Department of Economics and Research, National Association of Realtors®.

(2) PNEW = Sales price of new one-family houses sold; Source: U.S. Department of Commerce, Bureau of the Census, Construction Reports, C-27.

(3) PCOMB = Weighted quarterly average of PEXIST and PNEW, that is,

$$\frac{(PEXIST \times R) + (PNEW \times S)}{R + S} = PCOMB$$

where R + S are the number of home sales for existing and new homes.

(4) IPCOMB = Index of PCOMB, 1968 = 100.

(5) P1974 = Sales price of kind of new one-family house sold in 1974; based on ten important characteristics; Source: U.S. Department of Commerce, Bureau of the Census, Construction Reports, C-27.

(6) CPINOR = Consumer Price Index, all items less shelter component (all items 1968 = 100); Source: U.S. Department of Labor, Bureau of Labor Statistics.

(7) IPCOMNOR = IPCOMB/CPINOR.

(8) DSPINC = U.S. permanent disposable personal income plus undistributed profits (1972 constant dollars); seasonally adjusted annual rate; Source: M.R. Darby, "The Permanent Income Theory of Consumption—A Restatement," *Quarterly Journal of Economics,* Volume 88, May 1974. The series was developed from Darby's equation:

$$YP = 0.025*Y + (1 - 0.025)*(1 + 0.00949)*YP(-1)$$

where YP (1946 − 4) = 222.91.

(9) DSP72 = U.S. "current" disposable personal income plus undistributed profits (1972 constant dollars); seasonally adjusted annual rate; Source: Survey of Current Business.

(10) GNPDFR = Implicit GNP price deflator, personal consumption expenditures, seasonally adjusted (1968 = 100); Source: U.S. Department of Commerce, Bureau of Economic Analysis.

(11) BNDRTE = Yield spread between conventional mortgage yields on new homes and yield on AAA new issue utility bonds; Source: Federal Housing Administration and Board of Governors, Federal Reserve Board.

(12) MYBR = Yield spread between conventional mortgage yields on new homes and yield on three-months' Treasury Bills; Source: Federal Housing Administration and Salomon Brothers.

(13) TSTOCK = Total number of housing units, U.S.; Source: U.S. Department of Commerce, Bureau of the Census, *1970, Census of Housing: Annual Housing Surveys, 1973-1976*; quarterly interpolations by authors based on allocations of housing completions plus mobile home shipments.

(14) OSTOCK = Total number of owner-occupied housing units, U.S.; Source: U.S. Department of Commerce, Bureau of the Census, *1970, Census of Housing: Annual Housing Surveys, 1973-1976*; and current housing reports, *Housing Vacancies,* H-111; quarterly interpolations by authors.

155

Table 6A-1 continued

(15) RSTOCK   = Total number of renter-occupied housing units, U.S.; Source: U.S. Department of Commerce, Bureau of the Census, *1970, Census of Housing: Annual Housing Surveys, 1973-1976*; and current housing reports, Housing Vacancies, H-111; quarterly interpolations by authors.

(16) VSTOCK   = Total number of vacant housing units, U.S.; Source: See OSTOCK and RSTOCK.

(17) VSALE   = Total number of vacant housing units available for sale, U.S.; Source: See OSTOCK and RSTOCK.

(18) VSALE1   = Total number of vacant housing units available for rent, U.S.; Source: See OSTOCK and RSTOCK.

(19) TPOP   = U.S. civilian population; Source: U.S. Department of Commerce, Bureau of the Census, *Current Population Reports, P-20.*

(20) TPOP30   = U.S. Civilian Population, thirty years of age and older; Source: U.S. Department of Commerce, *Current Population Reports, P-25*; interpolations of quarterly estimates for each year by authors.

(21) TFAM   = Number of families, U.S.; Source: U.S. Department of Commerce, *Current Population Reports, P-20*; interpolations of quarterly estimates for each year by allocations of marriages as reported by U.S. Department of Health, Education and Welfare, *Vital Statistics of the US.* and *Monthly Vital Statistics.*

(22) THSHLD   = Number of households, U.S.; Source: U.S. Department of Commerce, *Current Population Reports, P-20*; interpolations of quarterly estimates for each year by authors.

(23) RINFL   = Actual rate of change in Consumer Price Index (CPI) minus expected rate of increase in general price level (EINFL); Source: U.S. Department of Labor, Bureau of Labor Statistics; University of Michigan, *Survey of Consumer Attitudes.*

(24) QTR 1/QTR 2/QTR 3 = Quarterly dummy variables.

(25) OPER1   = OSTOCK/TFAM.

(26) VSPER1   = VSALE/TFAM.

(27) OPER2   = OSTOCK/THSHLD.

(28) VSPER2   = VSALE/THSHLD.

(29) ONPER3   = OSTOCK/TPOP30.

(30) VNPER3   = VSTOCK/TPOP30.

(31) NPER1   = OSTOCK + VSALE/THSHLD.

(32) NPER2   = OSTOCK + VSALE/TPOP.

(33) NPER3   = OSTOCK + VSALE/TPOP30.

(34) IPER1   = $DISPINC_{t-1}/THSHLD_{t-1}$.

(35) IPER2   = $DSPINC_{t-1}/TPOP_{t-1}$.

(36) DSPER   = $DSP72_{t-1}/THSHLD_{t-1}$.

(37) GNPLAG   = $GNPDFR_{t-1}$.

(38) CPILAG   = $CPINOR_{t-1}$.

(39) CRNTLG   = $CPIRNT_{t-1}$.

7 The Outlook for Price Adjustments

Whether the recent escalation of house prices was generated by inflationary expectations or other causes of excess demand, or both, it signified a major market imbalance. Market imbalances are eventually succeeded by adjustments leading to an equilibrium position. Such adjustments rarely follow a smooth path in the sense that a new balance is established without some further disequilibrium. In the case of a price surge, especially if it is fueled by anticipated capital gains, prices may be under some downward pressure before stability is achieved or before price increases return to more "normal" rates.

Adjustments in the single-family house market are already taking place in the major urban centers of California where the price escalation began and was most acute. Since mid-1977, property turnover and mortgage loan applications have been declining. Builders and real-estate agents report that it takes longer to sell both new and existing homes. According to brokers' multiple listing services, the ratio of sales to listings has decreased sharply.[1] Even the volume of listings has diminished in many areas as owners who had placed their property on the market withdrew when their asking prices were not met. Purchase contract cancellations in projects under construction have been growing. Speculative buying, the "hot" news of 1976 and early 1977, has subsided. The media became silent on the subject. The price increase was moderating, and asking prices of existing homes were being reduced. As was mentioned in chapter 5, permit authorizations for new houses in California reached their peak in the first quarter of 1977, while nationwide starts of single-family units rose to new heights in the course of the year. The inventory of unsold new homes in the six-county area of Southern California was increasing.[2]

The recent softening of California markets is evident in declining rates of average price escalation reported locally or for the western region. In contrast, most of the national series show continued price acceleration in early 1978.[3] But areas outside of California, which had joined the inflationary parade later may also soon experience some adjustment in market conditions, and the practitioners will face the questions already raised in California: What will be the aftermath of the price surge and buying spree? Will it be a "soft" or a "hard" landing? These are crucial issues not only for builders and real-estate brokers but also for lending institutions and private mortgage insurance companies as well as the public at large.

It would be folly to attempt to forecast answers. Not only do local conditions vary but the uncertainties are too great to allow just one scenario.

Instead, this chapter seeks to specify and appraise the numerous factors bearing on future prices of homes. In the process, one can also identify the forces that are instrumental in the market adjustment itself.

Supply and Demand Variables in the Market for Homes

To begin with forces operating *within* the single-family house market, greatly expanded new construction has played the classic pivotal role in containing the rise in home prices by enlarging the supply. To be sure, construction could not augment the supply in specific built-up areas recently favored by well-to-do home shoppers such as Beverly Hills or West Los Angeles and in similar city districts elsewhere. Builders were able to offer equivalent property in more outlying areas, however. A strategic question for the future concerns the business psychology of builders. Will they overshoot the market, as they have typically done in the past, and thereby add to the competitive pressure on prices? If historical experience is any guide, they will. But there are some countervailing reasons why they may not. More severe municipal restrictions and the resulting shortage of buildable lots could tame builders' expansionary instincts.[4] The greater tendency of lenders to commit funds for limited sections of new projects and make additional commitments depending on sales experience could have similar effects. If so, the new supply that serves to moderate inflation of house prices would lose some of its force.

The volume of home construction will also be greatly influenced by the availability of funds for mortgage lending. The growth of savings deposits at financial institutions has been slowing down. For example, net savings flows into FSLIC-insured savings-and-loan associations in 1977, exclusive of interest credits, were $32 billion as against $34.4 billion in 1976, a decrease of 7.5%, while the comparable data for 1975-1976 showed an increase of 17.4%. When interest credits are included, net savings gains were about $50 billion in both 1977 and 1976, that is, there was virtually no change as against an 18% increase between 1975 and 1976. The deceleration worsened in the first six months of 1978. Net savings flows were only $21.8 billion inclusive of interest credits, compared to $27.8 billion in the same period of the preceding year, a decline of nearly 22%. The spread between average interest rates on S&L accounts and yields on medium-term securities has changed greatly in favor of the latter,[5] although it has been moderated by money-market certificates issued by associations since 1978. Meanwhile, the amount of outstanding loan commitments of the associations had doubled between early 1975 and late 1976 and stood at an unprecedented $24 billion in May 1978. The institutions resorted to larger borrowings, mainly from sources other than the Federal Home Loan Banks, to obtain the funds for meeting growing loan disbursements and commitments without impairing their liquidity. Total borrowings were about $28 billion at the end of 1977 as against $19 billion the year before and reached $34 billion in June 1978.[6] Mortgage loan commitments and purchases by the Federal National Mortgage Association accelerated at a fast pace in late 1977 and the first half of 1978,[7] indicating that loan originators experienced increasing difficulty in placing mortgages with private investors. Effective home mortgage interest rates have been creeping up since mid-1977 and within a year approximated levels exceeding the previous peaks of 1974.

These changes reveal considerable strain, which if continued, could lead to sharp curtailment of funds available for home financing and to tighter credit terms. Such a development usually forces builders to pull in their horns and reduce additions to the supply, with the result that competitive price pressures coming from new construction may be lessened. A decrease in the availability of mortgage credit could also constrain home purchase and for this reason dampen further price increases. As will be suggested later, the net outcome depends largely on economic conditions and the future course of general inflation.

The level of house prices may be affected negatively if some recent buyers for owner-occupancy discover that they have overextended themselves. The trade-off between larger current housing expenses and expected capital gains will not always work out as contemplated at the time of purchase. Some owners may find it impossible to cut down other consumption sufficiently to meet the periodic cash outlays for carrying high-priced property or may be unwilling to deplete their financial savings, or anticipated income gains will fail to materialize. Hence some recent home purchasers may be forced to sell to avoid foreclosure. Delinquency and foreclosure rates have so far remained low. However, since much of the construction of 1977 was presold before it was completed or even started, large groups of buyers have just moved into their new homes and have yet to experience the longer run impact of their actions on budgets. Buyers' realization of an untenable condition is more likely to come in 1979 or 1980 than in 1978. Further, the single persons and the "twosomes" or informal households who represented a growing percentage of recent home purchasers constitute a more volatile group of owners than do regular families.

To what extent resale by unstable or overcommitted buyers will affect the price level of homes depends on the incidence and urgency of financial difficulties as well as market conditions at the time of sale. The consequences could range from minimal to more widespread problems. However, few of the recent purchasers are likely to "walk away" from their properties or risk foreclosure. Most have made substantial downpayments that they are strongly motivated to protect. In a fairly large number of cases, the owners' parents or other responsible parties are cosigners of the mortgage note.

Adverse price effects in California could also result from the liquidation of speculative holdings. Some speculators have already resold their properties with or without the capital gains they anticipated. Others are faced with the recent softening of the market in California, and their strategy will largely depend on their overall financial capacity. Many of the well-to-do amateur speculators may extend their holding period in the hope for eventual capital gain, even in the face of the considerable costs of property held vacant or of the typically negative cash flows from rental. When they discover that their reservation prices for resale are not met, they may remain landlords much longer than anticipated. Others will need to sell promptly to realize any capital gain or minimize loss. Among the real-estate practitioners, the undercapitalized broker and salesperson may be forced into selling, especially if the same individual holds several properties. Altogether, one cannot dismiss the possibility of distress sales from these sources. However, the moderate overall volume of speculation suggests that the remaining disposition of short-term property holdings should have only a marginal influence on the general price level. The repercussions may be more severe in certain areas or projects where speculative buying was concentrated. In any event, the negative impact will be limited to California.

Another potentially adverse factor is the anticipatory character of recent purchases by owner-occupants to the extent that they were motivated by fear of inflation. These transactions were "borrowed from the future," that is, they would have occurred after 1977 in the absence of inflationary expectations. Hence future house prices may reflect a softening current demand for homes, other things equal. Finally, it is highly questionable whether the exchange of one owner-occupied unit for another—the main support of homebuilding in 1976-1977—can continue at the recent pace. More likely, the game of musical chairs will slow down at least for a while until the ranks of homeowners willing and able to switch to another house are replenished. An increase of first-time home purchasers can fill the gap only if builders are able to gear products and merchandising more closely to their needs. As the demand by owner-buyers weakens, builders will have a strong incentive to cater to first-time buyers. The poor sales record of the stripped-down, no-frills houses constructed in the early 1970s does not necessarily mean that such an effort would be unsuccessful under present conditions.

All these potentially negative effects on house price levels will be counterbalanced by continued strength of the underlying demand for housing and for single-family dwellings in particular. For several years to come, the number of people in age brackets forming families or other households will keep on increasing at fairly high rates, and so will the number of persons in typical homebuying age groups.[8] The upward trend of families with two earners is likely to continue, and it seems unrealistic to assume that the effect of this trend on the market has spent itself in recent years. Another favorable factor is the recent acceleration of rent increases. Many consumers who have been on the fence with regard to renting or owning may decide to buy a home if rents continue to escalate. Finally, the price surge for single-family units began at different points of time in different areas. It will probably decelerate in similar sequence. Hence the adjustment problems will appear in local succession rather than simultaneously, and their cumulative impact will be spread over time. For example, local mortgage lenders may experience an increase in defaults at various periods in various localities. If so, the result would not be tantamount to a wave of foreclosures that might threaten the stability of the home-financing system.

General Economic Conditions

Whether the potential strength of long-run demand for homes transforms itself into effective demand depends, of course, on developments in the economy at large. By the same token, these developments will greatly influence the severity of adjustments in the single-family house market to the recent price surge. Continued prosperity will reduce the number of recent homebuyers who find themselves under financial strain. Their income will have a better chance to increase, or the house market may be strong enough to allow resale of properties without substantial loss. Prosperity may even bail out speculators who are not under extreme pressure to sell. Continued economic growth would minimize loan defaults and their impact on lending institutions. A business recession would have the opposite effects.

The vast majority of economic forecasts project expansion through 1978, with a moderate increase of real GNP below the 1977 rate of 4.9%. Such an increase rests, among other things, on growing nonresidential fixed investment. If it is realized, the recent tightening of credit may become even more severe. Together with the need for financing a sizeable federal deficit, larger business demand for funds can "crowd out" the housing sector and, in the extreme case, lead to yet another credit crunch. Thus while continued prosperity would ease the adjustment of the single-family house market to the price escalation, a marked decline in the availability of funds for home financing could at the same time reduce sales potentials and thereby aggravate the adjustment process. As was shown in chapter 5, the 1975-1977 price surge in the market for single-family houses was made possible by an ample supply of mortgage funds. A reversal of this condition is likely to hasten the deceleration of price increases for homes.

Market adjustments will extend well into 1979 and 1980, and forecasts for these years are more divided and far more uncertain than for 1978. The possibility of a general business recession cannot be dismissed, and many forecasters consider it a strong probability. Alternatively, the economy may enter a period of more sluggish growth. If the current expansion continues through 1978, it will have lasted 15 calendar quarters, or nearly four years. This is well within the range of duration of previous cyclical upswings, including those that were prolonged by U.S. military engagements. Only the expansion of late 1960 to III-1969 lasted much longer. Such a comparison, of course, does not mean that the economy must or will turn down in 1979 or 1980, but it remains suggestive. Should a recession intervene, it would also aggravate the repercussions of the recent surge in house prices. In this case, the financial system could provide the funds for an active single-family house market, but consumer confidence would be impaired, gains in real income would be slowed or reversed, and the current demand for homes would shrink. Thus both economic contraction and continued expansion may have unfavorable effects on the adjustment of the residential sector to the price escalation, but for different reasons.

In all probability, however, the most crucial determinant of future house prices relative to their present level is the rate of general inflation and the inflationary expectations that it spawns. That increases in consumer prices and the GNP deflator accelerated materially in the first half of 1978 highlights the importance of this factor. Should accelerated inflation persist, renewed public apprehension over future prices could generate another buying spree in the house market, restimulate anticipatory purchases, and produce another upward thrust of home prices. Higher nominal mortgage interest rates would probably be as ineffective in stemming the tide as they were in the past few years. Under such a condition, the adjustment problems arising from the recent surge of house prices would be greatly diminished. However, sharply reduced availability of mortgage funds might have a restraining influence on further house price escalation, an influence that did not exist in the 1975-1977 period.

The Lesson of Previous Experience

Finally, it is instructive to review briefly the earlier experience of three areas that have completed a cycle of house price fluctuations under sharply varying economic conditions. One case pertains to Seattle. Heavily dependent on employment at the Boeing Company, the local economy benefited from a boom in the 1960s, accompanied by inmigration, and suffered a severe slump beginning in 1968.[9] Manufacturing employment decreased from a peak of 171,800 in that year to 104,600 in 1971, or by 64%. Total employment declined from its 1969 peak of 559,800 to nearly 490,000, or by 14.3%. The unemployment rate rose from 4.2% in 1968 to 12.4% in 1971 and was 10.8% in 1972.[10] Building-permit authorizations in the Seattle housing market area dropped from 23,377 dwelling units in 1968 to 5,681 in 1971, or by nearly 60%. Even the less volatile single-family house permits decreased by about 37%. How did house prices fare under this extreme adversity? According to the local Real Estate Research Committee, the average market value of existing single-family dwellings increased by over 13% between April 1968 and April 1969, still reflecting the previous Boeing boom, and declined by 3.5% in the next annual period. There was no change between April 1970 and April 1971. Market values increased moderately in 1972-1973 and more substantially thereafter, at annual rates of 8.3% in 1974, 6.1% in 1975, and 11.5% in 1976. Yet the Seattle economy recovered from its slump quite slowly. Total employment increased by 3.5% in 1974-1976 while manufacturing employment still declined by 8.8%. Unemployment was in the 9% range in 1975 and 1976. Thus negative effects of economic trouble on average house prices were relatively small and short-lived.

The second case is the condominium boom of 1972-1974 in the Miami, Florida, area (Dade and Broward Counties) and its aftermath. Sales of new condominium units increased from about 10,500 in 1971, already twice the volume of 1968, to 22,000 in 1973, and nearly 26,000 in 1974. According to local reports, the boom was accompanied by substantial speculative purchases. Sales dropped to about 12,000 a year in 1975 and 1976, while unsold units reached an unprecedented 6,000 units in 1974, remained at this level in 1975, and declined to 5,000 in 1976. The boom left a legacy of project foreclosures. The mortgage lenders that became involuntary owners resorted to large price concessions to reduce the overhang of unsold units, but the market adjustment was still incomplete by the summer of 1977. The market for single-family houses, subject to somewhat distinctive supply and demand forces, was affected in terms of declining sales in 1974 and 1975, but average prices continued to move up until 1976.[11]

The third case is the boom-to-bust course of residential construction in Orange County during the 1960s. As a consequence of overbuilding in the early part of the decade, new housing units authorized fell from over 30,000 in 1964 to about 12,000 in 1967. The decline was especially marked for multifamily dwellings. Despite the county's long-term population and economic growth, it took several years before the large rental vacancies and the builders' inventory of unsold houses were absorbed. Price and rent concessions were widespread. Homebuilders and sponsors of apartment houses suffered losses. To judge from the scanty sample for existing single-family houses, however, average prices merely ceased to rise in 1966-1967 and resumed their upward movement in 1968.[12]

The examples suggest that adverse local conditions *can* generate at least temporary price declines. They illustrate also the fairly long time required for market adjustments to work themselves out. However, the difficulties experienced in the three areas—the acute slump in Seattle and the extreme building excesses in Miami and Orange County—probably exceed any that may be expected for the United States as a whole or even for California and its major metropoles. Only catastrophic developments could produce problems of the magnitude encountered in the three cases. Also the adverse conditions in Seattle and Orange County occurred at a time when people did not anticipate general inflation. Altogether, then, market adjustments to the recent homebuying spree and the escalation of house prices are likely to be less severe than in any of the cases reviewed.

A Summary Judgment

We can now venture an appraisal of the outlook derived from supply and demand variables in the market for homes, conjectures on future business conditions and inflation potentials, and the record of boom-bust sequence in three local areas. The analysis suggests that the short-term adjustments resulting from the recent escalation of house prices will be of moderate proportions. In the aviation terms cultivated by California practitioners, the possibility of a "crash" or even a hard landing appears remote. In all probability, the bubble will deflate rather than burst. To repeat, the problems are localized and unlikely to be felt all at once throughout the nation, and their solution will be facilitated by continuous strength of the basic demand for single-family houses. On the other hand, it is difficult to subscribe to the expectation of a soft landing if it is meant to denote no problems whatever. Some recent homebuyers are apt to encounter financial strain. Defaults on mortgage loans are apt to increase. Distress sales by overextended owner-occupants and by speculators caught at the end of the line are likely to generate downward pressures on the level of house prices at least in some areas. The adjustment problems will probably be most acute in the major urban centers of California where the price surge was most pronounced and the rush into home purchase at times assumed an aura of hysteria. Also house prices in California have reached a level that seems to threaten further growth of inmigration, the one source of demand that could mitigate the aftermath of the price escalation. National corporations have found it increasingly difficult to transfer management or technical personnel from other parts of the country to the Golden State as candidates for transfer explore the cost of housing. Corporations and other institutions such as universities encounter similar difficulties in the recruitment of non-Californians for jobs in the state.

While the adjustment problems are not severe, their resolution will take considerable time. During the adjustment period, *average* house prices are unlikely to decline nationally or regionally, but decreases from peak levels will occur in individual cases and some local areas, especially in California. Barring a new surge of general inflation, the average rate of price advance in the near future will probably decline. If so, the capital-gain expectations of some recent buyers will fail to materialize. This point warrants some elaboration.

As indicated in chapter 4, the price expectations of recent home purchasers in two California counties were two to two and one-half times greater than their expectations on upward movements in the general price level. If such anticipations were to be realized, house prices would be twice as high relative to other prices within 6.6 to 9 years. Presumably, price increases of this magnitude would be accompanied by higher homeownership expenses for new buyers. As a result, periodic housing outlays as a share of income would rise significantly. Even if one were to make generous allowance for income gains during the relevant time horizon and introduced the questionable assumption of consumers being relatively insensitive to price shifts between housing and nonhousing, much of the higher income would be sopped up by increased housing expenditures. For example, consumers spending 20% of their income on housing initially would find this share to be 27% at the end of the period after house prices doubled and income, let us say, went up by 50%. About 40% of the incremental income would be spent on housing. If initially 25% of income was devoted to housing and the assumption of consumers' insensitivity to price shifts between housing and other goods and services held, the eventual income share of housing expenses would be 33%; 50% of the incremental income would go to housing. The evidence that consumers would be prepared to make these kinds of sacrifices for the sake of homeownership is extremely weak. Hence it is unreasonable to expect that price anticipations derived from the short-run experience of recent years can be validated in the longer run.

Beneficiaries and Victims of House Price Inflation

Any inflation is a powerful engine for redistributing wealth or economic welfare; it favors some groups of the population and hurts others. When the dust of the recent house price inflation settles, who will emerge as the beneficiary and who will be disadvantaged?

Without question, the vast majority of homeowners will be among the most favored groups.[13] Those who acquired their property before 1975 and still own it or sold it recently to move to rental accommodations have benefited from price appreciation and even greater appreciation of their equities. For households that have terminated ownership, the capital gains are realized. For pre-1975 purchasers who still own the same property, the gains are unrealized, representing increases in the "book value" of their asset, as it were. Only if house prices should decline to a level averaging much less than 1975 prices would some owners fail to obtain realized or unrealized gains, and such a decline could occur only under the most adverse national or international conditions. Of course, any such statement about gains or losses refers to group experience. If individual homeowners are caught by deterioration of their neighborhoods, for example, they will lose all or much of the benefit of capital appreciation or may even incur losses in resale.

Quite apart from realized or unrealized capital gains, homeowners of pre-1975 vintage have an enormous advantage through their position as debtors.[14] Their mortgage borrowings are being repaid in "cheaper dollars"—cheaper not only because of general inflation but also relative to their earnings except for those owners who live on truly fixed income.[a] Interest rates on long-term

[a]Even many types of retirement income such as social security and a large number of annuities under public and private pension funds have been adjusted to inflation although the adjustments frequently lag behind the rate of inflation.

mortgages contracted in the 1960s are far below the current rates and again typically absorb a smaller portion of the owners' generally increased income. The same is true for loan amortization payments. The magnitude of the benefits can be gauged by the fact that home mortgage debt represents by far the largest component of the total liabilities of households, personal trusts, and nonprofit organizations, the only category for which data are available. At the end of 1976, the $540 billion of home mortgages outstanding accounted for nearly 61% of total liabilities in the amount of $890 billion. Consumer credit of all types, with $224 billion outstanding, ran a poor second and did not generate any significant inflation benefits for borrowers since it is extended for shorter periods. Further, the home mortgage debt in 1976 exceeded slightly the long-term debt of all nonfinancial corporations, which are also among the main beneficiaries of inflation when they had issued bonds or similar obligations. Such an excess has been typical of the entire period since 1965.[15]

According to the analysis in chapters 4 and 5, some perception by the public of the advantages of homeownership under inflationary conditions has contributed to the recent increase in the demand for single-family houses and the attendant price escalation. However, the homeowners' gains from inflation are partially diluted by larger property taxes and, to a smaller extent, higher hazard insurance payments that are the direct results of the surge in house prices. Under prevailing law and practice, tax assessors must take proper notice of increased market prices, although observance of this requirement varies locally. Hence property assessments are rising at an accelerated rate, though with some lag, wherever price increases have accelerated. This trend alone leads to larger property taxes even in the absence of higher tax rates. It affects homeowners regardless of whether they have benefited from inflation. For example, those who own their property free and clear of debt—36% of all homeowners according to the *Annual Housing Survey* of 1976—do not now gain from repaying mortgage loans with cheaper dollars. Those who have the satisfaction of knowing that their house is worth more than they paid for it must still make the cash outlays for increases in real-estate taxes and hazard insurance. Thus there is not necessarily a balance of benefits and costs when subgroups of homeowners are considered. Higher assessments following the price surge have reinforced the pressures for property-tax relief or reform of the local and state tax structure. This has been an especially acute issue in California, leading to the voters' approval in 1978 of the referendum known as Proposition 13, which limits real-estate tax payments on all types of property to an initial 1% of the assessor's estimated market values and rolls the assessments back to 1975-76 levels.

The foregoing observations were limited to homeowners of pre-1975 vintage because the inflation-induced gains or losses of the more recent buyers can as yet not be gauged. The outcome depends on the future course of prices and the purchasers' ability to carry their typically augmented current housing expenses.

There is also no basis for assessing the redistribution of wealth through the short-lived speculation in houses. The speculators who got into the market early, sold promptly, and could resist the temptation to try it again have probably been rewarded with capital gains despite substantial transaction costs. The outcome may be quite different for those who joined the game later when the single-family house market in California began to soften.

Among the beneficiaries of house price inflation are homebuilders. In many areas and projects, at least, the extraordinary demand for single-family houses made it possible to sell at prices allowing more than normal profit margins. However, the practice of precompletion or even prestart sale at fixed prices has placed the burden of intervening cost increases on the builder unless he was protected by fixed-price arrangements with his contractors. The ability of California speculators to buy homes in new developments and resell them at a profit indicates that builders did not necessarily charge what the traffic will bear. Hence supernormal profits of builders have probably been of moderate proportions, not unlike those obtained in any construction boom. Recent sellers of land ready for site improvement or already improved are another favored group, benefiting from record prices for sites. But the characteristics of the group are unknown, and so are the dates of their land acquisition and their holding costs.

First-time housebuyers emerge without doubt as the principal group disadvantaged by the recent surge in house prices. Although this study attempted to rectify exaggerated views about their curtailed access to the market (chapter 3), the price escalation for existing as well as new homes will in all probability have a ratchet effect, that is, leave a permanent imprint on price levels even after market adjustments have been completed. The relationship between house prices and typical incomes of first-time homebuyers is likely to remain worse than it was three or five years ago. Hence it has become a live issue whether public policies should be redesigned to facilitate access of first-time purchasers to homeownership, and what directions such policies might take. This is one of the subjects of the final chapter that discusses a variety of policy questions posed by the recent inflation of house prices.

Notes

1. Multiple listing data in *California Real Estate,* various issues. As for the time required to sell existing houses, for example, the San Diego Real Estate Board reported that an average of 46 days elapsed between listing and sale in the fall and winter of 1977 as against 18 days in the spring and summer. The figures for San Jose, probably more subject to seasonal variations, were 76 days and 31 days, respectively (Communication of the California Association of Realtors).

2. The inventory in December 1977 was 16,556 units compared to 11,552 a year earlier. Most of the unsold homes were under construction at both dates

while the inventory of completed units remained low. (Real Estate Research Council of Southern California, report for the fourth quarter of 1977.) Still the increase of unsold units under construction indicates that precompletion sales were beginning to weaken.

3. Between October 1977 and April 1978, average prices of existing houses rose by 11.4% compared to 14.7% in April-October 1977 in the seven-county area of southern California. The figures for the nine counties comprising the San Francisco Bay area were 8.2% and 12.7%, respectively, and for Sacramento County 9.6% and 11.1%. (For sources, see table 2-5.) Review of the whole series of semiannual changes precludes any consistent seasonal fluctuations as an explanation of the declining rate of price increases. According to the reports of the National Association of Realtors for existing homes, average prices in the West rose at the same rate in the first half of both 1978 and 1977, that is, there was no further acceleration. Nationwide prices recorded an average advance of 14.8% in the first six months of 1978 as against 13.5% in the comparable 1977 period. For new homes currently sold, the U.S. Department of Commerce shows a price increase in the West of 15.4% in I-1978 over I-1977 following an increase of 17.9% between I-1976 and I-1977. The comparable data for the U.S. are 14.7% and 12.2%, respectively. According to the nationwide figures of the FHLBB, prices of new homes continued to escalate between the first half of 1978 and the first half of 1977 while a declining rate of increase was reported for existing units.

4. In August 1977 it was reported that lots were scarce and increasingly expensive in all but a few local markets and that water supply problems were becoming more severe, especially in the West and Southwest. (Release of August 22, 1977, of U.S. Housing Markets, a service of the Advance Mortgage Corporation, Detroit, Michigan.) The water supply difficulty may have been eased by substantial rainfall in the late months of 1977 and early 1978.

5. The average yield on 3-5 year Treasury notes was 6.58% in June 1976 and approximated 8% in the spring of 1978. Average interest rates at FSLIC associations on all savings accounts were 6.34% in July-December 1976 and 6.42% in July-December 1977. Treasury yields from Federal Reserve Bulletin, and all S&L data from Federal Home Loan Bank Board Journal and monthly releases of FHLBB on savings-and-loan activity.

6. The increase includes mortgage-backed securities issued by several large savings-and-loan associations. But short-term borrowings, payable in one year or less, rose at an even faster rate, from $6.5 billion at the end of 1976 to $12.0 billion at the close of 1977.

7. Press releases of FNMA.

8. The number of persons twenty-five to forty-four years of age is estimated to increase by 8.2 million in 1975-1980 as against 5.3 million in 1979-1975, and to rise by another 9.3 million in 1980-1985. For the age group twenty-five to thirty-four, the increase is estimated at 5.2 million in 1975-1980

compared to 5.6 million in 1970-1975 and at 3.7 million in 1980-1985. Thus the future growth is focused on the thirty-five to forty-four age group. U.S. Bureau of the Census, Population Estimates and Projections, Series P-25, No. 704, July 1977. The cited figures hold for all of the three series of projections issued by the Bureau of the Census.

9. The slump was caused by layoffs at the Boeing Co. due to cuts in the NASA space programs, the cancellation of the military SST plane development project, and declining 747 plane orders from commercial airlines.

10. All data are from reports of the Seattle Real Estate Research Committee. For a graphic account of Seattle's problems during the 1968-1970 period, see "Seattle under Siege," *Time Magazine,* January 4, 1971.

11. Data from materials kindly supplied by the regional underwriters of two mortgage insurance companies. For FHLBB price data for the Miami-Fort Lauderdale area, see table 2-4.

12. Reports of the Residential Research Committee of Southern California, seriatim.

13. For a summary of the wealth effects of inflation on different population groups, see John L. Palmer and Michael C. Barth, *The Distributional Effects of Inflation and Higher Unemployment,* Brookings Reprint 339 (Washington, D.C., The Brookings Institution, 1978), pp. 205-209. When households are classified according to age of head, the largest inflation-induced increases in real net worth occur among the group having heads aged twenty-five to thirty-four. When they are classified by current income, the middle and upper-middle groups gain more than the others. The authors stress in a note that the relatively young, middle-income household is one of the classic beneficiaries from inflation because the owner-occupied home dominates its assets and the mortgage dominates its liabilities. During inflation, the home increases in value while the mortgage loan does not.

14. The inflation-induced advantage of mortgage debtors has been obtained at the expense of creditors—in this case, mostly the depositors in savings accounts of financial institutions. See the discussion pertaining to table 5-17.

15. All data from the Flow of Funds Accounts of the Federal Reserve, specifically "Assets and Liabilities Outstanding, 1965-76," December 1977.

8 The Role of Public Policies

Among the shock effects of the recent escalation of house prices have been proposals for new public policies and reinforced pressures for adoption of old proposals. [Calls for government action range from local to federal measures, from antispeculation taxes to expanded subsidy programs to facilitate home purchase by moderate- or middle-income people, especially first-time home-buyers.]

A capital-gains tax to combat speculation has been discussed in California at the state level and locally for Los Angeles and San Francisco. For example, a bill introduced in 1977 in the state legislature as a comprehensive measure to reform property taxes in California contained a provision to impose a tax on all of the capital gain on the sale or exchange of single-family houses not occupied by their owners. The tax would range from 50% of the gain to 30%, depending on the length of the holding period.[1] No action had been taken by the time of this writing, however. A member of the city council of Los Angeles has proposed a graduated real-estate transfer tax for residential income property changing hands within one to three years, but the proposal was rejected by the city council.[2] The opposition argued that such a levy would exert upward pressure on rent levels and impede apartment building and that it would evoke methods of tax avoidance. A transfer tax of 5% on the full resale price of single-family houses irrespective of the holding period was also considered during the 1978 debate of the state legislature on property-tax relief. The transfer levy was designed as a partial offset to the revenue loss resulting from lower property taxes. The proposal was later modified to a 5% tax on the capital gain from resale of homes.[3] The final legislation contained neither provision. Even so, Governor Brown's "Urban Strategy for California," outlined in March 1978, includes legislation to impose a substantial tax on profits from the sale of certain classes of real estate held for only a short period of time. In this case, "primary residences" and properties purchased for rehabilitation are among the categories exempt from the tax.[4] The proposal indicates that the idea of an anti-speculation real-estate tax is kept alive.

In the framework of this study, comment on a special capital-gains tax on short holdings is confined to the single-family house market. As was shown in chapter 3, speculation in California during 1976-1977 was a passing phenomenon and a symptom rather than a significant cause of the price surge. Speculative activity elsewhere has been of minor proportions. Whether it will reappear in the future is highly uncertain. Imposition of an antispeculation tax now would be tantamount to locking the stable after the horse was stolen. Besides, ownership of short duration may be caused by circumstances such as job transfer, divorce, or death and can therefore not be easily equated with speculative intent. Hence the tax would be inequitable in some cases, or the control of exemptions would be difficult, with its costs absorbing a considerable part of the tax revenue. Speculators, clever people by definition, would discover means of tax evasion. In other words, the light would hardly be worth the candle. Finally, an antispeculation tax on single-family houses raises the serious question why it should be limited to one class of real property. This issue is germane to any capital-gains tax imposed on transactions in selected types of real estate.

Another policy issue is the activity of real-estate brokers and salespersons in buying and reselling homes on their own account. This matter comes already under the purview of California law. Briefly, the law provides that a broker employed to negotiate the sale of a property cannot purchase the property for himself unless he has made a full and fair disclosure to the seller of his intention to change his position to that of a principal and has received the seller's permission to do so. Brokers and salespersons who violate the rule face suspension or revocation of their license. Violations include among other things any "substantial misrepresentation."[5] According to the California Department of Real Estate, there has been no great influx of complaints on this subject during the 1976-1977 wave of speculation. Yet the general public seems to have been under the impression that some practices of brokers and their sales personnel in buying property on their own behalf bordered on unethical if not illegal conduct. Although no regulatory change may be required, steps to inform the ignorant public more effectively of existing rules would have been highly desirable in the heydays of speculation. As matters stand, constraints on real-estate licensees and cases of violation are periodically published in the *Real Estate Bulletin* of the Department of Real Estate, read solely by professional practitioners. When newspapers and other media devoted a great deal of attention to speculation, it would have been quite easy for the department to place stories or interviews about the law in media that reach a wider audience. Communication would have helped to close the information gap that may account for the relatively few complaints brought to the authorities. The department, aware of the need to educate the public in the intricacies of real-estate transactions, held "consumer clinics" in 1977 at a large number of community colleges, but this was only one of several potential means of disseminating the facts on brokers' legal obligations more widely.

Turning to the broader problem of the effects of house price inflation on the demand for single-family houses by moderate-income families, especially first-time buyers, some policy proposals call for official sanction of alternative mortgage instruments (AMIs) that vary from the prevailing fixed payment plan for the life of the loan. Although the recent price escalation has been associated with a growing volume of homebuilding and sales of existing houses, the proposals assume that this may not be the case in a continued inflationary economy and stress the reduced access of potential first-time buyers to homeownership. Besides, they are based on the inherent merits of offering consumers a choice of various home financing plans that take account of different stages in their life (and earnings) cycle.

There is a rich array of suggested AMIs and an extensive literature dealing with them.[6] In the context of this study, it is sufficient to focus on just one proposal that is definitely designed to facilitate home purchase under inflationary conditions. This is the graduated payment or "slow-start" mortgage plan (GPM), already the object of an experimental program conducted by the Department of Housing and Urban Development in conjunction with FHA-insured loans. Among other alternative mortgage instruments, the variable interest loan, already used extensively by state-chartered savings-and-loan associations in California, is neutral with respect to first-time or moderate-income homebuyers. The five-year rollover mortgage, quite common in Canada and adopted by some institutions in the United States, is in the same category since it serves merely to make interest rates over the life of the loan more flexible. The reverse annuity mortgage plan applies to elderly homeowners, and its discussion here would take us too far afield regardless of its merits. The price level adjusted mortgage would improve access of moderate-income people to homeownership by a low interest rate equal to the "real" rate and by adjustment of monthly payments and the outstanding loan balance to the changes in some price index. One of the admitted difficulties of this plan is the need of financial institutions to hedge a price-level adjusted asset with a similarly adjusted liability, that is, savings deposits would also have to be adjusted for changes in prices. This opens up the Pandora box of price adjustments for other fixed-money claims such as corporate bonds and long-term government obligations. Still another proposal is the deferred interest loan, under which interest payments are low initially and rise later, akin to the graduated payment mortgage.

Under the GPM, the mortgage contract provides for reduced initial monthly payments compared to those under the standard fixed payment loan by charging interest at a rate below the contract rate, and the payments rise over the years. If the contract interest rate for the life of the loan is 9%, for example, it may be set initially at 7½% or 3% and be stepped up until the early deficit in interest receipts by the lender is compensated by the subsequent surplus, or until the loan is refinanced or the property sold, in which case the deferred interest falls due. Thus smaller initial payments and larger subsequent payments would effectuate a "tilting" of the payment stream in favor of borrowers, just as the fixed payment plan produces a tilting effect for homeowners whose income increases because of inflation and/or seniority in their occupation. An example is shown in table 8-1 for a five-year and ten-year GPM.

In the context of this study, two points warrant emphasis. First the initial annual payments under the GPM plans are sufficiently reduced from those under

Table 8-1
Key Data for Two Graduated-Payment Mortgage Plans and the
Fixed-Payment Plan
($30,000 loans for 30 years at 9% interest)

	5-year, 7½% GPM[a]		10-year, 3% GPM[b]		Fixed-payment Plan, 9%	
Year	Annual Payment	Outstanding Balance	Annual Payment	Outstanding Balance	Annual Payment	Outstanding Balance
1	$2,188	$30,533	$2,408	$30,304	$2,896	$29,795
2	2,352	30,945	2,480	30,562	2,896	29,570
3	2,530	31,212	2,555	30,765	2,896	29,326
4	2,718	31,306	2,632	30,908	2,896	29,057
5	2,922	31,197	2,710	30,983	2,896	28,764
10	3,164	29,098	3,236	29,975	2,896	26,826

Source: Adapted from table 4 in Donald M. Kaplan, quoted in footnote 6 of text.
[a] Annual payments increasing at 7.5% per year.
[b] Annual payments increasing at 3% per year.

the standard fixed payment plan to evoke considerable response by potential homebuyers. The reduction is nearly 17% for the five-year GPM and 24% for the ten-year version. Should the graduated payment mortgage be widely accepted within a short period, the additional demand combined with the inelastic short-run supply for new homebuilding could lead to a considerable price increase for single-family houses. If so, the buyers' benefit from the GPM plan would be largely or at least partially canceled. Price effects will depend not only on the speed of GPM adoption but on conditions in the single-family house market. If the GPM plan had become operative in 1976, it would have added substantially to the inflation of home prices. If it had been introduced during the recession of 1973-1974, immediate price effects would have been more moderate. The influence of the GPM plan on the volume of house purchases would in any event be diluted. The GPM might affect the price of homes more than the net additions to demand.

In connection with its study of alternative mortgage instruments, the FHLBB has undertaken a national survey of attitudes and preferences of potential home loan borrowers. According to preliminary results, about 25% of the survey respondents expressed a positive reaction to the slow-start mortgage plan. As for price effects, the "median priced house increased by approximately 20 percent for the entire sample" under the GPM provision.[7] These findings suggest considerable potentials for both additional homebuying and price inflation should the plan become operative.

Second the mortgage balance increases for the duration of the GPM plan. The $30,000 loan shows an outstanding balance of $31,200 at the end of the fifth year in the five-year version of table 8-1, as against less than $28,800 under the prevailing fixed payment mortgage. In the ten-year version, the balance just equals the original principal at the end of the period, while it is reduced to $26,800 under the fixed payment plan. Negative amortization in the first five or ten years exposes the lender to considerably greater risk, especially since experience indicates that the incidence of defaults and foreclosures is bunched during the early years of mortgage loans. Of course, rising average market values of single-family homes would diminish or remove the lenders' additional risk, but financial institutions are unlikely to rely on perpetual inflation of house prices; moreover, average price increases will not necessarily apply to individual cases. Hence use of the GPM plan would probably be limited to loans insured or guaranteed by FHA, VA, Farmers Home Administration, and possibly state housing agencies. Even so, the plan reduces total cash flows to mortgage lenders. Under the fixed payment loan illustrated in the table, cumulative receipts from interest and amortization at the end of five years total about $14,500. They are only $12,700 under the five-year version of GPM and $12,800 under the ten-year version. Any widespread adoption of the slow-start mortgage would therefore diminish the supply of home mortgage funds, and, other things equal, raise the level of mortgage interest rates or lead to tighter noninterest terms of credit. Such an outcome would cancel some of the expected benefits to borrowers from the GPM plan. The proposal offers no program to stimulate savings flows to mortgage lenders so as to offset the decline of cash flows from GPM loans.

To summarize, the GPM plan has serious drawbacks when its consequences for the single-family house and mortgage markets are considered.[8] Proposals for more direct assistance to moderate-income homebuyers center on federal subsidies. The resumption in early 1978 of the Section 235 program with its interest subsidies was a significant step in that direction. During 1977, bills were introduced in the U.S. Congress to facilitate home purchase by middle-income people and specifically by young families. One of the bills, The Young Families Housing Act, authored by Senator Brooke with 18 cosponsors, provided for a new type savings account through which first-time homebuyers could accumulate up to $10,000 tax-free for downpayments, plus graduate mortgage payments to reduce cash outlays during the early years of mortgage loans.[9] A similar proposal developed by Kenneth T. Rosen under the label "Individual Housing Account" estimated the first-year revenue loss to the Treasury at about $600 million and the steady-state loss at $1 to 2 billion a year, based on the Canadian experience with its Registered Home Ownership Savings Plan. The special savings account would be available to households with adjusted gross incomes of $20,000 or less.[10]

Of course, additional subsidy programs will have potential market impacts similar to those outlined in the discussion of the GPM plan. They will also augment total mortgage loan requirements. The effects will vary with market conditions and with the speed of effectuating the programs. Concerning speed, the public's utilization of a rule providing tax exemption of savings accumulated for downpayment is beyond the control of government while outright subsidies can be limited by maximum total amounts appropriated each year. As for conditions in the housing market, the injection of subsidies may have a substantial impact on construction and land costs and on house prices in periods of strong demand and nearly full employment of available resources. The effects will be more moderate under conditions of slack. In the case of new construction, however, the leadtime is so long that subsidy programs enacted in periods of relatively low market activity are in danger of coming to fruition when real and financial resources are under strain. If so, they may have significant inflationary impacts.

Besides, increased subsidies for certain classes of homebuyers raise serious questions of equity. In view of the small scale of housing programs for low-income people, would measures to facilitate home purchase by middle-income or moderate-income households be in accordance with proper social housing priorities? Homeowners are already among the favored groups. They can deduct mortgage interest and property taxes from income when they itemize income-tax deductions, while the rental value of owner-occupied residences is not included in their income. This advantage has been somewhat diluted through recent upward revisions of income brackets for which standard deductions are allowed. Nevertheless, subsidies would be piled on subsidies if home purchase were further facilitated by federal expenditures and if federal revenue were reduced through itemized deductions by the same taxpayers who obtained homeownership through subsidies in the first place.

Instead of the palliatives of subsidies or alternative mortgage instruments that reduce initial loan payments, improved access to homeownership of first-time buyers or others of moderate means calls for two more fundamental policy changes. One is a truly effective containment of inflation. As was shown in this study, inflationary expectations have contributed to the recent escalation of house prices and the resulting disproportion between price increases and income gains. This means that large segments of the public have little confidence in the adequacy of past efforts to reduce the rate of inflation. Unless the monetary and fiscal authorities demonstrate their capacity to bring the rate down to the more tolerable level of 2-3% a year—the level at which economic decisions are no longer dominated by price anticipations—the single-family house market is likely to be affected by expected inflation. The recent price surge may be followed by a short-term reaction generating greater stability, but stability is likely to be succeeded by another price escalation as fears of inflation are revived. Hence the removal of inflationary expectations is the key to normalizing price behavior in the market for homes.

Of course, the significance of this point extends way beyond the single-family house market. An annual price increase of even 6%, if it can be held at this rate, produces vast unintended and inequitable redistributions of wealth. It benefits debtors at the expense of creditors including savers. It favors holders of certain variable-price assets over those of fixed money claims. As inflationary expectations gather momentum, they stimulate consumption at the cost of saving as spending units attempt to stay ahead of future price increases and seek means of avoiding the shrinkage of the real value of their financial assets. (Consumers increased their saving rate in the early 1970s because the *unanticipated* inflation of that period created grave uncertainties.) More generally, when business firms as well as consumers expect continued inflation, they attempt to allocate their resources so as to protect themselves against it. Resource allocation becomes less efficient on economic and social criteria. The recent experience in the single-family house market merely captured the consequences of widespread inflationary expectations for one segment of the economy.

In this connection, some side-effects of inflation on housing warrant attention. As was pointed out in chapter 7, higher market values of residential property eventually are translated into higher assessments for property taxes and therefore generate pressures for reduced tax rates. California's Proposition 13 must be seen as the bellwether of this movement. The growing public demand for rent control in many areas of the country also reflects the influence of inflation on housing markets. In fact, both homeowners and renters are calling for public measures that in their view will protect them against some of the consequences of inflation for their household budgets. In light of the difficulty of projecting the aggregate and distributional effects of selective measures to cushion the impact of inflation on various population groups, a policy directed at reasonable overall price stability would promise a more equitable and effective solution of the problem.

The other policy change requires a revision of recent restrictions on homebuilding. Whether the restrictions were prompted by environmental considerations, antigrowth sentiments, reluctance to commit local government funds to the extension of the infrastructure needed for residential development, or other factors, their inevitable result is to raise costs and prices. Delays in obtaining permits from multiple jurisdictions and in the preparation and review of environmental impact reports represent a good part of the costs. It is altogether contradictory to press for building restraints in the interest of the public and then to deplore the fact that the public cannot buy houses it can afford. A better balance must be established between the needs of those who presumably benefit from restrictions and those who suffer from them through the high cost of new homes. This point applies also to efforts to preserve prime agricultural land by limiting its conversion to urban use, exemplified by bills introduced in the California legislature in 1977.[11] If adopted, such a measure would reduce the effective supply of sites for residential development and reinforce price increases for buildable parcels.

While our analysis in chapter 4 suggested that restrictions have not significantly impeded the volume of homebuilding in the recent expansion, they may well have affected the price mix in favor of higher priced houses. More important, the restrictions will exert their full force in the future when builders can no longer resort to land inventories acquired in the past, for these will have been more or less used up. Under future conditions, then, the position of middle-income buyers in the new-house market may deteriorate further unless the constraints are relaxed. Such a deterioration would affect first-time purchasers not only directly but also because high prices for new homes would increasingly deflect their demand into the market for existing property and push up prices there until a new equilibrium between new and old house prices was eventually established.

Like any new movement, the advocacy of environmental controls and urban growth limitations has tended to ignore or minimize side-effects of its objectives if these are realized. The time has come for fuller recognition of such effects. The achievement of a better balance between environmental concerns and housing concerns is made difficult by local autonomy—the community bent on no growth can palm off the housing problem on neighboring places that are less restrictive but may in time react imposing more stringent controls of their own. Another impediment is the common misconception of the parties in conflict. The contest is not between the general public and greedy builders but rather between different parts of the public itself, usually the "haves," or those who are established residents of a community, and the "have-nots" who knock at the door of the community for admission. It is one of the traditional and at the same time one of the most difficult tasks of public policy to reconcile such conflicting group interests. Reconciliation is badly needed in the case at hand.

Notes

1. Senate Bill 154 and, in a slightly different version, Assembly Bill 999.
2. *Los Angeles Times,* March 22, 1978.
3. Bills introduced by Senator Peter H. Behr.
4. *Los Angeles Times,* Real Estate Section, March 12, 1978.
5. Sections 10176 and 10177 of the Business and Professional Code. The penalties apply also to broker licensees who fail to exercise reasonable supervision over the activities of their salespersons. In the spring of 1978, the California Department of Real Estate issued a draft code of ethics and professional conduct, but its provisions merely underscored the above sections and addressed themselves to other issues such as real estate license schools.
6. The discussion here draws on Franco Modigliani and Donald R. Lessard, eds., *New Mortgage Designs for Stable Housing in an Inflationary Environment* (Federal Reserve Bank of Boston, January 1975); Donald M. Kaplan, *Preliminary Staff Report on the Alternative Mortgage Instruments Research Study,* presented before the Subcommittee on Financial Institutions of the U.S. Senate Committee on Banking, Housing, and Urban Affairs, October 6, 1977, reporting

results of a study undertaken by the Federal Home Loan Bank Board; Kenneth T. Rosen, "The Housing Crisis and the Homeownership Incentive Plan," *Journal of the American Real Estate and Urban Economics Association,* Fall 1977; and David L. Smith, "Reforming the Mortgage Instrument," *Federal Home Loan Bank Board Journal,* May 1976.

7. Donald M. Kaplan, *Alternative Mortgage Instruments,* pp. 46 and 48.

8. The same is true for the "equity-adjusted mortgage" proposed by Kenneth T. Rosen, "The Housing Crisis."

9. S. 664, introduced in February 1977.

10. Kenneth T. Rosen, "The Housing Crisis."

11. Senate Bill 193 and Assembly Bill 1900. For a detailed description and critical review, see Frank G. Mittelbach, "Our 'Lost' Agricultural Land is Really No Loss," *Los Angeles Times,* March 19, 1978, Opinion Section.

**Appendix A
Tables on House
Prices Analyzed in
Chapter 2**

Table A-1

Average Purchase Prices of New and Existing Single-Family Houses in the United States, 1968-1977

(thousands of dollars)

| Period | New (Commerce Dept.) | | Existing | Fed. Home Loan Bk. Bd.[c] | | Fed. Hsng. Adm.[d] | |
	Actual[a]	1967 House[a]	NAR[b]	New	Existing	New	Existing
1968	$26.6	$25.9	$22.3	$30.7	$25.6	$19.7	$16.2
1969	27.9	27.9	23.7	34.1	28.3	20.7	16.8
1970	26.6	28.9	25.7	35.5	30.0	23.2	18.2
1971	28.3	30.3	28.0	36.3	31.7	23.9	19.0
1972	30.5	32.2	30.1	37.3	33.4	24.8	19.6
1973	35.5	35.6	32.9	37.1	31.2	24.6	19.1
1974	38.9	38.9	35.8	40.1	34.7	27.7	21.6
1975	42.6	42.9	39.0	44.6	38.2	32.5	26.2
1976	48.0	47.1	42.2	48.4	41.3	35.4	26.8
1977	54.2	53.0	47.9	54.3	47.5	36.8	28.9

[a]Actual: prices of new homes sold by builders. 1967 house: prices of kinds of houses sold in 1967; see chapter 2, footnote 3, for detail.

[b]National Association of Realtors, monthly reports on existing home sales, based on data received from over 140 Multiple Listing Services throughout the country. According to the survey description, these sources are located in, or adjacent to, standard metropolitan statistical areas, but comparisons of their sales reports with census data from the Annual Housing Survey show that, as a group, their experience is representative of the sales activity and prices that generally prevail in each region of the country. As for sample size, the 1977 data cover nearly 600,000 existing single-family homes. In the main, a transaction is reported when the sales contract is signed, but a number of the sources report "closings." See the association's *Existing Home Sales, 1976.*

[c]From monthly reports on terms on conventional home mortgage loans made by major types of lenders. The prices are weighted averages compiled from individual loan data reported by a sample of lenders on fully amortized conventional first mortgage loans secured by single-family residential property; excluded are interim construction loans, refinancing loans, junior liens, and federally underwritten loans. The sample of lenders consists of savings-and-loan associations, mortgage companies, commercial banks, and mutual savings banks. Data beginning in 1973 represent a "new series," which differs from the old in the following ways: (1) It reflects a revised and expanded sample of lenders. (2) It covers loans closed during the first 5 business days a month, rather than loans approved during an entire month, and closing takes place after approval. (3) The weights used in calculating the "new series" averages compensate for the varying sampling fractions used for individual sampling strata defined in terms of type of lender, lender size, and lender location, whereas the "old series" calculations reflected fixed lender-type weights but not adjustment for variation in sampling fraction. As a consequence, the "new series" gives greater weight to small lenders located outside major metropolitan areas. The 1972-1973 and 1973-1974 data are influenced by the transition from the "old" series to the "new" series.

[d]FHA reports on home mortgage characteristics, Section 203b.

Table A-2
Selected Characteristics of FHA-Financed Homes, United States, 1968-1977

	Average Lot Size (sq. ft.) (1)	Average Mkt. Price of Site (2)	Price per Sq. ft. of Lot (3)	Average Site/Value Ratio (4)	Improved Floor Area[a] (sq. ft.) (5)	Centrally Air-conditioned[b] (6)
New Homes						
1968	9,186	$4,161	$.45	20.7	1,202	23.5%
1969	9,580	4,214	.44	19.9	1,178	28.3
1970	8,611	4,961	.58	20.9	1,267	30.3
1971	8,558	5,066	.59	20.8	1,267	32.3
1972	7,731	5,307	.69	21.0	1,251	32.3
1973	7,502	5,051	.67	20.1	1,211	36.1
1974	7,458	5,372	.72	18.9	1,248	44.3
1975	7,972	6,329	.79	18.5	1,330	52.6
1976	7,983	6,963	.87	19.1	1,332	55.1
1977	8,104	7,282	.90	19.0	1,313	61.4
Existing Homes						
1968	9,531	3,599	.38	21.8	1,157	
1969	9,500	3,665	.39	21.3	1,157	
1970	8,606	3,919	.46	21.1	1,144	
1971	9,315	3,984	.43	20.3	1,172	
1972	8,429	4,193	.50	20.9	1,146	
1973	7,796	3,949	.51	20.2	1,102	
1974	8,069	4,451	.55	19.5	1,105	
1975	8,278	5,423	.66	19.8	1,161	
1976	8,200	5,641	.69	20.0	1,138	
1977	8,479	5,877	.69	19.5	1,138	

Source: FHA reports on home mortgage characteristics, Section 203b.

[a]For one-story structures.

[b]Percent of all units.

Table A-3
Average Purchase Prices of New and Existing Homes Financed with Conventional Mortgage Loans, 1970-1977, Eighteen Metropolitan Areas
(thousands of dollars)

Period	Atlanta New	Atlanta Existing	Baltimore New	Baltimore Existing	Boston* New	Boston* Existing	Chicago* New	Chicago* Existing	Cleveland* New	Cleveland* Existing	Dallas New	Dallas Existing
1970	36.8	32.3	33.5	26.1	43.6	35.4	39.5	33.2	39.6	30.7	39.8	36.7
1971	37.1	34.5	35.5	28.2	52.8	40.2	39.2	35.2	42.2	33.0	40.5	37.2
1972	40.2	36.6	37.2	30.3	50.9	40.4	40.7	38.2	41.2	34.0	39.9	38.4
1973	43.3	37.1	37.5	32.6	n.a.	42.9	40.3	36.6	37.4	33.6	41.7	36.6
1974	48.4	43.7	42.1	41.3	n.a.	43.8	44.9	42.3	41.8	37.4	46.2	40.8
1975	54.2	49.8	47.7	41.3	n.a.	45.1	46.8	43.8	48.9	40.4	49.3	46.9
1976	54.1	50.1	56.5	44.3	n.a.	48.5	51.2	50.1	53.3	43.4	53.6	49.7
1977	56.3	52.2	56.5	50.5	n.a.	50.3	61.4	57.2	61.1	46.1	56.7	48.8

Period	Denver New	Denver Existing	Detroit* New	Detroit* Existing	Houston* New	Houston* Existing	Los Angeles* New	Los Angeles* Existing	Miami* New	Miami* Existing	Minneapolis New	Minneapolis Existing
1970	34.4	25.7	39.2	31.6	34.8	36.6	39.8	35.7	31.4	29.1	35.1	31.9
1971	35.2	30.6	38.0	31.7	37.0	40.0	36.0	36.7	39.7	33.2	33.0	32.8
1972	33.0	30.7	36.1	30.8	38.6	40.5	37.7	37.5	40.6	33.9	33.4	33.9
1973	35.0	31.8	38.8	33.2	41.7	36.6	41.0	39.6	36.4	38.9	39.3	35.1
1974	39.1	37.2	43.7	37.0	43.1	50.9	47.1	45.6	37.8	42.9	42.6	38.8
1975	46.7	43.2	47.2	39.6	51.2	52.9	51.2	51.6	48.1	48.6	n.a.	46.1
1976	50.1	46.5	49.4	40.1	53.5	52.5	65.9	60.0	51.3	49.2	n.a.	49.8
1977	61.1	53.0	53.3	42.6	57.4	55.8	72.5	70.8	43.3	50.8	56.0	52.9

Period	New York* New	New York* Existing	Philadelphia* New	Philadelphia* Existing	St. Louis New	St. Louis Existing	San Francisco* New	San Francisco* Existing	Seattle* New	Seattle* Existing	Washington, D.C. New	Washington, D.C. Existing
1970	42.6	39.5	34.2	27.1	n.a.	n.a.	39.6	37.0	33.0	32.5	n.a.	n.a.
1971	42.2	41.3	35.8	28.8	n.a.	n.a.	33.7	36.2	34.1	31.9	n.a.	n.a.
1972	45.2	43.0	35.4	30.5	n.a.	n.a.	38.3	37.7	31.3	31.8	n.a.	n.a.
1973	49.1	46.8	38.9	31.6	38.2	23.8	44.5	42.3	37.5	34.3	45.1	45.4

Year												
1974	51.8	50.4	39.2	35.8	37.6	26.8	48.1	47.7	40.6	34.9	49.1	50.3
1975	55.3	52.7	47.9	39.2	46.9	28.4	58.7	53.1	n.a.	37.4	53.5	59.2
1976	59.8	55.3	49.8	41.2	47.2	30.1	64.7	60.1	49.9	40.5	59.0	61.8
1977	69.7	61.0	51.5	44.1	53.8	38.4	75.2	71.0	52.1	46.4	66.7	68.9

Source: See table A-1, footnote c. The areas designated by an asterisk are standard consolidated statistical areas; all others are standard metropolitan statistical areas.

n.a.: data not reported for several months of the year.

Table A-4
Average Annual Compound Rate of Change in Purchase Prices of New and Existing Single-Family Houses Financed with Conventional Mortgage Loans, 1970-1977, Eighteen Metropolitan Areas

Period	Atlanta		Baltimore		Boston*		Chicago*		Cleveland*		Dallas	
	New	Existing	New	Existing	New	Existing	New	Existing	New	Existing	New	Existing
1970-1972	4.5	6.4	5.4	7.7	8.0	6.8	1.5	7.3	2.0	5.2	a	2.3
1972-1974	9.7	9.3	6.4	16.3	n.a.	4.1	5.0	5.2	0.7	4.9	7.6	3.1
1974-1976	5.7	7.1	15.8	3.6	n.a.	5.2	6.8	8.8	12.9	7.7	7.7	10.4
1975-1977	1.9	2.4	8.8	10.6	n.a.	5.6	14.5	14.3	11.8	6.8	7.2	2.0
1970-1977	6.3	7.1	7.8	9.9	n.a.	5.1	6.5	8.1	6.4	6.0	5.2	4.2

Period	Denver		Detroit*		Houston*		Los Angeles*		Miami*		Minneapolis	
	New	Existing	New	Existing	New	Existing	New	Existing	New	Existing	New	Existing
1970-1972	-2.1	9.3	-4.0	-1.3	5.3	5.2	-2.8	2.5	13.7	7.9	-2.5	3.1
1972-1974	8.9	10.1	10.0	9.6	5.7	12.1	11.8	10.3	-3.5	12.5	12.9	7.0
1974-1976	13.2	11.8	6.3	4.1	11.4	1.6	12.8	20.2	16.5	7.1	n.a.	13.3
1975-1977	14.4	10.8	6.3	3.7	5.9	2.7	19.0	17.1	-5.1	2.2	n.a.	7.1
1970-1977	8.6	10.9	4.5	4.4	7.4	6.2	8.9	10.3	4.7	8.3	6.9	7.5

Period	New York*		Philadelphia*		Seattle*		St. Louis		San Francisco*		Washington, D.C.	
	New	Existing	New	Existing	New	Existing	New	Existing	New	Existing	New	Existing
1970-1972	3.0	4.3	1.7	6.1	-2.6	-1.1	n.a.	n.a.	-1.6	0.9	n.a.	n.a.
1972-1974	7.1	8.3	5.2	8.3	13.9	4.8	n.a.	n.a.	12.1	12.5	n.a.	n.a.
1974-1976	7.4	4.7	12.7	7.3	10.9	7.7	12.0	6.0	16.0	12.2	9.6	10.8
1975-1977	12.3	7.6	3.7	6.1	n.a.	11.4	7.1	16.3	13.2	15.6	11.7	7.9
1970-1977	7.3	6.4	6.0	7.2	6.7	5.2	n.a.	n.a.	9.6	9.8	n.a.	n.a.

Source: See table A-1, footnote c. The areas designated by an asterisk are standard consolidated statistical areas; all others are standard metropolitan statistical areas.
aLess than 0.5%.

Appendix B
Methods Used for
Locally Generated
House Price Data

The data for the three major California areas in table 2-5 and those for Seattle in table 2-6 are based on a fixed sample of existing homes that are appraised semiannually. The following description of methods used in the surveys for southern California holds for all areas except Montgomery County:

> Every six months (April and October) a formal appraisal is made of each of the sample homes by professional staff appraisers under the supervision of a Sub-Committee of the Real Estate Research Committee. This procedure includes a check of comparable sales and a discussion with real estate brokers in the vicinity of each sample. These appraisals are then reviewed by the Sub-Committee and finalized with a specific value assigned to each home. This information is then converted to indexes. The sample homes are intended to represent various areas and districts of each county and to represent various price ranges as well as age or year built. Only single family detached homes are included in the sample. The intent over the years has been to keep the same sample homes, but substitutions are made when necessitated by removal or when the market price may be artificially distorted due to unusual circumstances—such as freeways, new zoning or major additions to the property.

Since 1966, the southern California sample has included 153 properties, the somewhat more varying sample for the San Francisco Bay area over 200, and the Sacramento sample only about 30 cases. The Seattle sample was augmented over time to 100 homes.

The data for Montgomery County are based on a sample of actual transactions in the market for existing single-family houses. For each current sale, the sales price is compared with the purchase price of the same property at an earlier date. The method yields average ratios of resale prices to previous purchase prices grouped according to various time intervals. Thus resale prices in 1975 are computed separately as ratios of purchase prices of the identical properties in 1974, 1973, 1972, and back over the years. These are converted into an average ratio of resale price to purchase price. The same procedure is applied to 1976 resales, and the average ratio of that year compared to the average ratio in 1975 yields a measure of average price change, expressed in index form. The sample for recent years includes over half the sales of existing houses made through the Multiple Listing System, which appears to be the source for current resale prices. The earlier purchase price is obtained "from a real estate directory source, a compilation from deed records which show the date of recording."[a]

aFrom Alfred W. Jarchow, "Measuring Trends in Home Prices," *Valuation* (American Society of Appraisers), December 1973. This article presents a detailed discussion of the author's techniques. For a shorter version, see his article "Recent Trends in Home Prices," *Realtor,* June 1974. Since that time, cases in which the date of previous purchase was more than 15 years prior to current resale have been excluded. Also the upper and lower half-decile of relative price level changes are now excluded. (Letter from Mr. Jarchow of June 25, 1977)

Appendix C
The Price Data of the Community Analysis Bureau of the City of Los Angeles

The first two reports on "Housing Price Trends," issued in November 1976 and July 1977, indicate the citywide coverage of the price statistics. For the 1965-1975 period, "valid sales" numbered 175,633 or an average of 15,967 per year. For 1975, however, only sales during the first half of the year were included. The second report is based on data for 1975 through July 1976 or 19 months, with 45,313 "valid sales." The sales volume in the four subareas is not reported. Nevertheless, it can be assumed to be sufficient for measuring price changes.

While an appendix to the reports specifies technical criteria for "acceptance" of data, it is never made entirely clear whether the results reflect the universe of eligible sales transactions or are drawn from a sample.

The reports include maps of census tracts, which show house price increases relative to the rise in the CPI. To indicate the degree of pervasiveness of price increases and the extent of sublocal variations, it would be also useful to array numbers of census tracts by groups with specified rates of price rise. Since the reports of the Community Analysis Bureau represent a commendable pioneering effort, they should be developed without restrictions that seem designed to protect the anonymous source of the original data.

**Appendix D
Historical Price Series**

Table D-1
Home Prices and Annual Rates of Change, 1890-1947, Various Areas
(1929 = 100)

	22 Cities Owner-occupied Houses (unadjusted)		Washington, D.C. Asking Prices, Existing Homes		Los Angeles Asking Prices		Cleveland New Homes		Seattle New Homes	
	Index	Percent Change	Index	Percent Change	Index	Percent Change	Index	Percent Change	Index	Percent Change
1890	61.3	—	—	—	—	—	—	—	—	—
1891	55.3	−9.8	—	—	—	—	—	—	—	—
1892	56.3	+1.8	—	—	—	—	—	—	—	—
1893	58.7	+4.3	—	—	—	—	—	—	—	—
1894	68.4	+16.5	—	—	—	—	—	—	—	—
1895	62.1	−9.2	—	—	—	—	—	—	—	—
1896	53.8	−13.4	—	—	—	—	—	—	—	—
1897	55.5	+3.2	—	—	—	—	—	—	—	—
1898	59.1	+6.5	—	—	—	—	—	—	—	—
1899	56.5	−4.4	—	—	—	—	—	—	—	—
1900	64.6	+14.3	—	—	27.7	—	—	—	—	—
1901	54.2	−16.1	—	—	33.1	+19.5	—	—	—	—
1902	63.9	+17.9	—	—	41.5	+25.4	—	—	—	—
1903	64.9	+1.6	—	—	46.9	+13.0	—	—	—	—
1904	67.9	+4.6	—	—	48.5	+3.4	—	—	—	—
1905	59.5	−12.4	—	—	50.8	+4.7	—	—	—	—
1906	70.6	+18.7	—	—	53.8	+5.9	—	—	—	—
1907	77.9	+10.3	—	—	56.9	+5.8	35.4	—	—	—
1908	70.3	−9.8	—	—	53.8	−5.5	36.6	+3.4	—	—
1909	68.7	−2.3	—	—	53.8	0	40.2	+9.8	56.9	—
1910	74.2	+8.0	—	—	53.1	−1.3	43.9	+9.2	58.8	+3.3

Year										
1911	72.5	−2.3	—	—	55.4	+4.3	45.1	+2.7	56.9	−3.3
1912	75.3	+3.9	—	—	55.4	0	46.3	+2.7	64.7	+13.7
1913	75.3	0	—	—	56.2	+1.4	47.6	+2.8	62.7	−3.1
1914	78.1	+3.7	—	—	53.1	−5.5	50.0	+5.0	64.7	+3.2
1915	71.7	−8.2	—	—	48.5	−8.7	51.2	+2.4	66.7	+3.1
1916	78.5	+9.5	—	—	46.2	−4.8	53.7	+4.9	64.7	−3.0
1917	80.1	+2.0	—	—	46.2	0	58.5	+8.9	62.7	−3.1
1918	85.2	+6.4	66.5	—	50.0	+8.2	67.1	+14.7	66.7	+6.4
1919	93.7	+10.0	77.6	+16.7	58.5	+17.0	76.8	+14.5	78.4	+17.5
1920	102.7	+9.6	86.9	+12.0	89.2	+52.5	86.8	+13.0	88.2	+12.5
1921	100.4	−2.2	96.9	+11.5	103.1	+15.6	87.8	+1.2	86.3	−2.2
1922	101.8	+1.4	99.3	+2.5	110.0	+6.7	91.5	+4.2	99.8	+15.6
1923	103.3	+1.5	102.1	+2.8	138.5	+25.9	96.3	+5.2	100.0	+0.2
1924	103.5	+0.2	106.5	+4.3	146.2	+5.6	100.0	+3.8	117.6	+17.6
1925	108.9	+5.2	107.8	+1.2	140.0	−4.3	102.4	+2.4	109.8	−6.6
1926	104.5	−4.1	106.9	−0.8	125.4	−10.4	103.7	+1.3	107.8	−1.8
1927	100.6	−3.7	106.0	−0.9	116.9	−6.8	102.4	−1.3	99.9	−7.3
1928	102.1	+1.5	101.2	−4.5	109.2	−6.6	101.2	−1.2	102.0	+2.1
1929	100.0	−2.1	100.0	−1.2	100.0	−8.4	100.0	−1.2	100.0	−2.0
1930	95.7	−4.3	98.6	−1.4	93.8	−6.2	95.1	−4.9	88.2	−11.8
1931	87.9	−8.2	93.8	−4.9	85.4	−9.0	—	—	—	—
1932	78.7	−10.5	89.9	−4.2	68.5	−19.8	—	—	—	—
1933	75.7	−3.8	79.5	−11.6	58.5	−14.6	—	—	—	—
1934	77.9	+2.9	82.4	+3.6	57.7	−1.4	—	—	—	—
1935	—	—	86.9	+5.5	66.2	+14.7	—	—	—	—
1936	—	—	84.8	−2.4	70.8	+6.9	—	—	—	—
1937	—	—	91.4	+7.8	82.3	+16.2	—	—	—	—
1938	—	—	88.6	−3.1	84.6	+2.8	—	—	—	—
1939	—	—	88.5	−0.1	80.0	−5.4	—	—	—	—
1940	—	—	90.5	+2.3	76.9	−3.8	—	—	—	—
1941	—	—	96.0	+6.1	82.3	+7.0	—	—	—	—
1942	—	—	104.5	+8.9	86.9	+5.6	—	—	—	—
1943	—	—	110.6	+5.8	100.0	+15.1	—	—	—	—
1944	—	—	119.4	+8.0	120.0	+20.0	—	—	—	—
1945	—	—	139.8	+17.1	144.6	+20.5	—	—	—	—

Table D-1 continued

Year	22 Cities Owner-occupied Houses (unadjusted)		Washington, D.C. Asking Prices, Existing Homes		Los Angeles Asking Prices		Cleveland New Homes		Seattle New Homes	
	Index	Percent Change	Index	Percent Change	Index	Percent Change	Index	Percent Change	Index	Percent Change
1946	—	—	174.4	+24.7	213.8	+47.9	—	—	—	—
1947	—	—	169.9	-2.6	216.2	+1.1	—	—	—	—

Sources: For 22 cities, Cleveland and Seattle, see Leo Grebler, David M. Blank, and Louis Winnick, *Capital Formation in Residential Real Estate* (Princeton, N.J.: Princeton University Press, 1956), appendix C, pp. 344-351. The Cleveland and Seattle indexes reported by L. Grebler, et al., were derived from Frank R. Garfield and William M. Hoad, "Construction Costs and Real Property Values," *Journal of American Statistical Association*, December 1937, pp. 643-662. The 20-city index is based on yearly median of 22 city relatives for one-family owner-occupied houses. The Cleveland and Seattle indexes relate to three-year moving averages of prices paid for a new six-room frame house and lot.

The Los Angeles data are reported by Robert M. Williams, "The Relationship of Housing Prices and Building Costs, 1900-1953," *Journal of the American Statistical Association*, June 1955, pp. 370-376. For discussion of methodology of constructing the series, see also Robert M. Williams, "An Index of Asking Prices for Single Family Dwellings," *The Appraisal Journal*, January 1954, pp. 33-38. The author notes that asking prices and market prices follow a similar path between 1940 and 1953—a period for which such comparisons were available.

The Washington, D.C., series is derived from Ernest M. Fisher, *Urban Real Estate Markets: Characteristics and Financing* (New York: National Bureau of Economic Research, 1951), table G.

Table D-2

Estimated Values of FHA-Financed Single-Family Houses and Related Data, United States, 1940-1954[a]

(Section 203, Purchase Transactions)

Year	Estimated Values		Percent Increase		Value as Multiple of Annual Income[b]	
	Existing Homes	New Homes	Existing Homes	New Homes	Existing Homes	New Homes
1940	$ 5,179	$ 5,199	—	—	1.72	1.95
1941	5,400	5,238	4.3%	2.7%	1.79	2.08
1942	5,568	5,385	3.1	2.8	1.72	1.98
1943	5,844	n.a.	4.9	n.a.	1.67	n.a.
1944	5,809	n.a.	−0.6	n.a.	1.64	n.a.
1945	5,835	n.a.	0.4	n.a.	1.66	n.a.
1946	6,269	6,957	7.4	n.a.	1.72	1.92
1947	7,190	7,817	14.7	12.4	1.82	1.96
1948	8,075	8,965	12.3	14.7	1.87	2.03
1949	9,093	8,753	12.6	−2.4	1.92	2.04
1950	9,298	8,594	2.2	−1.8	1.92	2.04
1951	10,147	9,307	9.1	8.3	1.96	2.00
1952	10,424	10,194	2.7	9.5	1.92	1.95
1953	11,352	10,166	8.9	—	1.92	1.92
1954	11,919	10,847	4.9	6.7	1.91	1.94

[a]Until 1951, FHA reported only estimated values rather than sales prices. A test of the relationship between the two for 1951-1954 revealed that sales prices averaged about 5% more than the agency's conservative value estimates.

[b]Annual effective income determined by FHA, which excluded income held to be transitory.

Table D-3
Home Price Trends in Los Angeles County
(1960 = 100)

Year	Index[a]	Percent Change	Year	Index[a]	Percent Change
1944	46	—	1961	107	+4.9
1945	54	+17.4	1962	114	+6.5
1946	82	+51.9	1963	121	+6.1
1947	78	−4.9	1964	124	+2.5
1948	76	−2.6	1965	128	+3.2
1949	67	−11.8	1966	130	+1.6
1950	70	+4.5	1967	131	+0.8
1951	76	+8.6	1968	133	+1.5
1952	77	+1.3	1969	137	+3.0
1953	77	0	1970	141	+2.9
1954	78	+1.3	1971	145	+2.8
1955	83	+6.4	1972	150	+3.4
1956	87	+4.8	1973	159	+6.0
1957	92	+5.7	1974	178	+11.9
1958	94	+2.2	1975	208	+16.9
1959	98	+4.3	1976	259	+24.5
1960	102	+4.1	1977	341	+31.7

Source: Real Estate Research Council of Southern California (formerly Residential Research Committee of Southern California).

[a]Indexes are for October of each year.

Appendix E
Analysis of
Downpayments

The data on purchase price and downpayment come from a single source, the reports of the FHLBB on terms of conventional home mortgage loans. Table E-1 computes downpayment as a percent of price as a reciprocal of the loan-price ratios reported directly by the FHLBB and derives the amount of downpayment from this computation. The results of the procedure are portrayed in figures 3-1 and 3-2 in the text. As a variant, table E-2 arrives at the downpayment by deducting the loan amount, reported directly since 1970, from the purchase price. This procedure results in somewhat larger downpayments in amount and in relation to price, but changes over time in the two series are about the same. The differing results obtained from the two methods are explained by the fact that each of the averages is an arithmetic average (with appropriate weights) of the individual items. Consequently, the weight of each loan is influenced by the value of the characteristic used in the average, and a high-priced home would have more influence on the average purchase price than it would have on the average loan-to-price ratio unless the loan-to-price ratio was also an extreme. In addition, minor differences are due to rounding. (Letter of Richard C. Pickering, Director, Statistical Division, Office of Economic Research, Federal Home Loan Bank Board.)

The text uses table E-1 because its measure of downpayment is believed to be less subject to distortion resulting from variation in the mix of loans on high-priced and low-priced homes in the averages.

The FHLBB series on terms of loans was revised in 1973. The revisions, giving greater weight to small lenders outside major metropolitan areas, affect changes between 1972 and 1973 shown in the tables and may also affect comparisons in the text between the early and late periods. Inaccuracies of the latter comparisons should be of minor magnitude.

Table E-1

Average Downpayment on Purchases of New and Existing Homes in Relation to Purchase Price and Per-capita Disposable Personal Income, United States, 1968-1977

Period	Purchase Price		D.P. as Percent of Purchase Price[a]		Amount of Downpayment[b]		P.C. DPI[c]	D.P. as Ratio of P.C.DPI	
	New	Old	New	Old	New	Old		New	Old
1968	$30,700	$25,600	26.1%	28.5%	$ 8,013	$ 7,296	$2,930	2.73	2.49
1969	34,100	28,300	27.2	28.5	9,275	8,065	3,111	2.98	2.59
1970	35,500	30,000	28.3	28.9	10,046	8,670	3,348	3.00	2.59
1971	36,300	31,700	25.7	26.1	9,329	8,274	3,588	2.60	2.31
1972	37,300	33,400	23.2	24.0	8,654	8,016	3,837	2.25	2.09
1973	37,100	31,200	22.7	24.8	8,422	7,738	4,285	1.96	1.80
1974	40,100	34,700	24.2	27.6	9,704	9,577	4,646	2.09	2.06
1975	44,600	38,200	23.9	26.6	10,659	10,161	5,077	2.10	2.00
1976	48,400	41,300	24.2	26.2	11,713	10,821	5,511	2.12	1.96
1977	54,300	47,500	23.7	24.9	12,869	11,827	6,037	2.13	1.96

Source: Federal Home Loan Bank Board.

[a]Reciprocal of reported loan-price ratio.

[b]Computed from percent of downpayment and purchase price.

[c]Per-capita disposable personal income (U.S. Department of Commerce).

Table E-2
Variant of Table E-1, 1970-1977

Period	Amount of Downpayment[a]		D.P. as Percent of Purchase Price		D.P. as Ratio of P.C.DPI	
	New	Old	New	Old	New	Old
1970	$10,300	$ 9,000	29.0%	30.0%	3.08	2.69
1971	9,700	8,600	26.7	27.1	2.70	2.40
1972	9,200	8,500	24.7	25.4	2.40	2.21
1973	9,000	8,400	24.2	26.9	2.10	1.96
1974	10,300	10,200	25.7	29.4	2.22	2.19
1975	11,300	10,800	25.3	28.3	2.22	2.13
1976	12,500	11,700	25.8	28.3	2.27	2.12
1977	13,800	12,800	25.4	26.9	2.28	2.12

Source: Federal Home Loan Bank Board.
[a]Purchase price minus loan amount.

**Appendix F
Advertisements for
Unfurnished Homes for
Rent in Four California
Areas, 1976-1977**

Table F-1
Advertisements for Unfurnished Homes for Rent in Four California Areas, 1976-1977[a]
(January 1974 = 100)

	Contra Costa County			Santa Clara County			Orange County			San Fernando Valley[b]		
	1976	*1977*	*Percent Change*	*1976*	*1977*	*Percent Change*	*1976*	*1977*	*Percent Change*	*1976*	*1977*	*Percent Change*
January	85	142	67%	118	179	52%	138	231	67%	124	132	6%
February	103	180	75	145	220	52	128	252	97	130	163	25
March	133	178	34	148	239	61	143	253	77	114	118	4
April	139	187	35	143	248	73	137	247	80	101	173	71
May	151	164	9	156	216	38	141	243	72	121	154	27
June	154	142	-5	189	210	11	164	265	62	143	171	20
July	137	137	0	210	191	-9	175	232	32	133	182	37
August	138	143	4	206	171	-17	176	212	20	159	170	7
September	120	103	-14	188	165	-12	215	178	-17	144	130	-10
October	115	109	-5	192	154	-20	228	197	-14	153	142	-7
November	129	100	-22	194	151	-22	251	205	-18	153	138	-10
December	120	118	-2	196	147	-25	234	192	-18	138	140	1

[a]The monthly index numbers are not seasonally adjusted. Hence comparisons can be made only between identical months of 1977 and 1976. Nevertheless, it may be noted that Santa Clara County, Orange County, and the San Fernando Valley show significant increases in the course of 1976. The index numbers are derived from the count of advertisements during the first two weeks of each month in one major local newspaper for each area. Source: Citizens Savings and Loan Association Research Department, San Francisco.
[b]Part of the City of Los Angeles.

Appendix G
Rationale of
Speculation

This appendix illustrates profit potentials from speculation in the single-family home market under various assumptions in the 1976-1977 period. We present three types of cases. One concerns the "double-escrow"—that is, the purchase of a property followed immediately or shortly thereafter by its resale without taking delivery. The second case involves taking delivery of the property with positive cash flows during the holding period. The third case is a variant of the second and assumes negative cash flows during the holding period. For the sake of simplicity, case studies II and III are based on house prices in Los Angeles County in 1976 and 1977.

Case I: Double-escrow

The simplest case is the double-escrow technique. The buyer acquires a property from an ill-informed seller at one price and resells it immediately at a higher price, that is, he is really engaged in arbitrage. His risk is minimal. Little or no capital is required. The deposit he makes on the purchase presumably is compensated for by a deposit on the sale. He incurs some transaction expenses by sharing in the costs for title search, escrow, and other incidentals on both transactions. In addition to out-of-pocket transaction costs, one might include the imputed value of the speculator's time in alternate activities to arrive at a break-even point. Another factor influencing the prospective gain hinges on tax treatment of the gain.

Table G-1 presents a hypothetical illustration of the double-escrow technique. Given the assumptions, a substantial spread of $6,500 between the speculator's purchase price and the full information price at which he sells the property is sopped up by transaction costs, search costs and federal income taxes. Net profit after taxes is zero, and potential spe꜠ ꜠tors presumably would not be attracted to the proposition. A larger gap between purchase and anticipated sales price, reductions in transactions or search costs or a lower federal income-tax bracket would be favorable to speculation. Regardless of whether the assumptions on costs are realistic, the example indicates that transactions and other costs are of more than negligible consequence. A considerable difference between purchase and expected sales price is necessary before speculation in real estate becomes profitable.

Table G-1
Case I: Double Escrow

Purchase price	$50,000
Plus transaction costs of 3%	1,500
Plus imputed search costs	1,000
Net price "paid"	$52,500
Selling price	$56,500
Minus transactions costs of 6%	3,390
Net price received	$53,110
Gross profit ($53,110 − $52,500)	$ 610
Taxable profit (Gross profit + imputed search costs)	1,600
Ordinary income taxes (38% tax bracket − $1,600 × 0.38)	610
Net profit after taxes	0

Case II: Speculation Involving Some
Holding Period—Positive Cash Flows

In this example we examine how a speculator in Los Angeles might have fared assuming he purchased a home in April 1976 and sold it in April 1977. In this period the typical price for existing homes rose from $56,600 to $73,600.

To single out the return from speculation, we assume that the speculator divested himself of some assets on which he earned a return. This return is posited to be commensurate with the return on the home during the holding period. The discounted value of cash flows while holding is therefore the same for alternate opportunities. For the sake of simplicity, we further assume that transaction costs in disposing of other assets to purchase the home are zero or negligible, but transaction costs do apply when buying and selling the home.

The rise in home prices is attributed to a sudden increase in demand to hold houses as a form of investment and in the short run is disassociated from changes in rents and operating costs.

Table G-2 shows the after-tax discounted value of the capital value enhancement as of April 1, 1976. After taxes, the purchaser earned $6,866 strictly from the gain in capital value. This represents 12% of the initial purchase price. Assuming the property was purchased with a 20% downpayment or $11,320, plus buyer transaction costs of $1,641, the speculator's after-tax return on equity approximates 53%. The illustration also shows that the real return represents about 40% of the property price increase.

Table G-2
Case II: Speculation with One-Year Holding Period
(commensurate cash flow during holding period)

(1) Home purchase price, April 1, 1976	$56,600
(2) Plus settlement (transaction) costs (Buyer's share 2.9%)	1,641
(3) Total price paid	$58,241
(4) Home sales price April 1, 1977	73,600
(5) Minus settlement (transaction) costs (Seller's share 6.5%)	4,784
Net price received	$68,816
(6) Before-tax nominal cash gain ($68,816 − $58,241)	10,575
(7) Discounted value of the increase in home price minus seller transactions costs, April 1, 1976 ($17,000 − $4,784) × 0.917−9% discount rate)	11,202
(8) Discounted value of home price increase including seller and buyer transaction costs, April 1, 1976 (Item 7 − $1,641)	9,561
(9) April 1, 1976, value of capital-gains tax due April 1978. Assume:	
(a) Taxable gain of $12,097 (b) Investor is in 50% tax bracket, and capital-gains tax of 25% applies; recapture is $188. (c) Capital gain discounted at 9% ($12,097 × 0.25 × 0.839) + ($188 × 0.839)	2,695
(10) After capital-gains tax, discounted value of home price increase, April 1, 1976 (Item 8 − 9)	6,866

Case III: Speculation Involving Some Holding Period—Negative Cash Flows

In case II the assumption was made that the home purchaser earned a normal return on his investment during the holding period. The capital gain he obtained in this instance could be considered a pure windfall since he might have been induced to purchase the home in any event for long-term investment. A more realistic example of speculation would be one where negative cash flows are incurred during the holding period and the anticipated increase in capital value is the major gain sought. To determine the outcome, we must include the cost of holding and potential income-tax benefits in arriving at estimates of the speculator's return.

Table G-3 presents illustrative results with fairly realistic assumptions as they applied to Los Angeles during the 1976-1977 period. The speculator is assumed to rent out the property and to seek potential value enhancements

Table G-3
Case III: Speculation with One-Year Holding Period
(negative cash flows while holding)

	Assumptions	
(1)	Home purchase price, April 1, 1976	$56,600
(2)	Downpayment of 20%	11,320
(3)	Buyer settlement costs (2.9% of home value)	1,641
	Cash outlay (2 + 3) at purchase	$12,961
(4)	Return on operations	
	Rental income: $500 per month, 11 months	5,500
	Interest and amortization $45,280 for 25 years at 9% interest rate	4,560
	Property taxes $13.50 per $100 of assessed value (25% of market value) = $14,150 × 0.1350	1,910
	Maintenance and insurance	1,200
	Net cash from operations	($ 2,170)
(5)	Sales price	$73,600
(6)	Seller transaction costs of 6.5% of sales price	$ 4,784

Speculator's Nominal Cash Flow

(7)	Initial expenditures		
	Downpayment	$11,320	
	Settlement costs	1,641	
	Total		$12,961
(8)	Receipts on sale		
	Return of downpayment	$11,320	
	Return of amortization	505	
	Home price appreciation	17,000	
	Less settlement costs	4,784	
	Gross receipts		$24,041
(9)	Nominal return on speculative purchase and sale		
	Receipts on sale	$24,041	
	Minus initial expenditures	12,961	
	Minus operating loss	2,170	
	Before-tax cash return		8,910
	Capital-gains tax		3,212
	Net cash after capital-gains tax (excluding income-tax benefits from operations)		$5,698

Table G-3 continued

Speculator's Discounted Cash Flow (April 1, 1976)

(10) Present value (P.V.) of receipts on sale $24,041 at 9% per annum	$22,056	
Minus initial expenditures	$12,961	
Minus P.V. of capital gains tax due 2 years after purchase $3,212 at 9% per annum	2,703	
Minus P.V. of negative operating return $180.83 per month at 9%	2,068	
Present value April 1, 1976, excluding income-tax benefits		$4,324

Implied Income-Tax Benefits

(11) Operating statement for income-tax purposes		
Rental income		$5,500
Operating expenses		
Property taxes	$ 1,910	
Maintenance	1,000	
Insurance	200	
Interest on mortgage	4,055	
Depreciation (125% declining balance over life)	1,887	
Net return		($3,552)
(12) P.V. (April 1, 1976) of income-tax benefit (50% tax bracket)		
1976 tax return 0.75 × $3,552 × 0.5 × 0.917431	$ 1,222	
1977 tax return 0.25 × $3,552 × 0.5 × 0.84168	374	
Total		$1,596
(13) Present value April 1, 1976, including income-tax benefits ($4,324 + $1,596)		5,920

taxed at capital gains. Assumptions concerning initial purchase price, value enhancements, settlement costs, and so on, are the same as in case II. The major difference is that the speculator in case III experiences a net cash loss from operations of $2,170, which translates into a loss of $3,552 for income-tax purposes. The investor is assumed to be in the 50% tax bracket. The *nominal* net cash return on the property purchased in April 1976 and sold in April 1977 is $8,910 before and $5,698 after capital-gains tax (excluding ordinary income-tax benefits).

The cash gain discounted back to April 1976 including capital-gains tax amounted to $4,324 or 34% on the initial expenditures including downpayment and buyer settlement costs. Incorporating implied income-tax benefits from negative returns on operations raises the discounted return to $5,920 or 46% on initial expenditures.

In conclusion, speculators were able to earn a very handsome return in buying and selling homes during the period under consideration. However, a very significant share of home price increase was siphoned off by capital-gains tax and transactions cost and in case III by negative cash flows from operations. At the same time, given the assumed income-tax position of the speculator, a large part of the loss on operations was tax sheltered.

The cash yield to the speculator might have been improved substantially if some part of transactions costs were avoided. Selling the home without a real-estate agent would have increased the yield assuming the same market price had been attained at the time of sale.

Two types of potential costs were not considered in the illustrations. Specifically excluded were transaction costs in disposing of or acquiring alternate investments at the time of the home purchase and after the sale. Also we excluded prepayment penalties on the mortgage loan at the time of sale. These types of costs could be quite significant under certain circumstances.

In general, it would seem that substantial components of transactions and related costs are fixed in character. As a result, price increases more moderate than those during the period studied would quickly wipe out speculative gains or reduce them sharply. Equally important, if holding costs (that is, negative returns on operations) are substantial, potential speculators must carefully consider the probabilities surrounding anticipated capital gains. With considerable uncertainty over projected home price increases, this will normally discourage many speculators from entering the market.

Appendix H
Homebuyer Surveys in Contra Costa and Orange Counties, California: Methods and Responses

Survey Methods

The strategy for sampling recent homebuyers in Contra Costa and Orange Counties was circumscribed by severe resource constraints. These constraints called for predetermination of recently sold homes or recent homebuyers from an easily accessible source rather than sampling a larger universe, a share of which was involved in home purchase.

The study was based on lists of homes sold in the respective areas for purposes of sampling. These lists were not complete but are believed to include between 30 and 40% of home sales in the two years covered. Essentially, the samples were drawn from lists of reported first-quarter 1975 and 1977 sales.

We have no reason to believe any particular bias was introduced as a result of the lists covering only a portion of the total universe sampled. Potentially more troublesome might be problems associated with the fact that sales dates as indicated on the lists did not accord with the sales dates reported by respondents to the questionnaire. The problem here is not that the respondents reported an earlier date of sale than shown on the lists. This might be expected since some homebuyers consider the point in time they made a deposit or received loan approval as consummation of sale. The contrary happened, a large fraction of the sales dates reported by respondents fell in the period after the first quarter of the respective years (see table H-2). As will be shown presently, some decision rules had to be adopted in determining eligible responses by reference to date of reported sale and other criteria.

Sample Plan

At the outset it was decided that a mail survey would be used. Generally, mail surveys require high response rates before significance can be attached to results. Moreover, the response rate is not easily predictable and may vary across strata in samples. Without prior knowledge on these points, 1,000 sample points in each of the four cells were selected. This means that fractions of the lists or the universe sampled vary over time and by area. Therefore the samples cannot be pooled without weighting. Further, assuming that the samples were to be considered representative, the standard errors of the estimates will vary for any particular distribution of the sampled attributes. Generally, it turned out that in Contra Costa County the fraction of the universe sampled was higher and standard errors would be smaller than in Orange County in both 1975 and 1977. Since the samples are larger in 1977 than in 1975, the standard errors would be smaller for 1977 even though the universe of home sales had expanded significantly over the two years in both areas.

Each of the four strata was sampled separately. The total number of eligible transactions on the lists were enumerated, and sample intervals were determined to yield 1,000 sample points in the four cells. Tables of random numbers were used to establish starting points for sampling. No bias should result in the selection of sample points of eligible transactions from the lists.

The addresses of homes to be sampled were recorded on labels ready for mailing. The mailing of the questionnaires was completed over a short period, largely in September 1977. About two weeks after the initial mailing, postcards were sent out reminding prospective respondents to mail back the surveys. For Contra Costa follow-up postcards were sent out a few days earlier than for Orange County; this procedure may have contributed to a somewhat higher response rate in the former area.

Questionnaire Response

The course of events following the mailings is indicated in table H-1. Between 4.9 and 8.6% of the questionnaires were returned by the postal service with the comment "no such address." In addition, a very small fraction of the properties were reported as vacant. The rate of delivery by the postal service than ranges between 91.1 and 93.6%. The number of questionnaires delivered is the denominator for calculating the response rate. According to table H-1, the response rates in Orange County were 38 and 40% in 1975 and 1977, respectively, against 49 and 45% in Contra Costa County.

Screening of the questionnaires indicated that a surprisingly large number of respondents listed purchase dates other than the first quarter of the respective years. This issue, already mentioned, assumed more serious dimensions than anticipated. The question asked was "when did you purchase your home (month, year)." In retrospect, a more precise benchmark indicative of purchase date should have been sought—for example, date of deposit, loan approval, or close of escrow. A large fraction of the sales dates reported by respondents were after the first quarter of the respective years. This may be explained in part by some respondents' mentioning the date they moved into the home as the date of purchase. More significantly, the list of purchases sampled included a considerable number of transactions where escrows had not closed. In these cases the date of sale shown on the list was the estimated date of escrow closing.

Table H-1
Homebuyer Questionnaire Response

	Orange		Contra Costa	
	1975	*1977*	*1975*	*1977*
Questionnaires sent	1,000	1,000	1,000	1,000
Delivered by Post Office	936	924	933	911
Returned:				
Responses	352	365	459	411
"No Such Address"	49	63	62	86
Vacant	15	13	5	3
Response rate = # responses ÷ # delivered by Post Office	38%	40%	49%	45%
Editing process:				
Responses	352	365	459	411
Less:				
Date out of range	−124	−32	−148	−27
Renters	−21	−33	−31	−40
Not enough info	−20	−23	−	−5
Responses eligible for analysis	187	277	280	339
Response rates	Orange	39%		
	Contra Costa	47%		
	Total Sample	43%		

The problem was to distinguish situations where close of escrow might have been delayed for good reasons from situations where homes were sold or resold at a later date. Without other information to distinguish these situations, it was decided to use only responses reporting sales dates falling between July 1974 and June 1975, and between July 1976 and June 1977 for the analysis. As can be seen in table H-2, the number of responses with reported purchase dates before the first quarter of the respective year is small. Mostly these include cases of escrows closing earlier than expected and more generally situations where home purchasers had different perceptions on sales dates than those preparing the lists sampled. Concerning the cut-off date at the end of the second quarter of the respective years, the situation is more ambiguous. Some legitimate responses may have been removed from the sample, but there is no way of determining the number. We are reasonably certain that the preponderance of questionnaires removed from the 1975 samples involved cases where the homes were sold again. For example, in Orange County 75 of the 124 questionnaires removed for not complying with the decision rule reported sales dates in 1977; the same applied to 56 of the 148 questionnaires eliminated for Contra Costa County. Resource constraints inhibited a special study comparing 1975 transactions with the same owner occupant in 1977 to those sold or resold at a later date. Such a study may be called for eventually for its own sake and to examine possible biases.

Table H-2
Date of Purchase Reported by Recent Homebuyers

	Contra Costa County		Orange County	
	N	Percent	N	Percent
1975				
Third quarter 1974	1	0.4	4	2.2
Fourth quarter 1974	8	2.9	8	4.3
First quarter 1975	153	54.6	95	51.1
Second quarter 1975	118	42.2	79	42.5
Total	280	100.0	186[a]	100.0
1977				
Third quarter 1976	7	2.1	10	3.5
Fourth quarter 1976	10	3.0	25	9.0
First quarter 1977	196	57.8	122	44.2
Second quarter 1977	126	37.1	119	43.2
Total	339	100.0	276[a]	100.0

[a]One observation was excluded because precise data of purchase was not clear.

Reliability

No claim is made that the samples are statistically reliable. It is appropriate, however, to indicate the assumptions necessary for statistical reliability to be determined. First the list of sales from which the samples were drawn must itself be a representative sample of the universe of home sales and the purchasers. Second our method of sampling must be appropriate, and the sample points selected must accurately represent the properties included in the lists and their buyers. The third assumption concerns the delivery of questionnaires by the Postal Service. Although the number of questionnaires mailed back by the Service is small, this group might include a particular population. Aside from errors in recordation of addresses, which are likely to be distributed randomly, the "no-such-address" category might consist primarily of newly constructed homes that were not completed and occupied by the time the surveys were taken. However, this applies only to the 1977 returns. As can be seen from table H-1, the differences in the rates of failure to deliver questionnaires between 1975 and 1977 for "no such address" are relatively small.

The fourth assumption pertains to the response rate and states that respondents are not significantly different from nonrespondents. In the absence of a special survey of nonrespondents, this assumption is the most difficult one to check out. In addition, there is the aforementioned problem of questionnaires, returned largely in the 1975 samples, which were removed from the analysis because of the strong probability that the property was sold or resold at a later date. Finally, the exclusion of homes rented out by owners introduces the possibility of bias. As homes age, the chance of their entering the rental stock increases. Thus older and less expensive houses in the 1975 sample may have been particularly subject to change in tenure. In these cases, mailing questionnaires to the home addresses would not have yielded any responses unless, of course, tenants turned over the questionnaires to the owners.

Assuming the samples were representative of a universe of home sales, encompassing more than the properties on the lists, the size of this universe needs to be determined. (Ideally, of course, it would have been predetermined.) Since no accurate data on total home sales, however defined, were available for the periods and areas studied, estimates based on deed recordings were prepared.

We assume the samples were drawn from deed recordings whose distribution over time is approximately as shown on table H-2. From information based on actual deed recordings, we can make an estimate of the total number of deeds that comprise the universe. The estimated numbers of deed recordings in the universe were 15,828 and 28,163 in 1975 and 1977, respectively, for Orange County, and 6,346 and 10,471 for Contra Costa County. These recordings cover residential and nonresidential real-estate transactions. The distribution of the two categories is unknown, but trade sources suggest that in Orange County between 70 and 80% of deeds recorded were single-family home sales. If one selects the upper end of this range, the number of home sales in Orange County would approximate 12,662 in 1975 (15,828 × 0.8) and 22,530 in 1977 (28,163 × 0.8). For Contra Costa County the respective estimates based on the same assumption are 5,077 for 1975 and 8,377 for 1977.

Standard errors can be estimated using the formula

$$\delta = \sqrt{\frac{PQ\,(N-n)}{n\,(N-1)}}$$

where

N = size of universe
n = size of sample
P = percent of attribute in universe (assume 0.5)
$Q = 1 - P$

Given N as shown in table H-2, the standard errors at $P = 0.5$ are 0.036 and 0.03 for Orange County in 1975 and 1977, respectively, and 0.029 and 0.027 in Contra Costa County. At the 95% confidence level and $P = 0.5$, the formula suggests that true estimates would be ±7.2% for 1975 and ±6.0% for 1977 in Orange County. The Contra Costa County estimates would range between ±5.8% in 1975 and ±5.4% in 1977. Obviously for any P greater or smaller than 0.5 the standard errors of the estimates would be smaller.

Table H-3
Age of Household Head, Recent Homebuyers

| | Contra Costa County | | Orange County | |
Age	1975	1977	1975	1977
Less than 25	2.2%	6.5%	1.1%	4.7%
25-34	47.3	51.5	39.0	43.3
35-44	31.2	24.3	39.6	31.4
45-54	12.2	13.3	15.0	13.7
55 and over	7.2	4.4	5.3	6.9
	100.0%	100.0%	100.0%	100.0%
Median	35.0	33.5	37.5	35.6
N =	279	338	187	277

Table H-4
Household Size of Recent Homebuyers at Time of Purchase

| | Contra Costa County | | Orange County | |
No. of Persons	1975	1977	1975	1977
1	6.8%	9.2%	7.9%	12.7%
2	37.6	37.9	34.2	32.2
3	22.6	21.0	17.6	18.5
4	22.6	21.0	23.0	21.4
5	5.7	8.0	13.4	10.1
6 or more	4.7	3.0	4.8	5.1
	100.0%	100.0%	100.0%	100.0%
Median	3.2	3.1	3.4	3.3
N =	279	338	187	276

Table H-5
Distribution of Household Income, Recent Homebuyers

Income	Contra Costa County		Orange County	
	1975	1977	1975	1977
Less than $10,000	2.9%	—	1.1%	1.1%
10,000-14,999	9.8	10.7%	13.6	6.2
15,000-19,999	23.6	19.0	17.4	15.3
20,000-24,999	21.7	17.5	24.5	19.6
25,000-29,999	18.5	16.9	15.2	21.5
30,000-39,999	15.6	22.8	16.8	19.3
40,000-49,999	5.4	8.6	6.5	8.7
50,000 or more	2.5	4.5	4.9	8.4
	100.0%	100.0%	100.0%	100.0%
Median	$23,157	$25,828	$23,652	$26,814
Median home price/ income ratio	2.15	2.52	2.08	2.79
N =	276	337	184	275

Table H-6
Percentage of Recent Homebuyers, by Current versus Previous Year's Family Income and Current versus Expected Income

	Contra Costa County		Orange County	
	1975	1977	1975	1977
Percent with current income greater than previous year's income	82.3%	86.1%	84.0%	82.7%
N =	277	338	187	277
Percent expecting next year's family income to be greater than current year's	75.5%	74.6%	76.5%	71.0%
N =	278	335	187	276

Table H-7

Percentage of Homebuyers who Spend More, Same, or Less on Housing in Current versus Previous Home

Housing Expenditures in Current Versus Previous Home	Contra Costa County		Orange County	
	1975	1977	1975	1977
Much more	66.9%	65.2%	56.8%	66.8%
A little more	25.9	26.0	36.2	23.8
Same	1.8	5.3	3.2	5.4
A little less	4.0	2.7	2.2	2.5
Much less	1.4	0.9	1.6	1.4
	100.0%	100.0%	100.0%	100.0%
N =	278	339	185	277

Table H-8

Tenure of Recent Homebuyers in Previous Residence

	Contra Costa County		Orange County	
Previous tenure	1975	1977	1975	1977
Own	52.3%	61.2%	54.0%	71.6%
Rent	47.7	38.8	46.0	28.4
	100.0%	100.0%	100.0%	100.0%
N =	279	338	187	275

Table H-9

Percent of Recent Homebuyers Purchasing First Home

	Contra Costa County		Orange County	
First Home Purchase	1975	1977	1975	1977
Yes	42.5	34.4	36.9	21.0
No	57.5	65.6	63.1	79.0
	100.0	100.0	100.0	100.0
N =	280	337	187	276

Table H-10
Percent of Homebuyers Purchasing Newly Constructed or
Existing Homes

	Contra Costa County		Orange County	
	1975	1977	1975	1977
New home	25.4	26.0	34.1	28.8
Existing home	74.6	74.0	65.9	71.2
	100.0	100.0	100.0	100.0
N =	279	338	185	274

Table H-11
Relative Importance of Housing, Neighborhood, Location, and
Cost Components in Decision to Buy
(percent)

	Contra Costa County		Orange County	
	1975	*1977*	*1975*	*1977*
House				
Very important	81.1	84.0	85.3	79.5
Somewhat important	18.5	14.8	13.6	19.0
Not important	0.4	1.2	1.1	1.5
	100.0	100.0	100.0	100.0
Lot				
Very important	49.1	49.4	44.0	36.9
Somewhat important	45.4	42.8	44.5	52.0
Not important	5.6	7.8	11.5	11.1
	100.0	100.0	100.0	100.0
Neighborhood				
Very important	65.9	62.9	64.5	65.9
Somewhat important	32.2	34.4	33.9	32.2
Not important	1.8	2.7	1.6	1.8
	100.0	100.0	100.0	100.0
General location				
Very important	57.8	56.2	62.7	70.7
Somewhat important	39.3	40.2	34.6	28.3
Not important	2.9	3.6	2.7	1.1
	100.0	100.0	100.0	100.0
Cost				
Very important	72.1	78.5	74.3	60.5
Somewhat important	26.1	20.1	24.0	36.9
Not important	1.8	1.5	1.6	2.6
	100.0	100.0	100.0	100.0

Table H-12
Percent of Recent Homebuyers Satisfied with Current Home

| | Contra Costa County | | Orange County | |
	1975	1977	1975	1977
Satisfied				
Yes	91.1	89.6	90.3	88.0
No	8.9	10.4	9.7	12.0
	100.0	100.0	100.0	100.0
N =	280	335	186	276

Table H-13
Adequacy of Size of Home as Perceived by Homebuyers

| | Contra Costa County | | Orange County | |
	1975	1977	1975	1977
Size of Home				
Too large	16.8%	17.8%	14.7%	19.3%
About right	62.7	74.6	63.0	73.4
Too small	20.4	7.7	22.3	7.3
	100.0%	100.0%	100.0%	100.0%
N =	279	338	184	277

Table H-14
Percentage Distribution of Homes Purchased, by Number of Bedrooms

| | Contra Costa County | | Orange County | |
	1975	1977	1975	1977
Bedrooms				
2 or less	15.7	16.2	9.1	16.6
3	47.9	49.3	52.9	39.0
4	29.6	28.9	32.6	37.9
5 or more	6.8	5.6	5.3	6.5
	100.0	100.0	100.0	100.0
N =	280	339	187	277

Table H-15
Percentage Distribution of Homes Purchased by Number of Bathrooms

	Contra Costa County		Orange County	
	1975	1977	1975	1977
Bathrooms				
1	14.7	16.5	5.9	4.0
1.5	8.6	9.0	21.4	18.7
2	48.6	47.9	35.3	37.7
2.5	17.6	18.6	24.6	24.2
3 or more	10.4	8.1	12.8	15.4
	100.0	100.0	100.0	100.0
N =	278	334	187	273

Table H-16
Percentage Distribution of Homes Purchased with or without Separate Living Room

	Contra Costa County		Orange County	
	1975	1977	1975	1977
Separate Living Room				
Yes	95.3	93.1	94.7	93.4
No	4.7	6.9	5.3	6.6
	100.0	100.0	100.0	100.0
N =	276	333	187	271

Table H-17
Percentage Distribution of Homes Purchased with or without Separate Dining Room

	Contra Costa County		Orange County	
	1975	1977	1975	1977
Separate Dining Room				
Yes	66.9	66.9	61.8	69.9
No	33.1	33.1	38.2	30.1
	100.0	100.0	100.0	100.0
N =	266	314	178	256

**Table H-18
Percentage Distribution of Homes Purchased with or without
Family Room**

	Contra Costa County		Orange County	
	1975	1977	1975	1977
Family Room				
Yes	66.7	67.9	62.7	67.5
No	33.3	32.1	37.3	32.5
	100.0	100.0	100.0	100.0
N =	264	339	177	252

**Table H-19
Percentage Distribution of Homes Purchased with or without
Den/Study**

	Contra Costa County		Orange County	
	1975	1977	1975	1977
Den/Study				
Yes	22.8	21.8	26.1	33.0
No	77.2	78.2	73.9	66.1
	100.0	100.0	100.0	100.0
N =	228	248	157	218

**Table H-20
Typical Uses of "Extra" Bedrooms by Recent Homebuyers
(Includes Only Those Reporting Having "Extra" Bedroom)**

	Contra Costa County		Orange County	
Type of Use	1975	1977	1975	1977
Family or recreation room	7.1%	9.9%	8.0%	9.7%
Study or office	52.1	53.8	59.3	46.8
Sewing room	10.1	6.6	3.5	10.2
Guest room	17.8	20.8	23.9	24.2
Storage	8.3	3.3	3.5	4.8
Rental	0.6	0.9	0	1.6
Hobby room	4.1	3.8	0.9	0.5
Unused	0	0.9	0.9	1.6
Small business	0	0	0	0.5
	100.0%	100.0%	100.0%	100.0%
N =	169	212	113	186

Table H-21

Expected Increase in CPI in 1978, Recent Homebuyers

| | Contra Costa County | | Orange County | |
Percent	1975	1977	1975	1977
1-2	3.2%	6.2%	7.1%	5.1%
3-4	9.7	11.9	9.8	11.4
5	22.4	22.6	24.5	21.6
6-9	44.8	37.4	38.0	30.0
10 plus	13.4	11.3	12.5	20.9
Same or drop	0.4	1.2	0	0.4
Don't know	6.1	9.5	12.5	10.6
	100.0%	100.0%	100.0%	100.0%
Median	6.8	6.3	6.4	6.6
N =	277	337	184	273

Table H-22

Percentage of Homebuyers Who Would Consider Selling Home Immediately at Various Discrete Percentage Increases in Value

| Would sell with | Contra Costa County | | Orange County | |
appreciation of	1975	1977	1975	1977
0%	1.1%	0.6%	0.5%	0.4%
10%	0.4	0.6	1.1	0.7
20%	2.9	7.2	0.5	6.3
30%	5.4	10.2	2.7	9.6
40%	3.3	6.9	4.4	4.0
More than 40%	23.2	18.3	24.2	26.1
Would not sell	63.8	56.2	66.5	52.9
	100.0%	100.0%	100.0%	100.0%
N =	276	333	182	272

Table H-23

Opinions Concerning Local Business Economy: Recent Homebuyers

| | Contra Costa County | | Orange County | |
	1975	1977	1975	1977
Good times	20.4%	25.1%	29.4%	29.9%
Good some ways/bad others	60.6	58.1	54.0	49.6
Bad times	5.7	5.4	3.2	4.7
Uncertain	13.3	11.4	13.4	15.7
	100.0%	100.0%	100.0%	100.0%
N =	279	334	187	274

Appendix I
Tables on Sales and
Inventories of
Merchant Builders

Table I-1
Unsold Houses as a Percent of All New Single-Family Houses
in Seven-County Area of Southern California, December 1974
to June 1977

County and Completion Status	Dec. 1974	June 1975	Dec. 1975	June 1976	Dec. 1976	June 1977
Tract Developments						
Seven-county total						
Completed	25	20	22	20	15	7
Under construction	60	56	52	43	35	26
Total	36	33	38	36	31	25
Los Angeles						
Completed	24	18	16	23	17	7
Under construction	52	45	54	63	55	46
Total	35	29	38	51	47	43
Orange						
Completed	24	20	23	11	10	3
Under construction	57	57	41	31	22	17
Total	38	33	36	29	20	16
Riverside						
Completed	35	29	36	29	24	12
Under construction	53	55	63	41	34	13
Total	41	39	50	37	32	13
San Bernardino						
Completed	19	17	23	21	16	11
Under construction	67	68	57	42	45	34
Total	32	34	46	37	39	32
Ventura						
Completed	17	18	30	20	0	13
Under construction	62	45	40	20	15	4
Total	28	29	36	20	13	4
Santa Barbara						
Completed	19	13	0	20	14	0
Under construction	88	0	0	52	7	27
Total	42	13	0	51	10	24
San Diego						
Completed	28	22	19	18	15	5
Under construction	72	69	68	50	44	25
Total	37	34	36	37	33	22
Planned Unit Developments						
Seven-county total						
Completed	39	38	34	32	26	23
Under construction	87	81	80	48	43	22
Total	51	46	43	45	35	22
Los Angeles						
Completed	37	40	35	29	25	12
Under construction	93	82	78	66	68	29
Total	55	46	42	36	43	25

Table I-1 continued

County and Completion Status	Dec. 1974	June 1975	Dec. 1975	June 1976	Dec. 1976	June 1977
Orange						
Completed	38	33	30	25	16	21
Under construction	76	76	77	38	30	17
Total	45	42	41	33	28	17
Riverside						
Completed	44	37	44	40	30	50
Under construction	78	61	85	33	66	0
Total	50	41	51	39	41	14
San Bernardino						
Completed	38	46	47	10	0	0
Under construction	93	0	52	0	8	0
Total	46	46	49	10	8	0
Ventura						
Completed	51	35	23	25	17	0
Under construction	100	99	91	67	28	5
Total	63	49	41	40	24	5
Santa Barbara						
Completed	69	93	77	50	43	2
Under construction	98	100	83	55	39	42
Total	80	97	79	52	42	16
San Diego						
Completed	38	41	34	38	28	25
Under construction	75	86	84	57	50	41
Total	45	50	41	42	36	37

Source: Residential Research Council of Southern California, *Real Estate and Construction Report, Second Quarter 1977,* pp. 32-33. The source shows the underlying numbers of total units completed or under construction as well as the number of tracts and planned unit developments surveyed.

Table I-2
Merchant Builder Activity in the United States: Sales, Inventory,
and Marketing Period for New Single-Family Houses, 1963-1977

Year and Month[a]	Sales[b]	For Sale[b]	Inventory-to-Sales Ratio[c]	Median No. of Months on Market		
				Houses Sold[d]	Houses for Sale[e]	Difference for Sale/Sold
1963 Feb.	464	238	6.6	3.7	4.2	0.5
May	586	248	5.1	3.5	4.1	0.6
Aug.	570	264	5.6	3.1	4.2	1.1
Nov.	579	258	5.5	3.7	4.5	0.8
1964 Feb.	609	262	5.5	3.4	4.6	1.2
May	523	266	6.2	3.5	5.1	1.6
Aug.	582	258	5.4	4.0	5.3	1.3
Nov.	548	249	5.6	3.5	5.4	1.9
1965 Feb.	559	251	5.5	3.9	5.3	1.4
May	544	238	5.3	3.9	5.1	1.2
Aug.	615	232	4.6	4.1	4.6	0.5
Nov.	616	231	4.6	3.7	4.4	0.7
1966 Feb.	541	224	4.9	3.9	4.6	0.7
May	499	216	5.3	4.0	4.9	0.9
Aug.	377	208	6.8	3.9	5.7	1.8
Nov.	382	193	6.2	4.2	6.4	2.2
1967 Feb.	408	194	5.7	3.9	5.4	1.5
May	503	187	4.5	3.4	4.7	1.3
Aug.	504	181	4.4	2.8	4.1	1.3
Nov.	500	186	4.6	3.0	3.6	0.6
1968 Feb.	543	191	4.1	2.9	3.9	1.0
May	441	199	5.5	3.1	3.6	0.5
Aug.	507	206	5.0	3.7	4.2	0.5
Nov.	469	214	5.6	3.4	3.9	0.5
1969 Feb.	524	215	4.9	3.8	4.1	0.3
May	447	221	6.1	3.9	4.0	0.1
Aug.	422	223	6.5	4.0	4.3	0.3
Nov.	441	222	6.2	4.2	5.0	0.8
1970 Feb.	373	215	7.2	3.9	5.1	1.2
May	466	217	5.7	4.0	5.8	1.8
Aug.	515	218	5.1	3.1	4.9	1.8
Nov.	570	212	4.6	3.0	4.6	1.6
1971 Feb.	618	218	4.4	3.2	3.7	0.5
May	618	236	4.6	2.4	2.9	0.5
Aug.	659	254	4.7	2.9	3.2	0.3
Nov.	710	278	4.9	2.8	3.2	0.4
1972 Feb.	711	306	5.4	3.1	3.5	0.4
May	677	338	6.1	2.9	3.2	0.3
Aug.	773	375	6.0	3.3	3.8	0.5
Nov.	735	400	6.8	3.4	4.0	0.6
1973 Feb.	737	417	6.8	3.7	3.9	0.2
May	660	417	7.5	4.6	4.0	−0.6
Aug.	566	432	9.4	4.7	4.5	−0.2
Nov.	547	417	9.6	5.4	5.1	−0.3
1974 Feb.	539	420	9.6	5.3	5.3	0
May	590	399	8.0	5.1	5.7	0.6
Aug.	492	373	9.1	4.9	5.7	0.8
Nov.	450	350	10.3	4.9	6.2	1.3

Table I-2 continued

Year and Month[a]	Sales[b]	For Sale[b]	Inventory-to-Sales Ratio[c]	Median No. of Months on Market		
				Houses Sold[d]	Houses for Sale[e]	Difference for Sale/Sold
1975 Feb.	422	351	10.4	5.0	6.4	1.4
May	579	323	6.8	5.2	7.2	2.0
Aug.	566	319	6.8	4.1	5.2	1.1
Nov.	680	316	5.8	3.9	4.9	1.0
1976 Feb.	643	307	6.0	3.5	4.5	1.0
May	572	330	7.0	3.4	3.8	0.4
Aug.	652	336	6.3	3.8	4.3	0.5
Nov.	742	351	6.0	3.4	4.3	0.9
1977 Feb.	826	355	5.3	3.3	4.1	0.8
May	810	364	5.4	2.9	3.4	0.5
Aug.	818	389	5.8	3.6	4.0	0.4
Nov.	818	402	6.1	3.9	3.8	−0.1

Sources: Bureau of the Census and HUD, Construction Reports, C-25, "New One-Family Houses Sold and For Sale," seriatim. Revised data for 1973-1977.

[a]To reduce the scope of the table, benchmark data are shown for the midmonth of each quarter, while figure 5-2 presents figures for each month.

[b]Seasonally adjusted annual rates (1,000 units); "sales" for each month, "for sale" at end of month. Both categories include units completed, under construction, and not yet started.

[c]Ratio of homes for sale to homes sold; monthly rate, seasonally adjusted.

[d]From start to sale, seasonally adjusted.

[e]From start to end of month, seasonally adjusted.

Appendix J
Liquidation of Home
Equities in Recent
Years

According to the article "Housing in the Recovery" in the March 1977 issue of the *Federal Reserve Bulletin*, "it is estimated that in 1976 the net increase in long-term home mortgage debt of households exceeded the value of household net purchases of new and existing homes (including condominium units in multifamily structures) by about $15 billion. This increase compares with less than $1 billion in 1974 when credit conditions were relatively tight." According to the article, the data "suggest that homeowners have been liquidating large amounts of housing equities. . . ." Similar assertions have been made by others but, as will be seen, the Federal Reserve staff has pursued this subject most consistently over the past few years.

Upon inquiry, the authors received from the Federal Reserve staff table J-1, which differs from the figures in the *Bulletin* article because of revisions. According to the table, net additions to the home mortgage debt of households exceeded net home purchases of households each year since 1971, only slightly in 1974, but by substantial margins in 1975 and especially in 1976 when the excess reached over $22 billion. The last column in the table shows the Federal Reserve staff estimate of home mortgage funds raised for purposes other than house purchase, rising from nearly $8 billion in 1974 to $32 billion in 1976.

Among the statistical procedures specified in the footnotes to table J-1, the exclusion of land under new homes warrants attention. While treatment of the land component as an intrasectoral transfer may be appropriate for national income accounting, it becomes questionable when the value of net home purchases by households is compared with the net increase in the home mortgage debt. The land under new houses prior to construction is not held by households but by builders, except for units built on owners' land (either custom-built or "do-it-yourself" structures). Hence much of the land component represents a transfer from the business to the household sector. Moreover, increases in the home mortgage debt are partly attributable to the disproportionate price rise for the sites under new homes, paid by the homebuyers and included in the property appraisals determining the amounts of mortgage loans. Hence the value of net home purchases in the Federal Reserve estimates is understated, and the difference between net purchases and increments to the mortgage debt is overstated.

Instead of correcting the Federal Reserve estimates for the land component, table J-2 presents independent estimates derived from the data on the number and average price of new-home acquisitions assembled for this volume, plus

Table J-1
Federal Reserve Staff Estimates of Increase in Home Mortgage Debt
and Net Purchases of Homes
(billions of dollars)

	Increase in Home Mortgage Debt of Households[a]	Net Purchases of Homes by Households[b]	Difference between Debt and Purchases	Estimated Mortgage Funds Raised for Purposes Other Than Home Purchase[c]
	(1)	(2)	(3)	(4)
1970	$16.4	$18.7	$−2.3	$ 1.7
1971	28.4	25.2	+3.2	8.7
1972	39.8	32.0	+7.8	14.5
1973	42.1	35.9	+6.2	13.0
1974	34.7	34.3	+0.4	7.7
1975	42.6	31.9	+10.7	17.7
1976	66.1	43.7	+22.4	32.0

Source: David F. Seiders of the staff of the Board of Governors of the Federal Reserve System.

[a]Change in total 1-4 family mortgage debt outstanding (Federal Reserve Board), less change in 1-4 family construction loans outstanding (HUD).

[b]Household sector purchases of new homes (including condominium units in multifamily structures) and brokers' commissions on the sale of existing homes. The value of new-home purchases is based on F.R. Flow of Funds data derived from construction statistics for 1- to 4-family houses and excludes the land component, which is treated as an intrasectoral transfer. Purchases of mobile homes and expenditures on additions and alterations to existing homes are also excluded.

[c]Column 3 plus estimated downpayments on new homes purchased by households.

brokerage commissions on sales of existing houses (following the Federal Reserve definition of "net purchases" of homes). The use of price data means that both the land and the construction components are taken into account for the estimate of the dollar volume of purchases of homes sold by builders. The sources and procedures are given in the footnotes to the table, and only one more substantive item should be noted here. The available price or value data relate only to single-family homes, while the home mortgage debt covers 1- to 4-family dwellings. Hence column 8 of table J-2 adds the estimated sales value of new 2- to 4-family houses to net purchases, based on the data in table J-3.

The results of the alternative estimates show an excess of debt increases over net purchases of homes in 1972 and 1973 and a far more substantial excess in 1976. However, the near $11 billion for 1976 is less than half the $22 billion computed by the Federal Reserve staff. The 1972 and 1973 figures in our estimates are also lower than those of the Federal Reserve, and no excess appears for 1975 as against the $10.7 billion shown in table J-1. The results are not precisely comparable. The procedures for arriving at the two sets of data vary. Besides, the Federal Reserve staff includes and we exclude net purchases of condominium units. Nevertheless, the differences are large enough to suggest that the Federal Reserve staff estimates of the excess of debt increments over net purchases may be overstated.

Table J-2
Independent Estimates of Increase in Home Mortgage Debt and of Net Purchases of Homes in the Household Sector, 1970-1977

	New Homes Sold by Builders			New Homes on Owners' Land			Sum Clmn. 3 plus 6	Adjustment from Table J-3	Brokers' Commission on Sales	Sum Clmn. 7, 8, 9	Debt Increase	Difference Clmn. 11 & Clmn. 10
Year	Number (000)	Average Price (000)	Total (Billions)	Number (000)	Average Value (000)	Total (Billions)						
	(1)	(2)	(3)	(4)	(5)	(6)	(7)	(8)	(9)	(10)	(11)	(12)
1970	485	$26.6	$12.9	308	$18.6	$ 5.7	$18.6	$1.6	$ 2.5	$22.7	$15.3	−7.4
1971	656	28.3	18.6	378	19.8	7.5	26.1	2.3	3.4	31.8	27.0	−4.0
1972	718	30.5	21.9	401	21.3	8.6	30.5	2.7	4.1	37.3	43.2	+5.9
1973	634	35.5	22.5	434	24.8	10.8	33.3	2.7	4.6	40.6	44.0	+3.4
1974	519	38.9	20.2	380	27.2	10.3	30.5	1.9	4.9	37.3	33.2	−4.1
1975	549	42.6	23.4	361	29.8	10.8	34.2	1.9	5.7	41.8	41.4	−0.4
1976	646	48.0	31.0	406	33.6	13.6	44.6	2.8	7.6	55.0	65.8	+10.8
1977	819	54.2	44.0	440	37.9	16.7	60.7	3.9	10.3	74.9	99.6r	+24.7

Sources: Columns 1-3: Bureau of the Census, *New One-family Houses Sold and For Sale*, Construction Reports C25, seriatim. Column 4: Bureau of the Census, *Characteristics of New Housing*, Construction Reports C25, seriatim. Columns 5, 6: Authors' estimates. The average value of new homes built on owners' land is not reported. It was scaled down to 70% of the average price of units sold by builders to take account of the fact that the land component in this case clearly represents an intrahousehold transfer. The owners had acquired the land some time prior to construction. As for the construction component, it was assumed that the usually higher values of custom-built houses were offset by the usually lower values of "do-it-yourself" units. Column 8: From column 4 of table J-3. This adjustment is necessary because the data in the preceding columns are for new single-family houses, whereas the home mortgage debt relates to 1- to 4-family units. The computations in table J-3 assume that values of new 2- to 4-family dwellings relative to the values of single-family homes are proportional to the respective building-permit values. Column 9: Six percent of dollar volume of sales of existing homes reported by the National Association of Realtors. The amounts are overstated to the extent that some transactions occur without use of brokers, but they are understated to the extent that reported sales relate to single-family houses, exclusive of 2- to 4-family structures. Column 11: Federal Reserve Board data on home mortgage debt, without adjustment for changes in construction loans. Hence the figures vary somewhat from those in column 1 of table J-1.

r − revised.

Table J-3

Value of Building Permits for Private Single-Family Houses and for Two- to Four-Family Structures, and Estimated Additions to Net Purchases of Homes, 1970-1977

Year	One-Unit Houses[a]	2- to 4-Family Houses[a]	Clmn. 2 as % of Clmn. 1	Additions to Net Purchases of Homes[b]
	(1)	(2)	(3)	(4)
1970[c]	$11,486	$ 968	8.4%	$1.6
1971	17,284	1,541	8.9	2.3
1972[d]	21,430	1,909	8.9	2.7
1973	20,691	1,706	8.2	2.7
1974	16,774	1,024	6.1	1.9
1975	19,761	1,119	5.7	1.9
1976	28,997	1,795	6.2	2.8
1977	40,039	2,560	6.4	3.9

Source for building-permit values: Bureau of the Census, Construction C-40, seriatim.

[a]Millions of dollars.

[b]Percentages in column 3 applied to amounts in column 7 of table J-2, billions of dollars.

[c]1970 and 1971 based on 13,000 permit-issuing places.

[d]1972-1977 based on 14,000 permit-issuing places.

According to table J-2, the excess derived from our estimates increased dramatically to nearly $25 billion in 1977. An article, "Household Borrowing in the Recovery," in the March 1978 issue of the *Federal Reserve Bulletin* gives no specific figure for 1977 but adds other information relevant to the subject. It estimates the housing equity of households for the end of 1977 at more than $900 billion, or about double the estimated amount at the end of 1970. The Federal Reserve staff has since raised the 1977 figure to $993 billion (communication from David F. Seiders). These magnitudes, together with the mortgage debt on 1- to 4-family houses, make it possible to trace at least roughly the relationships between equity and debt in the 1970-77 period, as follows (billions of dollars):

Period	Home Equity	Mortgage Debt	Percent of Clmns. 1 + 2	
			Equity	Debt
1977	993	656[r]	60.2%	39.8%
1970	450	298	60.2	39.8
Increase 1970-77	543	358	60.3	39.7

If these benchmark estimates can be accepted, the relative equity and debt positions of holders of 1- to 4-family houses have been remarkably stable. The stability of such inventory data does not preclude excesses of debt increases over net purchases in individual years, which represent flow data. Nevertheless, the evidence of the benchmark estimates reinforces the impression that the Federal Reserve staff estimates of the excesses are overstated. If this is the case, the "liquidation of home equities," that is, the amounts of home mortgage funds raised for purposes other than home purchase (table J-1, column 4), is also subject to downward revision.

In sum, net liquidation of home equities has unquestionably occurred in some recent years. With the inflation of house prices, net cash proceeds of home sellers not or not fully reinvested in other homes have contributed to the process. For that matter, of course, an excess of net borrowing over net home purchases can occur in many other ways, including refinancing of existing first-mortgage loans, additional funds obtained through open-end first mortgages, loans taken out on debt-free property, and junior financing, often in conjunction with the consolidation of short-term consumer debt.

Further, use of single-family houses or, for that matter, other residential real estate as security for loans for nonhousing purposes is not necessarily an inefficient practice. A small businessman, for example, may find that he can obtain working capital for starting or maintaining or expanding his enterprise at lower cost and longer terms by mortgaging his home rather than through a commercial bank loan. Likewise, household borrowers and financial stability in general may benefit from the replacement of several consumer credit accounts with a less costly home mortgage of longer maturity. On the other hand, the use of mortgage borrowings for pure consumption purposes may be more hazardous. A staff paper of the Federal Reserve Board, which explores broader implications of the subject, makes the point that significant portions of recent mortgage borrowings against equity in existing homes went into consumption within relatively short periods of time. The paper implies that an adverse change in the house market could eliminate this boost to consumption and thus have a destabilizing influence on the largest component of GNP.[a]

The strategic question remains one of magnitudes. In the framework of this study, only a modest contribution could be made to the resolution of this issue. Much further research is needed to clarify the concepts involved in the measurement of net liquidation of house equities and improve the measurement itself. As matters stand, estimates will vary with the definition of the household sector, assumptions concerning intrasector versus intersector transfers, the selection of basic data, and procedures in adjusting the data to the purpose at hand. As an example of methodological problems, one may start from the premise that all purchases of existing and new 1- to 4-family dwellings, whether owner-occupied or rented, are attributable to the household sector and that the same is true for net changes in home loan borrowings outstanding. However,

[a]David F. Seiders, *Mortgage Borrowings against Equity in Existing Homes: Measurement, Generation, and Implications for Economic Activity,* Staff Economic Studies of the Board of Governors of the Federal Reserve System, 1978, pp. 26-27.

some purchases and borrowings may represent transfers to or from other sectors such as business or nonprofit organizations. Even a relatively small volume of such transfers in a given year can affect the results materially, especially when transfers to the household sector are followed by transfers from that sector, or vice versa.

Appendix K
Formula for the
Composite Index of
Borrowing Costs

Monthly mortgage payment per dollar of home price equals

$$\frac{\text{Loan/price ratio}}{\text{Present value of ordinary annuity*}}$$

where

$$\text{annuity} = \frac{1 - (1 + j/12)^n}{1 + j/12}$$

n = average maturity of mortgage (in months)

$j/12$ = effective *monthly* interest rate, where $1 + r = (1 + j/12)^{12}$,

$\quad\quad$ r = average effective *annual* interest rate.

*of n months at the effective monthly interest rate.

The three terms, loan/price ratio, average effective *annual* interest rate, and average maturity of mortgage (in years), were obtained from monthly reports of FHLBB on home loans by all major types of lenders. Because the *contractual* maturity is a component of the formula, the latter takes no account of loan repayment before the contractual term expires. Since the initial fees and charges that enter the effective interest rates are amortized over a ten-year period in the FHLBB data, this introduces slight inaccuracies. However, the use of contract interest rates alone would involve greater inaccuracies since initial fees and charges change more over time than do contract rates.

**Appendix L
Terms of Credit
Composite Index for
Conventional Home
Loans Made by Major
Types of Lenders in
Two California Areas,
1970-1977**

Table L-1
Terms-of-Credit Composite Index for Conventional Home Loans Made by Major Types of Lenders in Two California Areas, 1970-1977
(per dollar of house price; 1970 = 100)

Period	Newly Built Homes				Existing Homes			
	Effective Interest Rate	Maturity (Years)	Loan/Price Ratio	Monthly Payment	Effective Interest Rate	Maturity (Years)	Loan/Price Ratio	Monthly Payment
Los Angeles-Long Beach-Anaheim								
1970	100	100	100	100	100	100	100	100
1971	89	102	105	97	88	98	102	94
1972	86	102	106	95	84	99	104	92
1973	91	101	108	101	93	98	105	100
1974	105	102	105	108	108	99	102	108
1975	106	102	105	109	107	99	101	107
1976	106	103	102	106	104	100	101	104
1977-I	106	102	102	106	102	100	101	103
-II	105	103	101	105	102	101	101	102
-III	109	103	101	107	106	101	99	104
San Francisco-Oakland-San Jose								
1970	100	100	100	100	100	100	100	100
1971	86	101	105	94	85	104	104	91
1972	83	102	109	95	83	105	106	92
1973	89	102	104	96	91	104	106	98
1974	103	101	103	105	107	104	102	107
1975	103	103	103	104	105	105	102	105
1976	101	103	101	101	103	107	103	104
1977-I	101	103	101	101	101	108	105	104
-II	101	103	100	100	101	108	104	103
-III	104	103	99	101	104	108	101	103

Source: Underlying data from Federal Home Loan Bank Board.

Index

Asset prices, changes in house and other, 122-124
Atlanta, 26

Baltimore, 27
Baumol, W.J., 58
Beaton, William R., 86
Brooke, Edward W., 175
Builders' inventories: California, 89-93; United States, 93-95

Capital gains: expected trade-off against current housing outlays, 57; owner-buyers and, 40 *passim*
Chicago, 2, 26-27
Cleveland, 27, 32-33
Composite terms of credit index, 106-111, 235-238
Constraints on buyers, income and wealth, 39-51
Consumer income, 21-22, 103-104
Current housing outlays, 22

Dallas, 2, 26
Demographic changes, 100-103; net household formation, 102, 125; net migration, California, 102
Denver, 2, 26-27
Downpayment: analysis of, 197; Congressional Budget Office study, 51; relation to income, 53-54; relation to purchase price, 51-52

Equal Credit Opportunity Act of 1975, 101
Excess demand, 5; inflationary expectations as reasons for, 116-124; manifestations of, 89-99; reasons for, conventional approach, 99-116. *See also* Demographic changes; Consumer income; Mortgage loans; Restraints on new homebuilding

Farmers Home Administration, 49

Federal Housing Administration, 49
First-time buyers, 45-51, 73-74; Contra Costa and Orange Counties, 50. *See also* Homebuyers
Friedman, Milton, 58

General inflation, 3, 117; containment of, 8-9; expected and unexpected, 139; rate of, 7; "tilting" effect of, 44-45, 56
General price expectations, 118-121
General price level: changes in, 21; compared with house prices, 22
Graduated payment mortgage, 173-175

Home purchases: growth of, 37-39; investment and consumption components in, 121-124
Homebuyers: characteristics of, 71-74; current housing outlays of owner-buyers, 41; expectations of, 83-85; features of houses purchased, 74-76; first-time buyers disadvantaged by recent price surge, 167; in Contra Costa and Orange Counties, 69-87; income constraints on, 45-49; one-person households, 72; previous versus current residence, 76-79; price-income ratio, 73; reasons for purchase, 79-83; recent, 4-5; single persons, 101; survey of U.S. League of Savings Associations, 69; two or more earners, 73. *See also* Owner-buyers; First-time buyers
Homeownership, 49-51
House prices: California, 1, 3, 24, 27-28; historical sketch, 32-34; list of data, 13-14; local areas, 24-32; methodological problems in estimating, 11-13; nationwide movements in, 14-23; regional movements in, 23-24; reported by mortgage insurance companies, 27

Households, with two or more earners, 5-6. *See also* Homebuyers
Housing vacancies, 97-99
Houston, 2

Income tax, 45
Inflationary expectations, 43, 137-139; price anticipations of recent buyers overdrawn, 164-165; University of Michigan Survey Research Center, 6. *See also* Excess demand
Irvine Company, 1

Kansas City, 27

Lexington, 130
Liquidation of home equities, 229-234
Los Angeles, 14, 26-27, 29-34

Market adjustments, 7
Metropolitan areas. *See* names of principal cities
Miami, 2, 26, 163
Minneapolis, 2
Model of house prices: conceptual foundations, 129-131; methods to test, 139-143; regression results, 143-152; stock-flow relationships, 131-135; structure of, 135-139
Montgomery County, 14, 28-29
Mortgage insurance companies, private, 48-49
Mortgage interest rates: consumer incomes and, 55; nominal and "real," 54-57
Mortgage lending: California, 106-107; commercial banks, 104-105; mutual savings banks, 105; pools or trusts, 105-106; savings-and-loan associations, 104-107
Mortgage loans, availability and costs of, 104-112

New York, 26-27

Okun, Arthur M., 117
Orange County, 60, 92, 163

Outlook for price adjustments: already observed in California, 157; anticipatory character of recent purchases and, 160; availability of mortgage funds and, 158-159; influence of general economic conditions and, 161-162; lessons from experience in three areas and, 162-163; liquidation of speculative holdings and, 159-160; moderate adjustment expected, 164; new construction and, 158; overextension of recent buyers and, 159; strong basic demand and, 160; weakening demand by owner-buyers and, 160
Owner-buyers, 40-45. *See also* Homebuyers

Permanent income. *See* Consumer income; Model of house prices
Personal and per capita income. *See* Consumer income
Philadelphia, 27
Phoenix, 2
Policy issues, 8. *See also* Public policies
Portland, 27
Public policies: alternative mortgage instruments, 172-175; anti-speculation tax, 171-172; brokers and salespersons acting on own account, 172; effective containment of general inflation, 176-177; federal subsidies to moderate-income buyers, 175-176; revision of recent restrictions on homebuilding, 177-178

Recent movers, tenure changes of, 50. *See also* Homebuyers
Redistribution effects of house price inflation, 165-167
Restraints on homebuilding, 9, 112-116, 134-135, 177-178
Rosen, Kenneth T., 175

Sacramento, 14, 27
Saint Louis, 26-27

San Bernardino County, 93
San Francisco, 14, 26-27
Santa Barbara County, 93
Seattle, 2, 14, 26-28, 32-33, 162-163
Seldon, Maury, 86
Smith, L.B., 63, 133-135, 143, 146
Speculation, 2, 4; attempts to curb,
    60; and builders' pricing policy,
    61-62; "double escrow" procedure,
    58, 203-204; extent of, 59; Federal
    Home Loan Bank of San Francisco,
    response to, 2; functions of price
    arbitrage and, 64-66; index of, 60,
    202; market effects of, 62-64;
    rationale of, 203-208
Speculators, 58-66; professional and

amateur, 58, 62; rationale of, 62
Standard consolidated statistical areas.
    See names of principal cities
Struyk, R.J., 130, 138
Surveys: of consumers, University of
    Michigan, 6, 118-121; of home-
    buyers, Contra Costa and Orange
    Counties, 69-87, 209-221; U.S. League
    of Savings Associations, 69
Swesnik, Richard H., 86

Ventura County, 93
Veterans Administration, 49

Wallich, Henry C., 54, 57
Washington, D.C., 26-27, 32-33

About the Authors

Leo Grebler is emeritus professor of real estate and urban land economics at the University of California at Los Angeles. He is the author or coauthor of *Capital Formation in Residential Real Estate, Housing Issues in Economic Stabilization Policy, The Housing of Nations,* and other books dealing with housing and mortgage markets. His previous positions include service at Columbia University, the President's Council of Economic Advisers, and the Federal Home Loan Bank Board. He has been consultant to the Commission on Money and Credit, the Federal Reserve Board, the United Nations, and other organizations.

Frank G. Mittelbach is professor of management and urban planning and director of the housing, real estate, and urban land studies program at the University of California at Los Angeles. He is the author or coauthor of books and monographs on *Management in the Light Construction Industry, Residential Segregation in the Urban Southwest, Efficiency in the Housing Industry,* and *The Acquisition of Public Building Space,* among others. He has also served as advisor to the U.S. President's Committee on Urban Housing, The California Governor's Commission on Housing Problems, The U.S. Department of Housing and Urban Development, and the Federal Home Loan Bank Board. He is past president of the Western Regional Science Association.